Mega-Projects Unlocked

Mega-Projects Unlocked

The Insider's Guide to Winning, Managing, and Profiting from Alternative Delivery

Michael S. Shapiro, PE

Published by Game Changer Publishing

Paperback ISBN: 978-1-967424-41-2

Hardcover ISBN: 978-1-967424-42-9

Digital ISBN: 978-1-967424-78-8

GC GAME CHANGER
PUBLISHING

www.GameChangerPublishing.com

Dedication

I would like to dedicate my book to my beautiful wife, Deborah A. Block. She has been my source of inspiration, allowing me to focus on the creation of this book over the last four months. Deborah is also a graphic and fine artist and assisted me with developing the original concepts for the outstanding book cover. She is a woman of great talent, patience and provides me with the love and support that every husband wants and needs.

Thank you, Deborah!
Love, Michael

Mega-Projects Unlocked

The Insider's Guide to Winning, Managing, and Profiting from Alternative Delivery

Michael S. Shapiro, PE

Read This First

Just to say thanks for buying and reading my book, I would

like to connect with you! Both the link and the below QR code
will take you to my website: Https://msscllc.net

You can share your contact information, send me an email, or
read additional information that I share with you as a gift.

Scan the QR Code

Acknowledgments

Michael Shapiro has written a cogent primer on how to understand, participate, win and profit while employing Alternative Delivery (AD). AD projects require considerable time and resource commitments. Long lead times are required in identifying the right owners with the right AD process and assembling the right financial/construction/design team professionals. Michael walks us through the AD process in a stepwise fashion, providing real-world experiences to support his concepts and insights. Understanding the Owner's concerns, issues and potential needs must be systematically collected, validated and documented in a project e-notebook. The e-notebook will be refined and morphed to support the Qualification/Procurement/ Negotiation/Delivery processes.

Glenn Sadulsky (Former Vice President and
Alternative Delivery Design Director at AECOM)

Foreword

I want to introduce you to the author, my friend, and your guide into the labyrinthine world of Mega-Projects. I met Michael Shapiro many years ago when he accepted my LinkedIn connection request. I had just left my role as an executive in New York State Empire State Development.

Along with an outstanding team of other professionals and a Governor who was fully committed to ensuring that minority and women-owned businesses (MWBE) had a seat at the table of public contracting in the State of New York, we had just achieved a record-breaking 28% participation across all sectors of public procurement, which was a significant achievement in government and had not been accomplished until that time.

After meeting that professional milestone, my wife, Carline, and I started Brian Ansari and Associates Inc. I want to say I am not an engineer, a construction executive, a transit planner, or a cost estimator. But I do understand something about leadership, about what it takes to win in high-stakes environments, and—more importantly—what it means to build something lasting.

That is why I was honored when Michael Shapiro asked me to write the foreword to this remarkable and necessary book.

In a world increasingly defined by complexity, scale, and public scrutiny, few endeavors test an organization's skill, coordination, and resilience quite like a mega-project. These are not ordinary undertakings. They are ambitious, public-facing, billion-dollar-plus commitments that demand not only technical proficiency but strategic foresight, emotional intelligence, and operational excellence. They require more than engineers. They require builders of trust, architects of process, and stewards of vision.

This book is for those builders.

What Michael Shapiro offers in these pages is a rare kind of guidance—clear-eyed, practical, and born of experience. From the very first chapter, it's clear that this isn't just theory—it's a field manual shaped by real-world lessons from some of the most complex infrastructure projects in the United States. Through each chapter, he peels back the curtain on what it truly takes to pursue, bid on, and deliver Mega-Projects—not just technically, but relationally, strategically, and politically.

Chapter 2 is a masterclass in readiness. Long before a Request for Qualifications (RFQ) is released, the seeds of a successful pursuit must be planted: attending committee meetings, engaging the owner, preparing Go/No-Go assessments, and aligning internally as a team. The book emphasizes what those of us in any field know instinctively—success starts long before the spotlight hits.

In Chapter 3, Michael Shapiro addresses the assumptions and frameworks that underpin a winning proposal. Here, his insight shines especially bright: from team positioning and risk analysis to owner engagement and technical challenge readiness, he presents a robust structure to ensure that every submission is not just competitive, but compelling. The addition of real case studies—like the I-405 Express Toll Lane project in Bellevue, WA, or the SH 121 Toll Road in Dallas, TX—grounds these concepts in actual outcomes.

Proposal activities (Chapter 4) read like a leadership playbook. Topics like establishing a 30, 60, 120 day startup plan, estimating budgets, monitoring progress, and developing a winning execution strategy are given the attention they deserve. But again, the real value is in how Michael Shapiro integrates both process and people—explaining the "how" of project delivery while never losing sight of the "who."

As we move into project execution in Chapter 5, the book becomes a blueprint for leadership. Transitioning from pursuit to performance is a defining moment in any large-scale effort, and this chapter makes clear how essential strong principals, team mobilization, QA/QC processes, and owner alignment are. From safety planning to invoicing procedures to independent technical review teams—every detail is accounted for.

But what impressed me most, as someone outside the technical core of this work, was the humility and clarity with which Michael speaks to owners and developers directly in Chapters 6 and 7. These "How-To" guides distill years of hard-won experience into digestible, actionable wisdom. Whether you're an agency executive trying to diversify your program or a developer navigating the politics of Alternative Technical Concepts (ATCs) and design builder task group meetings, these chapters offer the kind of inside perspective that can only be shared by someone who's been in the room, asked the hard questions, and stayed for the answers.

Chapter 8 on best practices and training speaks to another deeply important truth: systems do not succeed unless people are equipped to lead them. Developing manuals, institutionalizing knowledge, and investing in ongoing learning are not just operational responsibilities—they are strategic imperatives. These are the investments that make excellence repeatable.

And finally, the book looks ahead. In Chapter 9, Michael outlines the forces shaping the future of the industry—from political shifts to funding mechanisms, from the evolving role of public-private partnerships to the lingering questions about what lies beyond the Infrastructure Investment and Jobs Act (IIJA). It is a powerful reminder that mega-project delivery is not just about what we have done, but about how we prepare for what comes next.

Throughout the book, there are dozens of case studies—well-chosen, detailed, and instructive. But it is not the case studies alone that make this book indispensable. It is the clarity of thought, the generosity of insight, and the strategic scaffolding that the author provides to help others replicate success. Michael does not just share what happened; he explains why it worked and how you can build on that knowledge.

For anyone engaged in the design, development, or delivery of infrastructure—whether you are a public official, a construction executive, or an emerging leader—this book is your advantage. It will sharpen your strategy, deepen your understanding, and, if you let it, challenge the way you approach large-scale work. Even for readers like me, outside the technical trenches, this book is a masterclass in high-stakes planning, relationship management, and disciplined execution.

I have had the privilege of watching Michael lead with integrity, humility, and a deep respect for the work and the people behind it. This book reflects that same ethos—rigorous, accessible, and built to last.

The world needs better infrastructure. But it needs better builders—those who understand that success is earned through vision, strategy, and unwavering execution. This book creates those builders.

Brian Ansari

President, BrianAnsari and Associates Inc.

Table of Contents

Introduction

So, who am I? I'm Michael Shapiro, P.E.—a professional civil engineer by trade. But beyond the title, I'm someone who's passionate about bringing ideas to life. I've built my career around business development, streamlining operations, and making sure projects don't just get done—they get done right.

I have 46 years of experience in operations, business development, project execution, civil engineering, professional services, and construction, AEC, with an emphasis on transportation, including highways, transit, and infrastructure. My focus in the AEC market has been for concessionaires, developers, contractors, engineering firms, and owner's representative services in both public and private sectors for transportation and infrastructure, including the highway and transit market.

I've lived in the Phoenix area since 1978. However, I had been traveling throughout the U.S. and parts of Canada for business development, operations, and project work for 17 years—until the COVID pandemic hit in 2019. I've worked in 36 states, and I have a strong understanding of the market, clients, and competition. I also bring excellent communication skills—verbal, written, and in presentations.

I am self-motivated, success-oriented, and highly organized. My 46 years in civil engineering have allowed me to take on many different roles.

Since 1987, I had highly successful progressive roles as department manager, office manager, assistant division manager, division manager, regional manager, deputy director, COO, capture manager, design director, design build manager, executive director, co-founder, practice lead, leader of a business line, owner, and member of the board of directors. I have worked for small- and mid-sized and very large organizations. These organizations have ranged in structure from privately held and family-owned to ESOP to publicly traded companies.

I am currently the owner of Michael S. Shapiro Consulting LLC. My focus is on business development, operations, and project execution for the AEC community. My strongest personal trait is my persistence.

I wrote this book to share my experiences that I have learned over my 32-year career in alternative delivery (AD), working on many AD Mega-Projects with many different roles, with the intent to provide what I see as best practices that can help my readers to better their experience in the AD Mega-Project space in North America.

This book is written for owners, contractors, subcontractors, lead designers, owner's consultants, subconsultants, third-party stakeholders, developers, and financiers.

I've been active in the AD marketplace across North America for the past 32 years. Over that time, I've worked on 51 AD projects with a combined construction value of $66 billion. My experience includes 12 Public-Private Partnership (P3) transportation projects valued at $28.3 billion, serving as the owner's representative on eight AD transportation projects totaling $9 billion, and leading design build efforts on eight transportation projects worth $7.3 billion. Additionally, I've been the lead designer on 26 AD projects with a total construction value of $12 billion, and I've provided DBE and Program/Project Management Consultant (PMC) services on seven projects totaling $34.2 billion. In all, I've contributed to 15 AD transportation Mega-Projects with a combined construction value of $52.2 billion.

There is some overlap between the work on P3 projects, the work on some of the projects representing owners, and the work on AD transportation Mega-Projects. I have been on the winning side of 25 AD projects with a construction value of $15.1 billion, winning 25% of the projects that I have gone after. With this as my background in AD and AD Mega-Projects, I have seen the projects from a 360-degree vantage point.

Through my experience, I have found that a systematic approach to business development by identifying your targets early and dedicating the necessary time and resources early and throughout the process can ensure greater success. Also, focusing on the execution of the project during the proposal efforts can take much of the guesswork out during the proposal phase as you move through the development of your schedule and pricing, negotiations, execution of the work, and close-out. The book describes the systematic approach in detail, citing best practices, and providing you with my experience and tools in making your AD project successful and profitable.

I also share my successes and failures through many case studies. I believe that you learn even more through your failures. I have specific chapters dedicated to the owner, the developer and developing an AD Best Practice Manual and Training.

Chapter 1
Background

Alternative delivery projects are relatively new in the U.S. They started in the 1990s. So we've really only been at it now for about 40 years.

In Europe, they started working on these 60 years ago. So we've started using a European and New Zealand model for doing these AD Mega-Projects. AD Mega-Projects can be a range of things. They can be Design Build. They can be what we call Construction Management/General Contractor (CM/GC). We can do what they call Construction Management at Risk (CMAR). They can be a Public Private Partnerships (P3s), which can have a Developer as the lead with the Design Builder supporting the Developer. A lot of those projects can be done both for public owners and for private owners. AD Mega-Projects are what I consider projects that have a construction value of over $1 billion.

We'll be talking about AD Mega-Projects mostly, but you can apply some of the practices that I discuss in this book, especially Chapter 8, to any type of AD project. My focus has been on AD Mega-Projects. We'll discuss some of the best practices, some of the tools, and the insights for success and profitability on alternative delivery projects.

Author's Background and Expertise

I have been in the AD field for 32 years.

CASE STUDY: 1,000-BED PRISON IN FLORENCE, AZ, FOR CORRECTION CORPORATION OF AMERICA

I started on my first AD project in 1993. That was a project that I did with the Correction Corporation of America, a private Developer that built, owned and managed correctional facilities. I was the lead civil engineer on the project. This is when I was with AECOM.

We first started out working on a master plan for a 1,000-bed private prison in Florence, Arizona. This was very similar to the CM/GC model, where both the designer and the contractor are reporting directly to the owner, and the owner is responsible for directing how everything goes. Correction Corporation of America and the Vice President we worked with, Gay Vic, were tremendous in working with both of us. He had a tremendous amount of experience working with AD on private prisons, and I learned a lot from Gay Vic through the process.

This was my first AD project. We did the master plan, which was very successful. We got everything approved through the agencies and then we went on to design and build the first 500 beds.

We scoped out the project completely throughout the master plan process. Mardian (contractor) prepared all of the construction cost estimates. We worked with the owner and our team to produce a complete schedule for the first phase (500 beds).

We agreed to the fees based on our understanding of the project's scope of work. By the time we developed the concept and design development drawings, we were pretty much in control of our destinies. We started advancing and constructing the first 500 beds.

Everything went along just fantastically. We were about three-fourths through building the first 500 beds when the Correction Corporation of America and Vic decided that they were going to change order the next 500 beds into our contracts. We negotiated that, we moved on and that was an incredible experience for someone who just participated in their first design build project back in 1993.

That project was totally successful, and we made a tremendous profit from it.

Since then, I have participated in 51 AD projects totaling $66 billion in construction value. This included 12 P3 projects that were valued at about $28.3 billion. I was in a leadership role on 30 of those AD proposals and efforts worth about $37.2 billion. We had a 25% win rate on those projects. That's a phenomenal win rate. Most of you are probably aware of that.

I had senior roles on 23 AD projects valued at about $14.9 billion. Except for one major claim project, the 22 AD projects that I was a part of the execution of, we had an (EBIT) earnings before interest and taxes and profitability between 10 and 19%.

Throughout my career on these AD projects, I have been principal in charge, project director, executive design director, deputy director, and chief operating officer (COO).

My partnerships and experience are with owners, developers, contractors, lead designers, and Minority Women-Owned and Disabled Business Enterprise (MWDBE) firms. I've worked on $15 billion worth of projects with Owners alone, mostly on program management or as a general consultant.

Systematic Business Approach

To work on these Mega-Projects, and especially these AD projects, you really must have a systematic business approach.

I always emphasize identifying your targets early. Most of these projects will take you a couple of years to understand and do your due diligence. You have to start a couple of years earlier, even before the Request for Qualifications (RFQ) comes out.

If you're going to really get to know the project, know it like the back of your hand and be able to work through the due diligence efforts. But the first thing you need to do is identify targets. You need to identify what projects you think you're the most well-suited for.

You could put together a multi-disciplined team where you may only have project management experience, but I don't recommend that. If you're going after a billion-dollar bridge project, you better have billion-dollar bridge experience. This is not the time to learn on an AD Mega-Project.

You have to be an expert in the subject. By the time you get into working on AD Mega-Projects, you better be an expert in AD. AD Mega-Projects are not for the meek and for the inexperienced.

Once you identify an early target project for your team, your firm, or your company, you can proceed. I talk about this in greater details later on in other chapters, but you need to go through that exercise.

You also need to ask yourself: *Hey, who's the best team? Who—and how—can we put together the best team to capture this project? Who's got experience with this owner? Who's worked on this type of project—whether it's a major highway, a major transit line, or a major airport? Who has the credentials? Who's actually done this kind of work before? Have I? Can I live* with—if I'm going to partner with a contractor—the contract they're going to offer me? Can I negotiate a fair contract? If I'm going to work for an owner, can we get a fair contract in place? Do I know the owner? Have I worked with them before? Have I been successful in working with them in the past?

There's a lot to consider before going after these projects. The early decisions you make will play a critical role in driving your success and profitability. Once that's settled, you need to prioritize your execution. You've got to focus during your proposal development—and then be ready to streamline the subsequent phases.

CASE STUDY: I-17, BETWEEN THOMAS ROAD AND DUNLAP AVENUE DESIGN BUILD FOR ADOT IN DOWNTOWN PHOENIX

Now, let me tell you about one of my first design build jobs. It was with the Arizona Department of Transportation on I-17 in downtown Phoenix—from Thomas Road all the way up to Dunlap Avenue.

It was about a six-mile corridor. We were adding auxiliary lanes, widening bridges, relocating utilities, building noise and sound walls, and reconstructing about three or four interchanges. Initially, the project was awarded to us as a design contract—we won it when it was planned to be a traditional design-bid-build job.

We secured that win—I was with AECOM at the time—in 1995. We began working on the design, and about 20% into it, we were collaborating with Terry Borland, the project manager at ADOT. He mentioned that the Director at the time, Mary Peters, was considering turning the project into ADOT's first design build effort. So, we continued moving forward with the design as they explored that possibility.

By the time we reached around 30% design completion, the decision was made: it was officially going to be a design build project. At that point, we weren't exactly sure what would happen next. We spoke with ADOT and with Terry, and they told us they would be issuing a solicitation for a general consultant to help develop all the procurement documents and define ADOT's approach to procuring design build work.

That shift felt like a big challenge—but also one we were well-prepared for. So, we made the decision to pivot and pursue that opportunity. We did have one concern, though: since we had already been working on the final design, we wondered whether that might limit the competition or create potential conflicts.

We talked to ADOT about our concern and asked, "What if no one else submits a Statement of Qualifications (SOQ)? Can we still be selected if we're the only ones?" They took that question to the Attorney General's office, and the decision came back that as long as we scored at least 70%, we could legitimately be awarded the contract.

And that's exactly what happened. No one else submitted—everyone assumed we were miles ahead of the competition. We ended up being selected as the general consultant, negotiated the contract, and got started.

One of the first things we decided to do as a team was to really dive into understanding design build and what was happening with it across the country. Back in the '90s, there weren't many examples to look at—but there were at least two strong ones. One was the San Joaquin Corridor Project in Southern California, which used a design build approach. The other was the I-15/US-80 project in Salt Lake City, where they were rebuilding these entire corridors in preparation for the upcoming Winter Olympics.

So, we decided to do a few site visits with the project teams on those earlier design build jobs to really understand how they handled their corridors—how they worked, what went well, and what didn't. We spent about a week visiting the San Joaquin project, and we brought along members from both ADOT and the Federal Highway Administration. Then we did the same in Utah, meeting with the project team and UDOT. We learned a lot—what worked, what didn't, and where the pain points were.

When we returned, we used those insights to craft our own strategy for how we wanted to approach procurement and define the boundaries for the design builders. We ended up writing all the procurement documents and developing the methodologies ADOT would use for future design build projects.

For this particular project, ADOT selected Granite/Sundt as the design builder. The project at that time had a construction value of $81 million— but in today's dollars, it would be closer to $350 million. Back then, it was still a fairly significant job.

We established a project office adjacent and along the I-17 project corridor and placed our whole team there. I had five people in the office—a small, tight-knit group. Granite/Sundt had their major project staff there too, along with their lead designer. We all worked closely together, shoulder to shoulder. Our team was hands-on with every review. If something went wrong in the field, our folks were out there working alongside the project manager and the design builder to solve it on the spot.

It ended up being one of the best projects I've ever worked on. One thing that really made a difference was the level of support from ADOT's leadership. Since it was their first design build, Mary Peters told Terry Borland, "If you need anything, call me directly, and I'll make sure you get it." That kind of backing was huge. Terry had a direct line to Mary and the department's leadership, and he was able to get decisions made and issues resolved in hours—something that normally might take days or even weeks.

That project turned out to be a great success. It was originally scheduled for 19 months, but we completed it in just 16. The job won a partnering award, and both we and the design builder made good money on it. The state was incredibly pleased with the outcome.

CASE STUDY: IH 635 MANAGED LANES P3 IN DALLAS FOR TXDOT

Fast forward to the mid-2000s—I was the proposal lead for AECOM on the IH 635 Managed Lanes P3 project in the Dallas District for TxDOT. It was a massive $2.4 billion construction job. We teamed up with Dragados-Williams Brothers Joint Venture (JV) on the proposal, and we also had strong support from our local Dallas team, which also included a number of talented DBE subconsultants.

The competing team came down to our team led by ACS, with Cintra and Ferrovial as our competition. We got about 75% through the proposal process when Williams Brothers unexpectedly withdrew from the competition, leaving the team in a tough spot. All of our local contractor relationships were tied to them.

To fill the gap, we brought in a joint venture made up of Kiewit, Zachry, and Granite. This change came pretty late in the game—again, about 75% into the proposal—but they stepped up in a big way. They were a strong team and made a huge contribution.

We ended up submitting a construction bid of $2.4 billion. Ferrovial's team, surprisingly, submitted a construction bid of just $1 billion. I was shocked—we all were. We had no idea how they got their numbers that low. Ultimately, TxDOT had no real choice—they had to award the project to Cintra, Ferrovial, and their team based on their construction bid.

But what was really interesting is that after negotiations and financial close, the actual construction value escalated to a point where it ended up being just $200,000 higher than our original bid. And yet, the contract still went to them.

It's very important in these jobs to understand your competition and how your competition will also move through these projects. Understanding how your competition is going to react to a project and how they're going to bid the project, and what they're going to do is really important, too.

I'm going to talk more about that in detail in some of the later chapters. But everything you can do up front to understand the challenges of a particular job—who your competition is and what you're likely to face—is incredibly important. These pursuits are expensive. I think, as a team, we ended up spending around $20 million just to go after that project. So these are things you really need to think about—very seriously.

Chapter 2
Tasks and Activities Prior
to the RFQ

1.   Identifying Your Targets

Everyone needs to recognize that alternative delivery projects take years to develop internally before going to an RFQ. The owner goes through a tremendous amount of information just to get it to the point where they can issue that RFQ. There are preliminary designs, conceptual designs, and environmental analyses.

They usually have stakeholder meetings. They will have community meetings. They'll meet with the local municipalities.

They'll meet with utilities. They'll usually hire consultants to help them through the process. This is even before they hire a program manager, management consultant, or general consultant.

There's a tremendous amount of activity that happens just to get to the point where an agency can say, "We're almost ready to issue an RFQ." So if you're serious about targeting a project, don't go after something that's already been in the works for two years—where you've missed the window to meet with the owner or participate in those early, formative activities. If you come in late, you'll be playing catch-up, and you simply won't be competitive.

Instead, focus on identifying projects early—projects that are just getting started—so you can be part of the progress from the beginning. You need to identify your targets very early, ideally when they first appear in the Capital Improvement Plan.

We'll dive into that more in another section of this chapter, but here's the takeaway: start your process at least two years before the RFQ is issued. That gives you time to build relationships, shape your strategy, and truly position your team.

CASE STUDY: SH 130 TURNPIKE EDA FOR TTA AND TXDOT

For example, we began working on the State Highway (SH) 130 Turnpike project at least two years before the RFQ was even released. That kind of early engagement made a significant difference.

We teamed up with Fluor on that project back in the early 2000s—around January 2000. The RFQ wasn't expected until 2002, but we were already aligned with Fluor well ahead of time.

We were actively meeting with the owner, who at that time was the Strategic Projects Office at the Texas Department of Transportation. We had a teaming agreement in place with Fluor, and they had already brought in their partners—TJ Lambredth and Balfour Beatty. Together, we were holding early brainstorming sessions to figure out the best approach for the project.

We were already analyzing our competition, engaging with key stakeholders, and participating in TxDOT's environmental process meetings. As a team, we developed a detailed SWOT analysis—identifying our strengths, weaknesses, opportunities, and threats. We also assessed our competition throughout the entire process.

This kind of work is something every team should be doing *before* the RFQ ever hits the street. And once you've done this groundwork, it's critical to capture everything in a centralized, digital workbook or database. I can't emphasize enough how important good note-taking is. Every time you attend a stakeholder meeting, someone needs to take clear notes—highlighting the key points and lessons learned—and those insights need to be shared across the team. Everyone should be on the same page.

The next step is participating in the early planning meetings, environmental reviews, and community engagement sessions. I've been doing this since around 1995 on nearly every major project I believed we had a shot at. That early involvement makes all the difference.

Some of the most recent examples were from when we were leading business development efforts with Walsh in Los Angeles between 2016 and 2018.

CASE STUDY: WEST SANTA ANA TRANSIT CORRIDOR FOR LA METRO

One particular project we targeted heavily was the West Santa Ana Transit Corridor Project—a $4.5 billion initiative that was being considered as a potential P3.

We began following the project closely around 2017. I attended nearly every public meeting and community engagement session held during the environmental process. I also participated in meetings with LA Metro and met many of the individuals leading the planning and environmental efforts. I connected with all of the consultants working on the project and identified who the ultimate project manager would be for LA Metro—it was Monica Born. She introduced us to several major stakeholders involved in the project.

We also identified who the opposition was, and through these meetings, we were able to get introduced to all the key players. That allowed us to schedule one-on-one meetings with most of them, which in turn gave us more opportunities to build a stronger team and gain a deeper understanding of the project and its true needs for successful delivery.

My advice to anyone pursuing large-scale projects like this—start developing your strategy early. Get your internal team engaged. Divide up responsibilities and meetings—it doesn't have to fall on just one person. Spread the work across the full team so that everyone involved in the pursuit is part of the process from the beginning.

2. Attend Committee and Board Meetings and Review Notes

Another important thing you want to do is attend community and board meetings—and make sure to review the notes and materials from those meetings.

CASE STUDY: SANTA ANA TRANSIT CORRIDOR FOR LA METRO

On that same West Santa Ana Corridor project, we attended all of Metro's committee and board meetings, starting very early in the process.

We didn't just show up—we reviewed all the agendas ahead of time. Often, the agenda itself might only be a couple of pages, but the supporting documentation could be 50 to 100 pages long. Those attachments were packed with background information, and reviewing them gave us deep insight into what was really happening behind the scenes.

So, what's the value in attending those meetings and reviewing all that material? You gain a tremendous amount of information. You learn who the project advocates are, who the opponents are, and who the most vocal participants tend to be. You start to understand the internal challenges the owner and their team are dealing with. By preparing ahead of time, you walk into those meetings almost as informed as the board members themselves.

That allows you to really listen for the key points, take meaningful notes, and absorb what matters most. And if you're inclined, many of these meetings have time set aside for public comment. Most of the time, the public is allowed about two minutes to each person to ask questions—and that's an opportunity to learn who is for or against the project and why. You can start to become known to the board, and from there, you may be able to set up individual meetings with board members or consultants.

In my experience, most board members are willing to sit down with you if you approach them respectfully and come prepared. The same goes for consultants—they're usually open to having a conversation, especially if you've shown genuine interest and done your homework.

3.   Meet with the Owner

Most of the owner's team is usually willing to sit down with you during this stage. Again, the key is information gathering—learning as much as you can about the project.

And once again, I highly recommend taking copious notes. Store everything in your digital workbook and share it with your team. There should be no secrets. If you're working with a team, every member should be fully aware of what's going on. Transparency leads to alignment, and alignment leads to stronger proposals.

The next step is setting up one-on-one meetings with the owner. I've been doing these meetings for upcoming projects since the early 1980s, and over the years, I've developed a strong ability to uncover what the owner's true "hot buttons" are—what they care most about—and gain a deep understanding of their project constraints.

CASE STUDY: WEST SANTA ANA TRANSIT CORRIDOR PROJECT FOR LA METRO

For example, on the same West Santa Ana Transit Corridor project, I had several meetings with Monica Born, who was the project manager for LA Metro. We stayed in contact throughout the entire pre-RFQ and pre-RFP process. During our conversations, we discussed how LA Metro was struggling to determine which delivery method to pursue—whether to go with traditional design build or a progressive design build approach.

They had started receiving a lot of feedback from contractors who were expressing frustration with the design build process. Many contractors felt they weren't seeing the profit margins they expected and believed that progressive design build offered a better model. Unlike traditional design build, where the scope is clearly defined up front, progressive design build starts with very little scope in place. The contractor is selected based on qualifications, and then works collaboratively with the owner to develop the scope, the cost estimates, and ultimately, deliver the project together.

It's a very effective delivery method—and it doesn't carry the kind of upfront pursuit cost we had on IH 635 Managed Lanes P3, where we spent $20 million just to go after the job.

Because LA Metro was still debating between these two models, the timeline for the project kept shifting. By the time I left Walsh in late 2018 and joined Brian Ansari & Associates in March 2020, I was still in discussions with Monica. Even after the transition, those relationships and insights carried forward.

And I continued discussions with them. However, in June 2020, she informed me that she was no longer going to be involved with the West Santa Ana project and that this project was going to move to June Susilo, who was now taking over as the PM. Fortunately, I knew June very well.

I had previously worked with June on other projects, and therefore was able to continue my contacts with her on the West Santa Ana Corridor job. We continued to meet with June, and she brought in others within her group. At that time, we decided to develop a construction management strategy.

June brought in her lead construction manager, and we were able to talk with Brad Owens and get his take on the construction management for the project. The point that I'm making here is any of the contacts you're making, if you're going to continue a relationship with that client, every contact you make is important. Every relationship you make is important.

It doesn't matter if the job changes or the PM should switch, you can still recover if you do your due diligence and you do it right. So again, on that one, we continue to take great notes. We continue to develop our digital workbook so everyone continues to learn from that project.

4. Meet Internally with Your Team

The next key step is to continue meeting internally with your team. You want to have a clear strategy for sharing your findings and insights throughout the pursuit process.

Start hosting internal meetings early—*formal* meetings—even before the RFQ is issued. During this phase, it's critical to conduct a SWOT analysis and an initial risk assessment. Take a close look at your team's strengths and weaknesses, analyze your competition's strengths and weaknesses, and use that information to develop a mitigation strategy that addresses potential risks.

CASE STUDY: NORTH MOUNT VERNON AVENUE OVER THE UPRR FOR SAN BERNARDINO COUNTY TRANSPORTATION AUTHORITY (SBCTA)

I'll give you an example. When I was with Walsh, we targeted a project with the San Bernardino County Transportation Authority (SBTA). It involved replacing an old wooden trestle bridge on North Mount Vernon Avenue that crossed over the Union Pacific Railroad (UPRR) and the historic San Bernardino Depot.

We had been in ongoing conversations with the client for several months, particularly with Paula Beauchamp, the Director of their Project Delivery Group. Through those discussions, we were able to learn all the nuances of the project directly from the source—giving us valuable insight that shaped our approach and strategy.

And then we formed a tentative team of experts with experience of people who worked with the San Bernardino County Transportation Authority (SBCTA), people who were experienced in bridge rebuilding. This was an old trestle bridge that was built over the railroad yard. Union Pacific was working right under that bridge.

That railroad was going to remain active throughout the project. We quickly determined that we'd only have limited windows to perform construction. Even dismantling and rebuilding the bridge required close coordination with the railroad operators. It was a relatively small project in terms of size, but it was highly complex.

We needed people with the right kind of experience—people who knew how to work with a unionized railroad like the Union Pacific. Fortunately, we found an excellent highway and bridge engineering team to bring on board. We walked the site together and began developing conceptual ideas to solve the key challenges.

Then we started holding internal team meetings. One of the first was a SWOT analysis and risk assessment session. That process helped us identify some critical gaps. We realized that our lead bridge engineer—while brilliant—might not fully meet the qualifications needed to get us shortlisted.

That led to an important question: *Do we need to find a different bridge engineer, or can we revise this one's resume to meet the RFQ criteria?* After reviewing his experience in detail, we discovered he actually had the qualifications—we just needed to rework his resume. Once we did that, we were confident we could get through the shortlisting process.

We also met with UPRR well before the RFQ was issued. That gave us insight into their concerns and priorities. In parallel, we held multiple meetings with the County of San Bernardino, met their consultants, and even held one-on-one discussions with their internal team.

These are exactly the kinds of things you should be doing well before an RFQ is released. We were also able to define early strategies for design, construction, financials, operations, and maintenance. And, as always, we captured all our notes in a centralized digital workbook to keep the team aligned and informed.

5.　Prepare Initial Go/No-Go Form

The next thing you'll want to do is prepare an initial **go/no-go** form.

If your company doesn't already have one, it's time to develop one. Most larger firms—whether contractors or designers—have a go/no-go process in place. This should be completed *before* the RFQ is even issued.

Your go/no-go form should capture essential details:

- The anticipated timing of the project.

- The estimated value.

- Your team's strengths and weaknesses.

- The key risks.

- Whether you believe the project is financially viable.

- Whether you've worked with the owner before.

- Whether you've successfully worked with your proposed team members.

Essentially, you want to lay out everything you know about the project—every inch of insight you can gather.

When you're working for a large firm, like when I was with Walsh, every go/no-go decision for a major project—especially design build—had to go through an executive risk committee. That's a standard practice for most major companies. It was the same at AECOM when I was there. On significant design build pursuits, the go/no-go form was submitted to the risk committee for review and approval.

It's critical to get buy-in from these committees early. You want to make sure they're aware of the opportunity and support the pursuit. As a project manager—or even as a project director or senior regional manager—you don't want to move forward on your own and risk overextending without executive approval. I had that responsibility at AECOM as a senior regional manager, and I made sure every major pursuit had risk committee backing.

CASE STUDY: LAX AUTOMATED PEOPLE MOVER P3 FOR LAWA

Let me share a case study that really illustrates this process.

When I was at Walsh, we pursued the LAX Automated People Mover project—a $1.6 billion P3 opportunity. We started the pursuit in June 2016 and continued through February 2017. We completed the first stage of our internal go/no-go process and received initial approval to move forward.

At that stage, there were six proposers who submitted Statements of Qualifications (SOQs) for the project. It was highly competitive, and our preparation through the go/no-go process played a critical role in helping us navigate that pursuit.

It turned out that all six firms were qualified to move forward on the $1.6 billion LAX Automated People Mover project. At that point, we revisited and updated our go/no-go decision.

Up to that stage, we hadn't spent a significant amount of money—just the cost of forming the team and submitting the SOQ. That probably came to about $100,000 to $150,000. But moving into the next phase of the pursuit, we were looking at a $50 million investment just to compete.

Now we had to ask ourselves: *With six qualified teams in the running, do we realistically have a one-in-six chance of winning this job? Do we have a competitive edge that clearly sets us apart from the others?*

Our team consisted of Walsh, Granite, and AECOM for construction and design, with Plenary, Walsh, and AECOM also serving as the developer. We all had prior experience working at LAX and strong reputations there. But we were up against a couple of highly motivated Spanish firms that were extremely hungry for the job.

We completed a second go/no-go evaluation. The conclusion? Our chances of winning had significantly diminished. Based on our internal review, the likelihood of success was estimated at just 15%.

After careful discussion, the joint venture—Walsh, Granite, AECOM, and Plenary—made the difficult but smart decision to withdraw. We drafted a respectful letter to Los Angeles World Airports (LAWA) informing them that we would not be advancing or submitting a proposal.

And honestly, it was the best decision we could've made.

When your chances of winning are only 15% and you're facing a $50 million pursuit cost, the risk simply doesn't justify the investment. This is exactly where the go/no-go process proves its value. It helps you make sound, data-informed decisions—before you're too deep in to turn back.

In that case, we had already invested nearly two years tracking the project before making the decision to pull out. We had no idea LAWA would qualify all six teams. That was a major lesson learned, and I'm glad I can share it here.

Now, the next thing I want to talk about is your initial discussions with teaming partners.

6. Initial Discussions with Teaming Partners

Engage with potential teaming partners as early as possible. You really can't afford to wait. Early engagement gives you time to assess their availability, strengths, and potential contributions. Start by building a matrix of findings and keep it updated for your internal team.

When you conduct your SWOT analysis (as discussed earlier), you'll begin to see where the gaps are:

- Do we have someone with the expertise in this area?

- Do we have relationships with the right stakeholders?

As these questions arise, work with your internal team to identify the holes. Once you've identified the gaps, collaborate to find ways to fill them. If you can't fill those gaps, it might be time to revisit your go/no-go decision.

The good news is—if you're early in the process—you still have time to pivot, partner, or bring in additional resources. That's the advantage of getting started early and being proactive about building your team.

7. Update Initial Go/No-Go and Submit for Approval

At this stage, you should update your go/no-go form with all the new information you've gathered. This includes:

- An updated budget estimate for the RFQ and proposal phase.

- Risk reassessments.

- Any major developments in team composition, project scope, or competition.

Resubmit the form to your executive team for approval. Skipping this step can have serious consequences. I've seen it firsthand—if you spend a significant amount of money on a pursuit without executive approval and lose the job, it reflects poorly on leadership and decision-making. This step protects you, your team, and the company.

8. Develop a Detailed Planning and Pursuit Document

Once your go/no-go form is approved, the next step is to develop a detailed planning and pursuit document. This will serve as your roadmap throughout the RFQ and proposal phases.

This document should include:

- A complete work breakdown of all phases.
- A budget for the pursuit.
- Your approved go/no-go form.
- All relevant documents from your digital workbook.
- A procurement schedule.
- A contract execution plan.

This planning document is critical. Don't wait until you're shortlisted to begin—start preparing now so your team is ready to move swiftly.

Establish a regular meeting cadence with your team. Determine how often you'll meet based on the pursuit schedule and workload. At this stage, weekly or biweekly meetings are typical. There's always something to address—gaps to fill, challenges to overcome, and strategy to refine. Having your full team engaged makes a huge difference.

9. Initiate and Negotiate Teaming Agreements

Start the process of initiating and negotiating teaming agreements with all your partners—even before the proposal phase begins. While you may not have final terms and conditions worked out yet, it's important to establish the framework early.

If needed, begin with a Memorandum of Understanding (MOU)—keep it short and focused (2–3 pages). It should outline:

- The roles and responsibilities of each partner.

- The general framework for collaboration.

- A commitment to move forward together pending further development.

Each agreement should be **tailored** to your role in the team:

- If you're the developer, have agreements with your design build team.

- If you're the design builder, you'll need separate agreements with your design team and major subcontractors.

Getting these agreements started early helps avoid last-minute confusion and aligns everyone's expectations from the beginning.

You're going to want to have it with all your major subcontractors. You don't want your major subcontractors in a teaming meeting with you, talking about how you're going to win strategies and things like that if you haven't entered into some type of confidentiality agreement. Your MOU should talk about confidentiality between the parties.

Your teaming agreements need to talk about the confidentiality between the parties. You don't have to have the dollar values in there right now, but conceptually on these types of projects, your designer is going to want to get paid probably a reduced multiplier and is going to want a success fee. You have to understand that going in, cause they're going to be doing real work for you.

They're not just going to be doing proposal work. They're going to be designing as you get into the proposal. They're going to probably advance the design of wherever you have it at least another 10%.

And you're going to want to have them look at your and their ideas, what you call alternative technical concepts. And that's going to take some time. Again, after you get all the teaming agreements done, those teaming agreements need to be signed, they need to be filed and they need to be put into your detailed planning document.

Also, you need to get that executed go/no-go form into that document, too.

10. Engage Your Proposal Team

The next step is to engage your proposal team. You'll need a dedicated lead—someone who can oversee the proposal process from beginning to end. This person will need to understand the format, requirements, and expectations of the RFQ and eventually the RFP. Early on, they'll be responsible for breaking down the RFQ and building a response matrix to divide and assign tasks.

Even at the SOQ phase, many owners require an extraordinary amount of documentation—sometimes hundreds of pages. It's simply not possible for one person to handle it all. You need an experienced proposal lead who has done this before and can manage the process smoothly.

Engage that person **before** the RFQ is issued. Bring them into team discussions, share your digital workbook and planning documents, and fully brief them on the work done so far—often years of preparation. Get their commitment early. You may even need to work with their supervisor to secure their time.

These pursuits become full-time efforts for the proposal team once they begin, and it's critical to lock that down early.

11. Strategic Planning Meeting with Team and Partners

Once teaming agreements are in place, schedule a strategic planning meeting with your internal team and external partners. Your proposal lead should help develop the agenda and may also bring in matrices or tools from past proposals with the same client.

During this meeting, cover:

- A project overview.

- Pursuit expectations.

- Team responsibilities.

- Assignment of tasks and deliverables.

Use this time to formally kick off the team's collective efforts. Keep up the due diligence, document every assignment, and circulate materials to ensure alignment. Begin building a running action item list, tracking what's missing, who's responsible, and when it's due.

If you haven't already, assign a pursuit manager—someone responsible for coordinating everything. This may not be your project manager, especially if you're a contractor (they're often tied up in the field). At AECOM, for example, we had a dedicated Alternative Delivery Group with experienced pursuit managers. I served in that role both at AECOM and Walsh, traveling nationwide to manage pursuits.

12.   Coordinate Team Assignments and Due Diligence

Your pursuit manager should now be coordinating all action items, meetings, and team responsibilities. These meetings can be virtual—they don't need to be face-to-face—but they must be consistent and well-documented.

Make sure your assignment tracker and digital workbook are up to date. Decide where to store your documents:

- Use a secure, shared platform like a G drive, Microsoft Teams, SharePoint, or another system your company supports.

- Implement check-in/check-out protocols to manage version control and transparency.

This centralized approach helps ensure everyone has access to the latest information and avoids duplication or confusion.

13.   Continue Participation in Stakeholder Meetings

Don't stop attending planning, environmental, community, and board meetings. You don't have to attend every single one personally—assign team members to represent your group, and make sure they're taking and sharing notes.

This kind of shared involvement not only spreads the workload, but it also builds ownership across your team. When everyone is engaged, they're more invested in the project. You'll see better collaboration, more creative input, and deeper insights as they participate in key conversations.

Keep populating your digital workbook with new findings, updates, and insights from these meetings.

14.   Ongoing Owner Meetings

Continue holding owner meetings for as long as possible. Once the RFQ is released, a "cloak of silence" often sets in, and you may be restricted from further direct contact.

So maximize the pre-RFQ window. These meetings are your chance to:

- Showcase your team's capabilities.

- Build trust and familiarity.

- Stay informed about shifting priorities or changes in schedule.

These can be virtual and just as effective—just be mindful of optics. If the owner brings two people to a meeting, don't overwhelm them with 20 from your side. Match the tone and size appropriately.

Ask smart, respectful questions:

- Is the RFQ still on track for release in the next 30 days?

- Has the scope or schedule changed?

- Are there new priorities or stakeholders involved?

If you're doing things right, the owner may begin asking you for input—that's a great sign. I've had multiple situations where we developed such a strong relationship before the RFQ that the owner began turning to us for advice. That kind of trust is invaluable, and it positions your team incredibly well for success.

Chapter 3
Assumptions for Preparing Your Proposal

1.   Overview of Proposal Preparation

The purpose of this chapter is to focus on your approach—and more specifically, how that approach impacts the profitability of preparing for and executing a complex project.

As we move into proposal preparation, we're going to make a few key assumptions:

- Your team is already well-positioned.

- You've gained meaningful insight into the client's priorities and major project influencers.

- You've engaged with community and political stakeholders.

- The technical aspects and challenges of the project are clearly understood.

With those assumptions in place, I want to shift focus to team preparation and positioning. And to do that, I'll walk you through a case study.

This case study will highlight how our team's early positioning and pre-RFQ efforts led to us being short-listed and pre-qualified for the RFP. I'll break down the strategies we used and spotlight some of the key actions that helped us submit a strong SOQ.

CASE STUDY: I-395 CORRIDOR AND SIGNATURE BRIDGE P3 IN MIAMI FOR FDOT

The project I'll be referencing is the I-395 Corridor and Signature Bridge Project—a P3 we pursued in Miami for the Florida Department of Transportation (FDOT). I was the design sponsor, responsible for proposal oversight, and officer in charge for STV (Lead Designer) on this project.

We worked on this proposal from November 2015 through November 2016. In early November 2015, Odebrecht, the Lead Design Builder invited us to Coral Gables, Florida, to have a preliminary discussion about being the lead designer on the team. Odebrecht had already established strong relationships with the local FDOT district.

They had already completed several successful projects for FDOT, as well as for other FDOT districts. They had also done a tremendous amount of pre-positioning and due diligence—not only with the agency, but also with key stakeholders, third parties involved in the project, and the consultant community.

MDX (Miami-Dade Expressway Authority) was another agency involved in the project, and Odebrecht had also partnered with them. In fact, Odebrecht had a strong track record with MDX, having both current and previous contracts with the agency.

The project was valued at approximately $850 million, making it what I would consider close to a Mega-Project—and in many ways, it truly was one.

The scope included the reconstruction and addition of general-purpose lanes on both MDX and I-395, as well as modifications to the interchange with I-95. One of the signature elements of the project was a landmark bridge over Biscayne Boulevard, along with long stretches of precast concrete segmental bridges and approximately 30 other bridge structures.

One particularly interesting historical note: the original I-395, built in the 1960s, actually bifurcated (split in two) a historic black (minority) community—dividing and disrupting the neighborhood for decades.

The project was going to raise I-395 within that community so it no longer would be bifurcated, and it had a linear park element that would be built below the bridge and the structures. The procurement and the project also included presentations and reviews for an aesthetic design review panel made up of diverse stakeholders who would also be part of the selection process. Odebrecht also had two JV partners.

They had Zachry and Traylor Brothers, both great general highway and and bridge firms. I had previously worked with both of these contractors on past projects and proposals when I was with AECOM. Both were an excellent choice as partners, with Zachry doing many large highway projects and Traylor Brothers doing many large bridge projects, including signature bridges.

STV did our due diligence on Odebrecht, and everything came up all right, including running a Dun & Bradstreet report to look at their financials and payment profile. We interviewed with the joint venture in mid-November and received an MOU and a draft teaming agreement later that month. Legal and I reviewed and commented on the agreement.

We negotiated what we could, signed the teaming agreement and we were on board. Brian Flaherty, who was my boss at the time, and I immediately brought on a large project proposal manager, Jim Kramer. Jim Kramer had originally worked with Parsons, another major design firm, and had worked on many major bridge projects and a lot of alternative delivery projects.

Jim really filled all of the internal lead positions for our design team. We also started talking with Wantman Group in Florida about bringing them in as a joint venture partner. They were a fairly large design firm that had great local experience.

So prior to our first brainstorming meeting with Mauricio Gonzalez, who was the lead for Odebrecht, we developed an agenda for the brainstorming session and distributed the agenda to all of our attendees. The agenda included introductions, the makeup of the project team, and the goals for the pre-RFQ phase and other activities for the session. So we had our first strategy session with Odebrecht JV and key members of the STV team in early December 2015.

We discussed other local and experts that Odebrecht had been talking with to bring to the design team. That included Corven Engineering for the viaduct precast segmental design, CSA Group for traffic, Bernard Zyscovich for architectural elements, Lakes Engineering for structures/approaches, FR Aleman & Associates for ITS, survey and lighting; Terracon for geotechnical, and Fernandez Beraud for landscape architecture. Several of these firms were already DBE, and at that meeting, we performed a SWOT analysis to determine the strengths and weaknesses, opportunities, and threats to our team and our competition.

From that analysis, we determined that we still needed another partner for highway engineering, a signature bridge firm, an architect, a bridge lighting specialty firm, a peer review firm for the segmental bridge, and someone for the design of temporary towers and falsework. Based on that analysis and the expertise of our firms, we brought on Wantman Group for the highway design, Schlaich, Bergemann and Partners (SBP) for the signature bridge design and Dissing+Weitling for the bridge architecture.

Dissing+Weitling had worked with SBP on many signature bridges. We brought on Brilliant Lighting for the bridge lighting, DiBari Innovative Design for lighting projections, Janssen Spaans Engineering, Inc. for the peer review for the segmental bridges, and CE for the temporary towers and falsework.

Odebrecht agreed with STV on Wantman and Corven Engineering doing a design JV, so we entered into a design JV there. At the brainstorming session, we developed a detailed activity list outlining all the key actions required from that point forward until the RFQ was issued. This list included the specifics of our due diligence efforts and identified everyone we planned to meet with—stakeholders, third parties, the aesthetic design review panel, past consultants, and owner representatives.

We also outlined a range of strategic and technical tasks, including:

- Brainstorming and developing potential Alternative Technical Concepts (ATCs).

- Generating early concepts for the signature bridge.

- Developing a baseline project schedule.

- Conducting a site visit with the full team.

- Performing a comprehensive SWOT analysis.

- Creating a detailed organizational chart.

- Gathering resumes for key personnel.

This planning phase was crucial to ensure we were aligned, proactive, and well-positioned once the RFQ was officially released.

After the initial brainstorming session and once all the design subconsultants were brought on board, Jim Kramer, our project manager, developed a comprehensive spreadsheet detailing the design scope for each bridge. It identified every design element and clearly outlined which firm was responsible for what. We reached an agreement with Odebrecht and the design subconsultants on how to divide up the design responsibilities.

I drafted MOUs for each of the design subs, attaching our draft design agreement with Odebrecht. All of the design subs and STV signed off on the MOUs. This process was completed by mid-December 2015.

Shortly after the MOUs were finalized, we held our second brainstorming session. Jim Kramer and Mauricio collaborated with the team to craft the agenda, and all key team members were invited to participate.

The agenda included:

- Team introductions.

- A review of the overall schedule and upcoming activities before the RFQ was issued.

- Initial concept development for the signature bridge.

- A status update on our due diligence effort.

- Early ideas for Alternative Technical Concepts (ATCs).

- Development of a team marketing document.

- Resume updates for Odebrecht's marketing package (and more).

During the meeting, we walked through each item in detail. We then split into task groups focused on signature bridge design, ATCs, and the marketing brochure. Each group scheduled its work independently while aligning with the master schedule.

As the signature bridge concepts took shape and the team brochure neared completion, we began engaging with:

- Key stakeholders.

- Third parties.

- The Aesthetic Design Review Panel.

- Past consultants.

- Owner representatives.

- And individuals we believed were likely to be on the selection committee.

We introduced our team to each group and asked a critical question: *What are your hot buttons?* Understanding what matters most to your client and stakeholders is essential. It allows you to tailor your approach, strengthen your team, and ensure you're aligning with their top priorities.

From there, we met with the Aesthetics Review Committee, continuing our outreach and alignment efforts. We asked them what their goals were and what their wants were for the signature bridge. Nowhere else did it really say that. I mean, there's been a lot of discussions with a lot of things written, but getting that information directly from them was a key to successfully coming up with the concept that they would like and buy into.

We also met with five of the team members on the review panel, so we really covered all of them. We asked what they liked and didn't like.

We took copious notes, produced those notes, and distributed it to all of the internal members of the team. We continued these meetings and made sure if they only had five people at the meetings, we didn't have any more than five people at the meeting.

Each task group refined what they were doing based on the meetings and the input that we continue to have with the stakeholders, third parties, the aesthetic design review panel, the consultants, the owner's reps, and the people who would most likely be on the selection committee throughout the period.

At our next meeting with the Aesthetic Design Review Panel, we presented our initial concepts for the signature bridge and received excellent feedback. We had developed four or five early ideas—most of them were rough, almost like napkin sketches, which was intentional. We didn't want to appear locked into a single concept too early in the process.

By showing a range of conceptual ideas, we invited input—and that openness paid off. The panel responded positively and offered helpful suggestions. One key piece of feedback was, *"We'd love to see something a little more striking—maybe some lighting on the bridge, something a bit more showy."* That kind of direction was exactly what we were looking for.

The most important takeaway from these sessions? Create open dialogue. Don't do all the talking. In fact, in our meetings with stakeholders and the aesthetic review panel, they probably did 70% of the talking—and that was by design. You gain so much more by listening.

As we continued refining our ATCs and bridge concepts based on this feedback, we also began drafting our SOQ. Thanks to our early positioning and thorough pre-RFQ efforts, we were able to submit a strong, well-informed SOQ—which ultimately got us short-listed for the RFP.

Just as importantly, that early groundwork gave us a clear head start and allowed us to move forward quickly and confidently once the RFP was officially released.

2.   Team Preparation and Positioning

The next topic we're going to cover is team preparation and positioning, with a focus on pre-RFQ achievements.

At this stage, your team should already be fully assembled. You've submitted a SOQ, and your team has been short-listed or pre-qualified to receive and respond to the Request for Proposals (RFP).

The next critical step is to engage subject matter experts, or SMEs. For those who may not be familiar, SMEs are highly experienced professionals with deep technical knowledge in a specific area. Depending on the nature of the project, this could include:

- Aesthetic bridge design.

- Tunnel engineering.

- Geotechnical analysis.

- Traffic systems and ITS (Intelligent Transportation Systems).

- Drainage and stormwater management.

- Highway geometry.

- Construction operations.

For example, if we're working on a bridge project, we may bring in someone who specializes in aesthetic bridge design. If it's a tunnel project, we'll look for someone with 20+ years of tunnel engineering experience. The key is to align your SMEs with the specific technical challenges of the project.

CASE STUDY: I-405 EXPRESS TOLL LANES DESIGN BUILD IN BELLEVUE, WA, FOR WADOT

Let me give you a concrete example. I was the Project Manager for both the SOQ and proposal for the I-405, 6th Street to I-5 Express Toll Lanes project in Bellevue, Washington.

This was a design build project valued at approximately $174 million, pursued between May 2011 and early 2012, during my time with AECOM. The scope included express toll lanes in each direction, located in the median of the general-purpose lanes, as well as direct connector ramps at major interchanges.

One of the significant challenges of this project involved sloughing high-cut slopes, complex drainage issues, and a large reconstructed interchange that included braided ramps and a long-span bridge.

We were teamed with Kiewit, and had already worked with them successfully on the I-405 Kirkland Phase One project in Kirkland, WA for WADOT. Many of the same team leads and subconsultants returned for this pursuit, creating continuity and strong working relationships. In fact, Kiewit and AECOM began collaborating nearly a year before the RFQ was issued—a testament to our proactive strategy.

During the pre-RFQ phase, we launched an early brainstorming session focused on identifying major ATCs. We invited SMEs from across the country, each with extensive experience in design build and express toll lane projects.

These SMEs specialized in areas such as:

- Interstate highway geometrics.

- ITS and advanced traffic systems.

- Geotechnical engineering.

- Bridges and structural work.

- Drainage and hydrology.

- Construction staging and operations.

Before the brainstorming meeting, team members were tasked with developing initial ATC ideas. We held a full-day session with key staff, during which we presented the project to the SMEs. While it's helpful to provide SMEs with background materials in advance, you can't assume they've absorbed everything. So, we always present the context in detail.

We walked them through:

- Existing site conditions.

- Corridor constraints.

- Key risks and opportunities.

- Google Earth visuals of the project area.

From there, we moved into our ATC presentations, which covered various technical areas: geometrics, ITS, drainage, bridge design, traffic operations, signage and striping, and geotechnical concepts.

Following the presentations, we held a group discussion and brainstorming session to refine and expand on the ideas. This collaborative exchange between the core team and the SMEs was critical in shaping our technical strategy moving forward.

The SMEs engaged in a great deal of discussion and provided valuable suggestions—particularly related to risk and constructability. It was truly a worthwhile day.

Toward the end of the session, all suggestions were documented, and an action list was developed. This was followed by meeting notes and supporting documentation that were shared with all parties.

The outcome of the brainstorming session was significant: we were able to eliminate the braided ramps and long structures, and we developed several suggestions to modify the geometry, minimize deep cuts, and establish a program to evaluate sloughing and the existing cut slopes.

Armed with this groundwork, once we were short-listed and received the RFP, we were able to present our ATCs to WADOT during one of our one-on-one meetings. We received initial feedback and proposed additional soil testing in the deep-cut areas to gather more data.

This was incredibly helpful.

WADOT allowed us to engage in this process—something many owners do not permit. They supported the one-on-one format and honored our request for additional information. Remarkably, they completed the testing and provided the data in less than three weeks from our initial request.

That information enabled us to conduct more detailed analysis of the cut slopes. In fact, we were able to develop alternative designs to stabilize those slopes. The revised geometry also allowed us to shift the alignment further away from the problematic slopes, reducing the severity of the cuts.

Taking this proactive approach early on greatly strengthened our proposal and put us in a more competitive position.

3. Risk Management and Analysis

Start with your first cut at risk management—even at the pre-RFQ stage, conducting a preliminary risk assessment can be extremely valuable. Once your team is organized, sit down together and walk through the entire project scope. Evaluate every discipline and potential risk area—whether it's political, technical, environmental, or related to existing conditions.

This includes:

- Utilities.

- Railroad coordination.

- Right-of-way issues.

- Permitting and regulatory constraints.

- Community or political opposition.

- Contractual and legal risks.

Everything should go into your risk register. If it's a known issue—even if it's vague or unresolved—log it. This is likely your team's first pass at formal risk assessment, so the focus should be on identification, not analysis. Get everyone to participate. You'll refine the details later, but at this stage, just list everything out.

Once the risks are captured, meet with your technical leads to review and begin evaluating operational risks—both during construction and post-completion. From there, move toward building a mitigation strategy for each item.

Create a scoring matrix on the right side of your risk register:

- Is the risk critical?

- Can it be controlled or mitigated?

- Is it going to be costly?

- What's the likelihood and impact?

This early scoring system will help guide your strategy and decision-making.

Be sure to document everything from the risk discussion. Then, invite your Subject Matter Experts (SMEs) to review the risk register. If there are items you're uncertain about, bring in the relevant SME, ask for their input, and incorporate their feedback directly into the register.

Once your risks are outlined and mitigation plans are in progress, revisit your go/no-go decision form. Use the updated information to guide this next round of decision-making.

At this stage—before the SOQ or proposal is submitted—your financial investment is still minimal. Most of the work is based on internal efforts and due diligence. If you discover a fatal flaw, this is the best time to acknowledge it. Either develop a strategy to overcome it or accept that it may be a no-go.

If you're pursuing a Public-Private Partnership (P3), your next step should be developing a financial strategy.

Engage your financial team and developer early. In most P3s, the winning team is selected based on the lowest net present value (NPV). If your NPV isn't competitive, you simply won't win.

Ask yourself and your team:

- What's our financial model?

- How are we structuring the bid to optimize NPV?

- What can be adjusted or innovated to reduce lifecycle costs?

Your financial strategy is often the key differentiator in a successful P3 pursuit.

CASE STUDY: NORTH MOUNT VERNON AVENUE CROSSING OVER THE UPRR IN SAN BERNARDINO COUNTY FOR SBCTA

Let's look at a smaller project where we applied this risk strategy. This was the North Mount Vernon Avenue crossing over the Union Pacific Railroad (UPRR)—a project I mentioned back in Chapter 2.

We performed our risk assessment before submitting the go/no-go form, well in advance of the RFQ. I served as the proposal manager for Walsh on this pursuit.

I developed the initial risk assessment, identifying major risk categories:

- Technical

- Political

- Environmental

- Third-party stakeholders

- Community and owner dynamics

- Contractual and cost risks

- Safety

- Unknowns

- Schedule constraints

Each risk entry included:

- A description of the risk

- Proposed mitigation measures

- A rating of severity and likelihood

- Known and unknown elements

One of the more significant risks involved construction and operational constraints imposed by UPRR. Because of their active rail operations and strict requirements, we had to anticipate potential delays, limitations on work hours, and special permitting needs—all of which were captured in the risk register.

If you remember this project, we were building over a Union Pacific Railroad yard that remained fully operational throughout construction. We had very limited windows during which we could place sections of the bridge over the railroad during the day. Each section had to be completed before we could move on to the next, due to strict constraints set by the railroad. We weren't able to shut the railroad down. The operator's constraints allowed us to close the original bridge during construction, but doing so meant we needed to find a way to get people from one side to the other. A large portion of that could be managed with shuttle service.

One of the ideas we proposed to the owner was to hire a bus during the construction period to transport pedestrians, as this was a highly used pedestrian bridge. That solution was discussed early and became part of our planning approach.

We also addressed several environmental unknowns:

- Hazardous materials.

- Archaeological concerns.

- Horizontal and vertical clearance issues during construction.

- The need to obtain environmental approvals and permits.

- The requirement is to secure an MOU with Union Pacific Railroad.

- Gaining site access for pre-construction services.

- Identification of underground and overhead utilities.

- Gaining community and stakeholder support.

We also considered contract-related and budgetary risks:

- Would the owner's contract be acceptable? Fortunately, we had worked with this owner before and were familiar with their contract terms.

- Could we bring the project in at or under the owner's budget?

- Would our proposed ATCs provide equal or greater value to the project?

- Would the ATCs be approved?

- Could we meet the owner's schedule?

All of these items were added to the risk register.

The risk matrix was shared with all project team members in advance of the risk assessment brainstorming meeting. It was uploaded to our Share-Point folder for the proposal, and team members were asked to populate each column with as much information as they could and add any additional known risks.

At the brainstorming session, the group reviewed the risk matrix and discussed whether any risks had not been identified. Additional risks were added. We went through each risk and each column in detail, made necessary modifications and reached an agreement on how each risk would be managed.

Mitigation measures were then turned into action items, with each item assigned to a responsible party and given a target completion date.

The initial risk assessment and action item list were included as an attachment to our go/no-go submittal to the executive team for further review. Remember, we continuously update our go/no-go assessment as we learn more about the project—which is exactly how it should be. This process continues up until the receipt and review of the RFP.

Our thorough pre-RFQ risk assessment allowed the team to mitigate major risks early and use the risk register as a proactive tool—before we began work on the proposal. This contributed to a more confident go/no-go decision and enabled us to move forward sooner. It also gave the executive team greater confidence in our preparation and understanding of the project risks, resulting in a faster approval process.

Additionally, it helped us get in front of the owner during a one-on-one meeting to discuss specific risks. That dialogue gave us valuable alignment and showed the owner that we were taking the process seriously.

CASE STUDY: SH 121 TOLL ROAD P3 IN DALLAS FOR TX-DOT

Next, I want to discuss financial strategies for a P3 project—specifically, the work we did on the State Highway (SH) 121 Toll Road in Dallas, which had a construction value of $580 million.

A key meeting took place in June 2005 before the RFP was issued. It included the developer, the design builder, and the lead designer.

That was Macquarie, the developer, Kiewit Abrams, the design builder who were in a JV and AECOM the lead designer. The teams were led by Chris Voyce of Macquarie, Mark Hildebrand of Kiewit and myself, Michael Shapiro. We knew from our due diligence and in talking with the TxDOT's Strategic Group in Austin, led by Phil Russell, that Alternative Financial Concepts (AFCs) were going to be part of the RFP.

We spent the day brainstorming financial strategies. Chris Voyce explained his ideas of the AFCs and asked us to consider what could be improved on the operations and maintenance (O&M) side. He also emphasized the importance of planning for the handback period—what we would need to do to ensure a smooth transition at the end of the concession.

Most P3 projects—like this one—have a long-term O&M period. In this case, the term was 50 years. Most P3s also include handback requirements, which can vary depending on the element of work. For example, TxDOT requires a 50-year life expectancy on structures at handback, whereas pavement may only require an additional 10 years, and so on.

Some of the concepts we explored were also part of our technical strategy. While I don't consider myself a final authority, I do have extensive experience in identifying creative alternatives—different ways to "skin a cat," so to speak. Some of these concepts can serve as technical approaches to improve cost and performance.

For instance:

- Do you need to build out the entire facility up front?

- Or can the initial construction meet the requirements of early traffic volumes?

- Can the future phases of the build-out be deferred and delivered later, reducing upfront financing needs?

When we discussed this concept, Macquarie's O&M team shared insights into the elements that typically drive long-term costs and challenges. These included:

- Structures.

- Pavement.

- Drainage.

- Erosion protection.

- Lighting.

- Landscaping.

- Intelligent Transportation Systems (ITS).

- Revenue collection systems.

At that point, it was agreed that each element—and the requirements for handback—needed to be clearly identified and evaluated. I stated that our team would collaborate with the construction leads and Macquarie's O&M team to develop concepts and strategies for phasing construction. This included looking at designing structures for a 100-year life, exploring pavement design alternatives, and developing maintenance strategies for each asset class identified by Macquarie's O&M staff.

We also agreed that a life-cycle-cost analysis would be conducted during the proposal phase for each of these elements, taking into account initial capital costs, ongoing operation and maintenance costs, and handback obligations.

As a group, we brainstormed the elements of work to be evaluated. I mentioned that our team would start analyzing traffic volumes—both during the initial 10 years and over the full 50-year life of the toll road. This analysis would help us better understand the demands on initial construction, future build-out needs, and the long-term O&M strategies and costs leading up to handback.

Our team committed to starting that analysis immediately.

An action item list was created, assigning each task to a responsible party along with a target completion date. A tentative schedule was developed for each element of work. We also discussed and agreed upon follow-up meetings to track progress.

It was agreed that analyzing different financial and technical strategies early on would enhance our proposal's competitiveness and profitability. The more time we invested up front, the more value we could generate on the back end.

As always, meeting minutes were generated along with the action item list and schedule, and distributed to all parties involved.

4. Owner Insight and Engagement

The next item I'd like to talk about is the owner's insight and engagement. As mentioned previously, understanding the owner's hot buttons and having knowledge of what issues are most critical to the client is key to success. Equally important is understanding the stakeholders who influence the engagement and what their hot buttons are.

Those insights are vital. In today's environment, engaging with the community and political entities is essential to gaining understanding and achieving success on any project.

CASE STUDY: I-17 FOR THOMAS ROAD TO DUNLAP AVENUE DESIGN BUILD FOR ADOT IN DOWNTOWN PHOENIX

So, I'm going to highlight what we did on the I-17 Design Build project from Thomas Road to Dunlap in downtown Phoenix. That was a design build project in Phoenix, and it remains one of the most successful examples of owner insight and engagement. It's a very unique story.

This design build project was unique in many ways. My background with ADOT went back many years to 1979, but I really began working closely with them on the East Papago Freeway in 1991 while with AECOM. Through that work, I got to know many of the top people at ADOT, including Steve Jimenez, head of the Maricopa Regional Freeway Program, and one of his project managers, Terry Bourland.

I came to know Terry extremely well and worked closely with him on many construction issues that arose, helping solve a number of problems. I also developed a strong professional relationship with Steve and Terry over time.

I was the quality engineer on the I-17 Thomas to Indian School Road project with AECOM, which was ADOT's first auxiliary and HOV lane project. I also chaired a 12-member technical committee for ADOT, tasked with providing auxiliary lane design guidelines for Maricopa County freeway projects—both for auxiliary lanes on existing freeways and for use in new freeway design. The I-17 from Thomas to Dunlap Road project involved adding auxiliary lanes from Indian School Road all the way to Dunlap Road, so my background with ADOT was a perfect fit for this effort.

This project was originally structured as a traditional design-bid-build. We won the project back in 1996, and I served as project manager for AECOM.

Prior to the issuance of the RFQ, our team conducted thorough due diligence and held multiple meetings with ADOT staff, including the PM,

Terry Bourland, Resident Engineer, John Akins, and all leads for traffic, lighting, structures, O&M, drainage, and utilities. We met with Terry several times, learned the key issues and goals of ADOT, and identified the most active stakeholders on the project.

We also met with third-party reviewers and partners, including the District office for the Federal Highway Administration (FHWA). We submitted an excellent SOQ and were selected for the project's design. We developed the scope of work and fee proposal and negotiated both with Terry and Ron Thomas, who led ADOT's Consulting Services at the time.

We had progressed to about 30% design when ADOT made an internal decision to shift the project to a design build model. That decision was made by Mary Peters, ADOT's Director at the time. I had known Mary since her early days as a secretary for Verne Doyle, the former head of Consulting Services. Terry kept me informed throughout the process, even before the final decision to move forward with design build was made. He encouraged us to continue progressing with the design work.

Terry informed us that ADOT would be seeking a general consultant (GC) to support the agency in developing the design build procurement documents, answering technical questions from prospective design builders, participating in pre-proposal and proposal meetings, working with selected contractors, supporting the design build office, conducting design reviews, and providing construction administration services.

I asked Terry whether ADOT could simply convert our existing design contract to the GC role. He followed up with Mary and the State Attorney General, who determined that the GC contract would need to be advertised separately.

I reminded Terry of our team's design build expertise, which we had built up over the previous three years, and emphasized that we were very comfortable taking on the GC role. However, we began to hear rumors that no other firms were planning to compete for the GC contract. That was a concern for both me and my leadership team. I asked Terry whether we could still be selected if no other firms submitted.

Terry again consulted with Mary and the attorney general. They concluded that as long as we scored 70% or higher, we could be awarded the contract.

During this time, I also discussed promoting Eric Crowe as the deputy project manager. Eric was already serving as project engineer, and I believed he was the right person to support the GC role. Terry agreed, and Eric became the Deputy PM. He and Terry developed a strong working relationship. Eric, who had experience as a traffic engineer, project engineer, and resident engineer, did an outstanding job on the project.

We also brought in John Patterson, a long-time ADOT resident engineer who had recently started his own firm. Back in 1996, his company was only about a year old. He's now celebrating 25 years in business, next year.

Through our final design efforts, we maintained strong relationships with ADOT and FHWA personnel. We began discussions with them to understand the constraints and opportunities tied to the GC contract. We outlined our approach to developing the procurement documents and addressed the unique requirements of the scope of work in our SOQ. We emphasized our capabilities and the advantages we brought to the table.

As we suspected, no other firms submitted an SOQ for the GC contract. Our score was well above the 70% threshold, and we were selected as the general consultant. Eric and I worked closely to finalize the scope of work and proposal for the GC role, gathering input from our subs and key staff members. We then entered negotiations with Terry, Eric, and Ron.

Our working relationship was extremely strong, and the four of us collaborated very well. Once under contract, we began moving forward in the GC role.

In conclusion, understanding and addressing the owner's hot buttons was crucial to the success of our SOQ and fee proposal for the GC procurement. We were able to tailor our strategies specifically to the project's needs, which led to a compelling SOQ, well-aligned scope of work, competitive fee proposal, and ultimately, successful negotiations.

During the debriefing, Terry told us we scored 95%. It was an incredibly successful pursuit.

5.   Technical Challenges and Expertise

I want to talk a little about technical due diligence. On every one of these projects, it's not just the politics, the strategy, or the stakeholders—you also have to understand the technical challenges you'll face.

Every job has its own unique technical challenge. I've worked on literally hundreds of projects. Every single one, no matter how big or small, has had its own unique set of challenges, and they're all different. So sitting back and saying, "I'll wait until the RFP comes out before understanding the technical challenges," is way too late. You've got to understand those challenges early on, way up front. You've got to prepare, and you've got to get your team ready.

You have to assemble a team that can take on those specific technical challenges. If you're not able to exceed the expectations of the owner and offer a solution that's even better than what the owner envisions, you're probably not going to get selected. So once you start identifying the technical challenges for your specific project, that's when you need to start assembling your technical experts.

Those experts may be within your firm or outside of it. When I was with AECOM, I had access to 40,000 people. I didn't reach out to all of them, of course, but since I was the Deputy Design Director of our alternative delivery group, I got to know every office and the talent across North America. I became familiar with who the subject matter experts were—whether it was tunnels, ITS, or any other area—and I knew who to call.

And that's what it takes. You reach out to the best of the best and the brightest of the brightest. That's what I did.

So get your experts lined up early for your project. Help them learn about the project. Get them involved from the beginning. Don't wait until the last minute to engage your SMEs. You'll be amazed at how many ATCs they can come up with.

Some of these technical experts may not be design build or P3 experts—but that's okay. You're looking for technical depth and insight. I was fortunate to have a lot of experience with alternative delivery, so I could fill in a lot of gaps myself—but you can't do everything alone, especially on a Mega-Project. These projects are just too complex. You need experts to help guide the way.

I already discussed one case study back in Chapter 3—the I-405, 6th Street to I-5 Express Toll Lanes project—so I won't spend too much more time on SMEs here. That was a great example of how to use technical experts effectively.

So now I'll move on and talk about go/no-go approvals and the next steps. We had conducted a thorough go/no-go evaluation.

6. Go/No-Go Approval and Next Steps

We went through the approval process with the executive team to get the green light to move forward with the proposal. After completing our initial analysis, we were granted a "go."

The next step after that is initial proposal planning. At this stage, our team is ready to begin preparing a comprehensive and competitive proposal.

But before fully diving in, you'll want to conduct another go/no-go approval process. This one should happen after reviewing the RFP in detail, especially the contractual language.

CASE STUDY: LAX AUTOMATED PEOPLE MOVER P3 PROJECT FOR LAWA

I've already walked through an example of this with the LAX Automated People Mover P3 project, which is a great illustration of how this second go/no-go process works in real time.

If you remember, in that case, all six pre-qualified firms were invited to move forward in the proposal process. But after evaluating the full scope, we made the decision to no-go the project. That was a critical decision.

Why? Because we estimated that our team would have had to spend $50 million just to prepare and submit the proposal. When you're only looking at a 15–20% chance of winning, it's just not a smart move to invest that level of resources. Sometimes, knowing when to walk away is as important as knowing when to move forward.

7. Key Proposal Considerations

We're going to focus on profitability. There should be an emphasis on the approaches that ensure profitability and project success.

Some of those approaches involve evaluating what you do during the proposal phase, as it has a significant impact on your profitability down the road. Remember, you're not only submitting a technical proposal on every alternative delivery job—you're also submitting a bid. And that bid has to be firm.

Unless you're pursuing a progressive design build, the owner is going to expect a lump sum price that takes the project from start to finish. So you have to define everything during the proposal efforts.

Now, it's impossible to finalize everything. If the owner provides a 10% design document, and you can take that to 15% or 20%, you're doing well. There's simply not enough time to do a full engineering deep dive within the short RFP window.

Most RFPs allow maybe five to seven months. Occasionally, you get longer—sometimes up to a year—but if you're working on a billion-dollar project, there's no way to take that design to even a 30% level. That would be an enormous amount of work.

If you can squeeze out another 5% to 10% of design development to refine technical aspects, that's typically all you can hope for. On a billion-dollar project, just that extra 5% to 10% of design can cost anywhere from $500,000 to $2 million. Everything comes down to understanding what has real value.

As you look at profitability, you need to ensure that as you prepare your job, you're not missing anything. Don't leave anything out. Make sure all elements of design and construction are covered.

Typically, on these projects, we set up task groups as we move through the proposal process. These can be organized by discipline or by specific activities. You can also set up dedicated task groups just for scheduling or estimating.

We tend to include estimators in those task groups. That way, if we're developing ATCs or considering alternative concepts, we can run cost comparisons. We also conduct value analysis.

As I mentioned previously, value engineering is critical. Including value engineering in your proposal helps demonstrate that any changes you're proposing still deliver equal or greater value. Owners won't accept compromises. You need to show that every ATC adds at least equal, if not better, value.

During the proposal effort, start building out your execution strategy. Look at your last job—you don't have to reinvent the wheel. If you've done a similar job before, pull out that execution strategy and build on it. Every project is unique, so add in the details specific to this one.

Outline what needs to be done for execution. Include a 30, 60, 120 day startup plan. On most alternative delivery projects, the better your start, the better your finish. Without a 30, 60, 120 plan, you risk falling behind right from the start.

You need your team to hit the ground running.

Now, let's talk a little about preparing for the RFP response. Ideally, as you've been working through the SOQ and pre-proposal phase, your team has been figuring out how to respond to the RFP.

Are you going to have your entire team in one office? That's often not practical. On some proposal responses, the design side alone had 60 or 70 people working. Then you add in the contractor, and for a P3, the developer, and suddenly you may have 200 to 300 people involved.

It's hard to find space to house 300 people for six months. What I try to do is get the core team—maybe 50 to 60 people including the contractor and developer—into a single office. The rest of the work is done from satellite offices.

You'll also need a solid communication plan. That's usually handled through platforms like SharePoint, Google Docs, or, on some projects, even round-the-clock engineering services.

For example, on the SH 130 Tollroad (P3), we had an entire team doing geometrics and earthwork out of our Australia office. We developed ideas during the day in Austin, and by the time we wrapped up, we transferred the work to the Australia team. When we came in the next morning, the work was ready for review and presentation.

All of these collaboration methods need to be carefully planned. How is your team going to work together across time zones, offices, and functions? These decisions can make or break your proposal efficiency.

8.   Next Steps in the Process

The next thing I'm going to talk about is the next steps in the process. We'll talk about proposal development, collaborations with SMEs, and risk and financial adjustments.

As you begin your proposal, you need to start drafting and refining both the proposal itself and your proposal plan, including a proposal management plan. You'll want to get your proposal lead identified and in place. Your full team should be lined up and ready to go.

You're going to start shredding the RFP—breaking it down to understand every requirement. You'll need to determine how the technical proposal needs to be formatted and responded to. You'll begin forming your task groups, assigning group leads, and defining how each group will operate. All of this should be clearly documented in your proposal work plan. At the same time, you should be developing your budget, identifying your resource needs, and setting your schedule for completing the proposal.

You'll also want to collaborate with your SMEs. Some SMEs may not be working full-time on the job, but for certain disciplines—like tunnels— you absolutely need a full-time SME dedicated to the work. Tunnel expertise is critical.

In other cases, you might have an SME with specialized experience, like someone familiar with Federal Highway Administration requirements. If FHWA compliance is a major factor on your project, bring that person in. Have them:

- Review the work your team is doing.

- Challenge assumptions.

- Identify fatal flaws.

- Offer alternative approaches.

Sometimes, we're so deep into a project that we miss obvious issues— this is where the perspective of a seasoned SME can be invaluable. They can spot things we can't.

So, get your SMEs involved. Make them part of the team. Schedule them to participate at critical milestones. Make sure they're engaged in brainstorming sessions and are providing meaningful input.

Next, you need to continuously assess your risks and financial considerations. Keep updating your risk register as the proposal progresses. Make sure each risk is clearly defined and that you've developed a mitigation strategy for each one. As you dive deeper into the proposal, new issues may arise.

For example, maybe you hadn't looked closely at the geology yet—and now you're discovering geological challenges. Bring in your geologist to evaluate and propose mitigation strategies.

If there are hazardous materials on site, bring in your environmental and hazmat specialists. Figure out what has to be done:

- Do you need to remove it from the site?

- Can you encapsulate it?

- What's the best and safest option?

If there are archaeological issues, evaluate the right approach:

- Can you reroute around the site?

- Do you need to excavate?

- Preserve?

- Recover?

These are all things that need to be evaluated during the proposal stage.

If you're working on a P3, your financial team must be involved in everything. Every design and construction decision has financial implications, and your financial experts should be engaged in tracking those impacts in real time.

They have to work with the investment communities. They need to consider Private Activity Bonds (PABs), which are tax-exempt bonds issued by state or local governments to help finance private projects that serve a public purpose. They also need to consider Transportation Infrastructure Finance and Innovation Act (TIFIA) loans, which provide low-interest federal financing for major transportation projects.

They should have a full menu of all available financing tools on the table so that we can remain competitive and offer the best possible net present value when we submit our proposal.

Chapter 4
Proposal Activities

1. Position Your Team for Success and Profitability
Objective

The first thing we're going to need to do as we start our proposal activities is figure out how to position our team for success and profitability. The objective here is to set a strong foundation for our proposal efforts—focused on success and focused on profitability.

As I mentioned when wrapping up the last chapter, one of the best tools I've used—and one that's worked well for my teams—is creating a proposal work plan. This should be a comprehensive plan outlining the entire scope of work for the team throughout the proposal process. Make sure to include your full budget allocation.

Depending on your role, you should be creating a tailored proposal work plan:

- If you're the developer, you need your own plan because you're leading the schedule.

- If you're the design builder, you need your own plan.

- If you're the designer, you need your own plan as well.

Each one of these should feed into the next:

- The design builder's work plan should feed into the developer's.

- The designer's plan should feed into the design builder's.

- If you're the designer and have subconsultants, they should also create their own work plans.

- If you're the design builder your major subcontractors should have their own work plans.

Everyone involved needs a work plan. Without it, no one truly knows where they're going. That's why this is one of the very first steps.

If you've done enough of these projects, you probably already have a skeleton of a proposal work plan to start from. I use a very simple, fill-in-the-blank type template. If you're going after a highway project—especially a P3—and you've just completed a similar one successfully, use that as your starting point.

Yes, the team members might be different. The technical aspects and scope of work might change. But the structure will be similar. You don't have to start from scratch every time, but you do need to customize the plan for the specifics of the new project.

Every project will have:

- A different scope of work.

- A different budget allocation.

- A different schedule based on the RFP and project expectations.

Collaboration

The next step is collaboration. Collaboration is critical to developing a successful proposal. The relationship between the proposal manager and the project manager is key. The proposal manager sets the stage for how the proposal will be developed. But the project manager has to be involved—even if they're full-time on another project. I understand that's where revenue is generated, but you still need to bring the project manager into the proposal process.

If that project manager is going to eventually take over this job and deliver the profits you're expecting, they need to understand how the proposal came together. They don't need to be involved full-time—10% of their time is often enough—but they need to have a voice and some visibility.

If you leave them out and then hand off the job after winning, it's going to be a difficult transition. No matter how good they are, it will take time for them to catch up. I once had to replace a project director, and I spent three to four months transitioning the new person into the role. If I hadn't done that, it would have set the whole team back. So take it seriously. That small time investment up front will be worth it in the end.

Also, make sure your proposal work plan includes the following:

- All technical disciplines

- All key contractors

- All key subcontractors

- All key consultants

- All SMEs

List them in the plan. Give them time. Even if someone isn't full-time, like an SME, give them a budget. Make sure they're included in the schedule, and they know when they need to participate.

You'll likely need to include MWDBE firms (minority, women, and disadvantaged business enterprises) in your project as well. There are some fantastic MWDBE firms out there—include them in the proposal. Have them actually participate in proposal development. If they're going to be a key part of the delivery team, use that to your advantage.

Identify them early in the proposal and make them part of the team. You'll see how much stronger your proposal becomes.

Components to Include

Include critical planning elements like a SWOT analysis. You've probably already done one or two, but once the RFP hits and the shortlist is confirmed, do it again. Your competition is now clearly defined. Take another look at your position:

- Are you missing anything?

- Are there any new gaps?

- Have your strengths or weaknesses changed?

Re-evaluate your win strategy:

- What's going to make your team stand out?

- What are the winning themes?

- What can you do to win?

Every job will have a different win strategy. Figure it out early. Your proposal manager can help—they're usually very good at developing win themes.

Also, determine:

- Who's doing the writing?

- How is the writing going to get done?

- Who's handling the graphics?

- Who's responsible for production?

- Who's covering the technical aspects?

Get your technical work groups lined up. Keep them manageable—five to six people with one lead is ideal. Larger groups can get unmanageable. Let the leads assign tasks as needed, but don't make your workgroups unnecessarily large.

You don't want to have 20 people in a workgroup. You're going to be out of control. Five to six people in a workgroup is big enough.

So you're going to figure out all the technical aspects you need to be looking at. Under positioning your team for success and profitability,

CASE STUDY: PURPLE LINE SUBWAY EXTENSION SECTION 2 FOR LA METRO

I'm going to talk about the Purple Line Subway Extension. This is an example of a team that was successfully positioned for both from the start of the proposal effort.

They had incredible strategic collaboration between the proposal manager and the project manager, and that set the stage for a great bid.

The Purple Line Subway Extension Section 2 was done for Los Angeles Metro (LA Metro). That proposal effort took place from January to June of 2016—so, six months total. I was the design director and the proposal development lead working for Walsh.

Our team was a joint venture of Walsh and Strabag as the design builder. Arup was our lead designer, and we had many subcontractors reporting to the JV, as well as subconsultants reporting to Arup. This was a very complex tunnel section of the Purple Line Subway—approximately three miles long with three large underground stations running through Beverly

Hills, which meant significant stakeholder involvement. The construction value of this project was $1.9 billion.

As I've said before, it's rare for your project manager to be available full-time during proposal development. This was true here as well. Our project manager was working full-time on the Crenshaw/LAX LRT project for LA Metro, about 15 miles from our regional office. We worked on the Purple Line proposal out of our LAX regional office. Our team frequently visited the Crenshaw project office, and we were fully responsible for both efforts.

I worked on the Crenshaw/LAX project myself, and we made sure the project manager was available when needed throughout the proposal. That Crenshaw project was a $1.3 billion job with one mile of tunnel and two underground stations. They had just broken through the tunnel during our proposal work on the Purple Line.

This gave us excellent insight—while the Purple Line had a different location and geology, we benefited from the experience of dealing with:

- Tunneling.

- Traffic conditions in LA.

- Political dynamics.

- Local community relationships.

Understanding LA politics is critical. Without it, you're at a disadvantage. We were fortunate to be actively delivering the Crenshaw/LAX job while bidding the Purple Line job.

There was a strong joint effort between the proposal manager and project manager. Our proposal manager, Matt Shepard, came from our Texas office and was outstanding. Our proposed project manager didn't need to be involved full-time, but when needed, he was there and fully engaged.

The project manager was also heavily involved when we developed the risk register, detailed execution schedule, fee estimate, bid, and escrow documents. He contributed valuable lessons learned from the Crenshaw/LAX job, including:

- Contractual issues.

- Legal and administrative considerations.

- Political and community factors.

- Stakeholder and third-party relationships.

- Constructability challenges.

- Production rates achieved on Crenshaw.

He also attended all estimating sessions and final bid reviews and played a major role in scheduling. It was a highly collaborative effort.

Our team was positioned for profitability from the start because of this collaboration among the proposal manager, project manager, and bid manager. The bid manager on the Purple Line was also the bid manager for the Crenshaw/LAX job. That continuity, combined with experience in pricing and working with major subcontractors, made the proposal process smooth and ultimately positioned the project for success.

The next item I want to cover is the development of the proposal work plan, continuing with the Purple Line Subway Extension as the example. The proposal work plan was crucial in aligning all stakeholders and ensuring no critical elements were overlooked.

We did significant due diligence before the RFP was even issued. This included:

- Meetings with the owner, stakeholders, and third parties.

- Risk assessment.

- Site visits with the project team.

- Attendance at LA Metro board and committee meeting.

Our leads for the Walsh proposal team: Bill Heathcott (VP and Regional Manager), Matt Shepherd (Proposal Manager), and Dustin Darby (Proposal Lead).

For Strabag: Bert Postma (Lead)

For Arup: Richard Prust (Vice President and Design Lead)

We also had Louis Peck as our tunnel lead—an SME from San Francisco with extensive national and LA-area tunnel experience.

Matt and Dustin developed the proposal work plan, which was comprehensive and covered:

- Detailed scope of work.

- Budget allocation.

- Schedule for all tasks outlined in the RFP and beyond.

The work plan organized:

- Task groups and their members.

- Weekly meetings.

- SWOT analysis.

- Win themes.

- Writing assignments.

- Graphics and production.

- Technical elements.

It also included:

- DBE participation and outreach.

- Technical proposal efforts.

- Fee estimate and escrow document development.

This thorough planning ensured alignment across the board and laid the foundation for a strong, responsive proposal.

It also included a section on ATCs, constructability reviews, the purpose of the task groups, and how the meetings should be conducted. Many of the ATCs were originally generated out of the task group meetings and then fully coordinated and refined within the task groups. We held a separate coordination meeting outside the task groups between the regional proposal managers and the technical leads to ensure alignment—this took place weekly.

One hand has to know what the other hand is doing at all times on these projects. The proposal effort was a complete collaboration among all members of the team. It included participants from:

- Walsh's LAX regional office and several other offices.

- Strabag's regional office in Toronto and headquarters in Austria.

- Arup's LA office and other locations.

- Subcontractors, consultants, and SMEs.

All of these contributors were active in task group meetings and helped develop and refine the ATCs.

The proposal work plan was uploaded to Walsh's SharePoint site so the entire proposal team stayed informed. A contract book was also created by Bill and Matt to track everything that needed to be addressed contractually. This included:

- Prime agreement.

- Teaming agreements.

- Joint venture agreements.

- Design agreements.

- Legal reviews.

All of these items were built into the proposal schedule.

We held a proposal kickoff meeting to review the proposal work plan and outline the meetings that would occur throughout the proposal effort. Task groups met weekly. There was a joint effort between the proposal manager, project manager, and bid manager to coordinate and outline all the upcoming activities, and all of this was captured in the proposal work plan.

The development of a comprehensive proposal work plan was crucial in aligning all members of the proposal team and ensuring that no critical elements were overlooked—including disciplines, subcontractors, and SMEs who all contributed to the success of the proposal.

2.   30, 60, and 120 Day Startup Plan

Let's go on and talk about the 30, 60, 120 startup plan. So really, what's the key? What's the purpose of that plan? It's to ensure that none of the critical startup activities are overlooked. There's usually a tremendous amount of startup activity, especially on an AD Mega-Project.

My current startup activity template includes about 45 items. That's a lot to cover. So get that checklist done. Use a similar project you've worked on before—ideally with the same owner. If you've done a job for that owner, it's a great idea to pull out the old checklist and use it as a foundation. Then keep adding to it as needed.

Try to get a solid first cut at the checklist. Usually, the proposal manager takes the lead and then shares it with the project manager and the bid manager for review. You'll continue to update the checklist as you develop your bidding strategy and refine your estimate. A few things always get missed in early versions, so it's important to revisit it regularly.

Everything on the checklist that you develop should be priced and should be scheduled. You should even include close-out activities—maybe not a full close-out plan, but at least the basics. Someone needs to start working with the person responsible for close-out early on. That person should have a role on your startup team to ensure the close-out process begins within the first 30, 60, or 120 days—not at the end of the project.

You'll also need to:

- Finalize the prime contract.

- Set up the project office.

- Mobilize staff and resources.

- Complete the QA manual and project management plan.

- Secure office space and get equipment in.

There's no shortage of startup activity to plan for.

The first time I developed a startup checklist was back in 2011. We called it the Design Build 90-Day Startup Checklist. At the time, it had about 33 items. Don Graul, who led the Alternative Delivery Group at AECOM at that time, shared that document with us. He had also developed a mobilization plan, which he sent me soon thereafter. I incorporated a few additional items based on his version. Any resource that helps shape your checklist is a huge advantage.

CASE STUDY: I-405 EXPRESS TOLL LANE DESIGN BUILD IN BELLEVUE, WA, FOR WADOT

We used the updated checklist on the I-405 Express Toll Lane project in Bellevue, Washington, where I was the proposal manager for AECOM. We reviewed the checklist against the RFP requirements, the prime contract, and our draft design agreement with Kiewit. We made a few modifications, but it served as a solid foundation for building our startup plan and ensuring everything was priced appropriately for execution.

Beyond design and construction phase services, we used the checklist to develop our integrated project schedule. That's key. Get your startup activities into your actual schedule—don't just add a single line that says "Startup Activities." That's not helpful. Break it down. Show when each task starts and finishes so everyone knows what they're responsible for and when.

Over the years, I've continued to update that checklist. As of November 2024, it's now called the **Alternative Delivery 30, 60, 120 Day Startup Checklist** and includes 45 items (this checklist is my gift to you for buying this book and can be downloaded by scanning the QR code at the beginning of the book). It's grown significantly since the original 33. I've used it on every single one of my proposals. It consistently helps us get ready to execute the work once we've won the project.

Our team walks into execution with a plan—and the right resources—for those first 30, 60, and 120 days. That smooth startup is critical to success, especially on AD Mega-Projects. It sets the tone for the rest of the job and positions us for profitability.

If you have a strong 30, 60, 120 day startup plan and you follow it to a tee, I guarantee the project will be successful. But if you don't have a plan, and you're still scrambling four, five, or six months in, your project is already behind.

You've got to get it done in the first 120 days. I guarantee it.

3. Framework for Startup Plan

So this startup plan is critical. You're going to develop it during the proposal. Try to get it 90–95% complete if you can. There will always be things to refine once you win the job, and we'll talk about that more during execution. But you need to start creating that plan during the proposal efforts.

You've got your checklist—that's the framework for the plan. Now you need to put the meat on the bones. If you're a firm that's never used a startup plan before, you'll probably need to get your team bought into the concept. Once they see how successful it can be, they'll get on board.

But you might hear questions like:

- "Why are we starting this during the proposal?"

- "Who cares what we're going to do at execution?"

- "We're just trying to get through the proposal."

You need to be firm that the only way to be successful on any AD job is by having a startup plan. That way, everyone knows exactly what needs to be done, and you can allocate the effort, time, and resources needed to get the job started correctly.

It's absolutely necessary to get your job running within 120 days. After four months, the job better be clicking. Having a well-thought-out startup plan in place is essential. It will also ensure that, when you put your estimate together, everything is accounted for—travel, people, time. You'll likely need a separate team just to handle the startup on an AD Mega-Project. You can't rely on your existing core team—you'll need a dedicated "SWAT team."

The critical people you need buy-in from include your executive team. The way to earn that buy-in is by showing them the startup activity checklist and what it allows you to do. Once selected, you'll finalize and execute the post-selection plan and begin implementing it.

You should:

- Host a startup meeting to align the team.

- Track progress weekly (just like during the proposal and project phases).

- Hold separate meetings specifically for the startup team.

That startup team will be bigger than you think. On an AD Mega-Project, you might have 20 to 30 people just for startup. There are a ton of tasks to handle.

One activity will be the Quality Assurance/Quality Control (QA/QC) plan and getting the quality manual started. That takes time. And without an approved quality manual, your designers—who are usually first to begin—won't be able to start work. Some owners won't allow you to begin without a submitted and approved design quality plan.

You can build your quality plan in phases, but you still need an outline that defines what the full plan will include. Even if you have a quality plan from another job, it must meet the current owner's requirements. Most owners have specific guidelines. Even if your company has its own quality plan, it may not be acceptable to the owner.

So, during the proposal, review the documents that define what the quality plan must contain and how it should look. If the owner asks for a preliminary quality plan for the proposal, you'll need to submit one. If not, you still need to know how to build and price it. Some owners may say you can use your firm's plan—but that's rare. Most want a plan tailored to their structure and standards.

4.   The QA/QC Process

Now let's spend a little time talking about the QA/QC process. The Quality Assurance/Quality Control plan is a formal document outlining the processes, procedures, responsibilities, and standards required to ensure that the design, construction, and proposal deliverables meet the owner's requirements, technical specifications, and contractual obligations.

A lot of people don't think about QA/QC during the proposal phase, but if you don't have one in place, you're likely to miss things—or say things you shouldn't. You need a second set of eyes on everything that goes out.

The QA/QC process during the proposal phase of an AD project is essential. It should mirror the process used during execution. There's very little difference.

During the proposal phase, you're:

- Preparing the technical proposal.

- Advancing the design.

- Conducting constructability reviews and phasing.

- Developing ATCs.

- Doing value engineering.

- Furthering your risk assessment.

- Developing an integrated project schedule.

- Working with task groups.

- Estimating, bidding, and preparing key documents that set the tone for success and profitability.

So, even if the full quality management plan has not been developed yet (as it would be during execution), QA/QC must still be applied at every level.

Each firm and team member must follow their organization's quality standards to ensure that:

- All documents and deliverables have been reviewed.

- All outputs are properly coordinated and integrated.

This is crucial because each design component (even preliminary ones) must align with the broader project. For example:

- Your bridge design must coordinate with roadway elements.

- It might intersect with track or utility infrastructure.

So blinders don't work—you can't just focus on "your piece." You must see how it fits into the whole.

That's why I also recommend conducting interdisciplinary reviews at key proposal milestones.

Assign a Quality Assurance Manager (QAM) at the start of the proposal phase—one for the lead contractor and one for the lead designer. These QAMs should:

- Provide leadership, tracking, auditing, monitoring, and ensure compliance across the entire effort.

- Report directly to the project manager for the design builder and the lead designer.

Also, a qualified reviewer must be assigned to every document or calculation. They must:

- Sign off as the reviewer, along with the originator.

- Be experienced in the type of work being reviewed (e.g., bridge, roadway, drainage design, etc).

- Understand the work plan and all requirements.

The QC documentation must show:

- The process used for quality control.

- What items were checked.

- Comments made by the reviewer.

- Any disagreements and how they were resolved.

- How the final version was approved.

That's how you maintain quality, avoid surprises, and set your team up for long-term success.

Once that's done, the QAM can quickly review that document and determine whether it meets the QA/QC process and requirements for the project. Without having that all documented, they have no idea—whether we've done a good job or even any job at all.

So I'm going to take you through a case study now. It's just one of many, but I want to highlight that every AD proposal I have been on or led has had a QA/QC process in place.

CASE STUDY: US 60 FROM I-10 TO GILBERT ROAD DESIGN BUILD FOR ADOT

The first project where I was truly aware of how impactful this process could be was US 60 from I-10 to Gilbert Road for ADOT. That proposal took place from 2000 to 2001. It was a $185 million design build, widening, and reconstruction project.

- The proposal team included Flatiron and FNF as the constructors in a joint venture as the design builder, and AECOM as the lead designer.

- Each firm had its own subcontractors or subconsultants.

- Jan Bohn was the project manager for the Flatiron FNF JV.

- I served as the proposal oversight and officer-in-charge for AECOM.

At the time, I led the Phoenix office in implementing AECOM's ISO 9001 program, and it was the first AECOM office to get certified. That experience gave me a lot of credibility on the QA/QC side of the business.

Both Jan and I made sure that all the QA/QC processes were fully implemented and followed. The QAMs were responsible for tracking, auditing, monitoring, ensuring compliance, and reporting directly to both Jan and me. Through this process, we uncovered one major gap.

- Task groups and disciplines were doing well in following the QC process, but an individual decision or change within one of the task groups was not being shared across the broader team.

- Those impacted by the change weren't being informed, which meant potential ripple effects were not being accounted for.

To fix this, Jan, the QAM, and I developed a process for conducting interdisciplinary review meetings whenever a change occurred. I had been using a version of this process for years, but it hadn't yet been implemented on the US 60 proposal.

This meeting was structured as a workshop:

- The individual or task group initiating the change would present it to all discipline leads and task group leads.

- Everyone would provide input, feedback, and flag any issues.

- Any discovered issues would be addressed during the meeting, and the team would decide whether or not to move forward with the change.

- The author of the change would document the entire discussion and final decision.

This process worked extremely well, and I've continued to use it on all of my AD projects since. It's incredibly efficient—you can resolve major issues in under two hours, and it works every time.

The benefits of a rigorous QA/QC process during the proposal phase are well documented. The lessons learned from the US 60 proposal were shared with Greg Sautter, who led the ISO 9001 program at AECOM. Greg distributed that documentation to both corporate and regional leadership, and it eventually became the standard practice at AECOM.

5. Review and Validate the Proposal Outline

It's very important that you get a proposal outline that details everything that's going to go into the proposal.

The first thing I usually do is get the team together and conduct a team meeting to go over the initial proposal outline. I'm always looking for feedback from all team members. Invite your entire team to this meeting—developer, the design builder, designer, subcontractors, your proposal manager—make sure everyone is involved.

What you're really doing is identifying potential gaps or overlaps in the plan. Gaps can cause major issues down the line. Overlaps can lead to duplicated work. You want to streamline the process, and since time is limited, it's critical to:

- Fill any gaps.

- Eliminate overlaps.

The next step is making assignments and approvals. You'll assign tasks to develop the detailed scopes of work, expanding the proposal outline. Then, you'll review, modify, and approve each of those scopes.

Once you're done, you'll have an outline that the entire team can follow, and everyone will understand the direction the proposal is taking.

6.   Estimating Budget and Resource Allocation

Once you've got a feel for your plan, get your leads, your management team—everyone—to start thinking about what they need for a budget. Every person, every discipline lead, every segment manager, and every proposal manager is going to be involved. They'll need to dedicate staff and resources, and that's going to happen at every level.

Develop a template for budget development. This can come down from your design builder, or you can take the lead yourself if you're the designer. Create it for the entire team and share it with the design builder to align efforts.

Have your team prepare both hour and fee estimates from all relevant parties. Make sure everyone understands the teaming agreement. If you're a designer, you'll probably be working at a reduced multiplier—typically around 1.8 or 1.65. If you win the project, you'll receive a success fee, which we can discuss more later.

Everyone must contribute to the budget. Once the estimates come in:

- Consolidate all budgets into a single, unified estimate.

- If you're the proposal manager, review each estimate for accuracy and consistency.

- Ensure each scope of work aligns with the proposal outline.

Once everything is consolidated, start developing the proposal schedule. It must meet the project's requirements and be agreed upon by the full team. If I'm the designer, I like to have my own design schedule, which I always resource-load once we've agreed on hours and dollars. I use it for tracking earned value, billing, and progress.

Adopt a proposal schedule for the entire team. It should include:

- Pink team review.

- Red team review.

- Gold team review.

- Timeline for completing estimates and bids.

- Assembly and submission deadlines.

Float all of this in your schedule. Everyone should be aware of it and agree to it—especially your executive committee, since they'll be plugged in at different points. Whether you're the design builder or lead designer, your executive team needs to be involved. It's a critical part of the process.

That schedule becomes the anchor for everything you're working toward. I recommend updating it at least monthly. If you've lost time on a task, figure out how to recover. If you're on track, keep pushing forward.

7. Monitoring Proposal Progress

Just like on a regular job, you should be monitoring how your proposal efforts are progressing in the same way you monitor the execution phase of projects. You might keep it a little simpler, with fewer tasks, but the approach should still be systematic.

Once all your proposal tasks are laid out in the schedule and estimate, you can start resource-loading that schedule. It's important to match your schedule with the estimate so everyone knows their budget.

Then, you'll create a cash flow curve to show planned spending from the start of the proposal to the finish. Most cash flow curves have an "S" shape. If yours doesn't, you may have a mistake somewhere.

Track your progress—ideally bi-weekly. Weekly tracking is usually too much of a burden. Biweekly gives you enough time to gather meaningful updates without overloading the team. Reach out to your discipline leads, proposal managers, and subcontractors.

A simple method is to distribute a paper or PDF version of the schedule for discipline leads to mark their percent complete. That gets sent back to whoever is managing the schedule—typically a project controls group that handles the schedule, budgets, and reporting.

Track physical progress and key project indicators bi-weekly:

- Are you spending according to plan?

- What's the earned value?

- Compare earned value to the original cash flow curve.

If your earned value is below your planned cash flow, you're likely off-track. If it's above, you're in good shape. Ideally, your report should include three curves: spending, earning (earned value), and original budgeted cash flow. If spending is low and earned value is high, you're performing well.

If not, assess what's causing delays or cost overruns. This kind of monitoring is the only way to stay on schedule and within budget.

CASE STUDY: SH 121 TOLL ROAD P3 IN DALLAS FOR TX-DOT

Let's look at a case study on monitoring proposal progress: the SH 121 Toll Road P3 in Dallas. Our proposal phase lasted from June 23, 2005, to April 28, 2006—a long P3 effort with a $580 million construction value.

Key project facts:

- Developer: Macquarie.

- Design builder: Kiewit Abrams JV (with Kiewit taking the lead).

- Segments: Five, from Denton Creek to the North Dallas Tollway interchange.

- AECOM role: Lead designer, with me serving as proposal design manager.

After reviewing the TxDOT RFP, we developed major ATCs, defined the scope of work, and prepared fee estimates. Our scope included the written technical proposal, preliminary engineering design, project management, and coordination across all five segments.

Proposal estimate:

- 2,167 hours.

- $1,577,000.

Stephanie Belluomini, our project controls lead, created an Excel-based timesheet system with a detailed WBS. Everyone, including subconsultants, submitted their timesheets weekly. Stephanie also developed a tracking report comparing hours and dollars spent to budget, using percent-spent metrics and linking the data to our MS Project Schedule.

She maintained the baseline cash flow curve and used it to generate KPIs each month, and spending reports weekly (weekly reports did not contain earned value, only the monthly report):

- Earned value.

- Actual spending.

- Variance against budget.

I shared this progress with the design team weekly and monthly. Each month, discipline leads entered their physical percent complete, which I reviewed and adjusted before finalizing. This formed our earned value report and monthly invoices, which we reviewed in detail with Kiewit Abrams.

Kiewit also received a weekly summary showing hours charged, work completed, and individual WBS-level effort. I met with Rob Anderson from Kiewit each month to discuss progress, invoices, earned value, and any concerns. This helped expedite payment and strengthen communication.

Our use of tools like the proposal timesheet, resource-loaded schedule, design team tracking report, earned value reports, invoicing, and cash flow management helped us stay on time and on budget. These KPIs and consistent communication allowed us to manage the proposal effort efficiently and effectively.

8. Value Engineering and Risk Assessment

Sometimes, if you don't have the right people looking at value engineering (VE), and you rely only on your design disciplines, your design manager, or your construction staff, you may go astray. The owners are looking for value. If you're going to submit an ATC, you've got to prove that what you've done will give the owner equal or better value.

How do you do that if you can't demonstrate it? Owners will ask, "Show us how you've done it. Show us that it doesn't reduce the value." That's why I recommend bringing in a specialist who can conduct a structured VE work plan and workshop. There aren't a lot of VE-certified professionals out there.

I've had the opportunity to work with one exceptional specialist over the years—Renee Hoekstra. She's run her own firm for over 30 years and does VE workshops worldwide. I've had her work with many teams, and I also conducted this kind of work myself.

If you have the right person to facilitate the VE workshop, it's amazing how quickly and efficiently it can be done. It usually doesn't take more than a week to conduct a very thorough VE and risk assessment workshop.

The outcomes from such a workshop include:

- Documentation of findings that guide all ATCs and risk assessments.

- Identification of financial challenges and cost-saving opportunities.

- Clear alternatives with measurable benefits.

Let me walk you through a case study to show how one of these VE workshops functions. This wasn't tied to a proposal but still illustrates the process well.

CASE STUDY: TH 252/I-95 VE STUDY FOR MNDOT IN MINNEAPOLIS

I was one of the SMEs for the Trunk Highway (TH) 252/I-95 VE Study for MnDOT in Minneapolis. The workshop took place July 8–14, 2019, and wrapped up in just six days. The project had a construction value of approximately $300 million. The VE study was conducted by Renee Hoekstra of RHA.

Renee, a certified VE specialist, also facilitates risk assessments and partnering workshops and does an excellent job in all three areas. Before the study began, an FTP site was made available with project technical data. There were three SMEs on the study team. Each of us reviewed the materials in advance and submitted memos to Renee outlining our initial observations, risks, and information requests.

Below outlines what took place each day of the VE Study.

Day 1:

- Overview of the VE process by Renee.

- 3.5-hour site visit.

- 2-hour presentation from the designer.

- Discussion of project goals, VE objectives, constraints, KPIs, risks, and the cost model.

Day 2:

- Functional analysis of the project.

- Brainstorming of ideas and alternatives.

Day 3:

- Recap and additional brainstorming.

- Evaluation of ideas using a two-step screening process.

- Narrowed 51 ideas down to 6 alternatives.

Days 4–5:

- Development and costing of selected alternatives.

- Finalization of alternatives.

- Preparation for the outbrief presentation.

Day 6 Outbrief Meeting:

- Presentation of all 51 original ideas in table format.

- Final presentation of 3 selected alternatives.

Examples of the selected alternatives:

- Alternative 21: Reduce crossroad capacity
  The baseline had all crossroads under the mainline bridges designed with five lanes. The alternative adjusted the lane count based on projected peak traffic volumes to reduce unnecessary capacity.

- Performance score: 0.75.

- Estimated savings: $500,000.

- Benefit: Reduced maintenance, no additional risks.

- Alternative 32: Balance earthwork by lowering crossroads
  In the baseline, the mainline went over the cross streets
  (66th Ave, Brookdale Ave, and 85th Ave), requiring large
  embankments. This created a need for 690,000 cubic yards of
  borrow.

- The alternative suggested lowering the crossroads to reduce
  embankment needs.

- Benefit: Significant reduction in borrow and haul costs.

This case study highlights how structured VE workshops, when led by skilled facilitators, can uncover substantial savings and improve project feasibility—both in design and execution.

The alternative proposed lowering all of the cross streets by five feet, which would, in turn, allow the mainline profile to be lowered by five feet. This reduced the amount of embankment fill required and generated additional excavation material that could be reused for fill embankment—thereby reducing the need for imported material and minimizing haul requirements.

This alternative had several benefits: reducing the height of noise walls, reducing or eliminating the need for retaining walls, allowing more room for drainage and multi-use areas, and lowering construction truck traffic.

The risks associated with this alternative included the possibility that we might not be able to lower the crossroads by five feet. Other risks included:

- Potential underground utility relocation requirements.

- Additional right-of-way potentially needed for fill.

- The water table possibly being higher than estimated (we had
  estimated 18 feet, which may not allow for lowering the cross
  streets as planned).

This alternative received an overall performance rating of 3.5 and had an estimated cost savings of $570,000.

- Alternative 42: Lower TH 252 to balance earthwork

The baseline scenario required 690,000 cubic yards of borrow material for the entire project. Importing this material was costly and required additional hauling.

The proposed alternative involved lowering the mainline of TH 252 between The interchange at 66th Avenue and Brookdale Drive, and Brookdale Drive and 85th Avenue.

This would reduce the embankment fill required and create excess excavation material that could be reused for fill, reducing the need for imported material and associated hauling.

The benefits of this alternative included reduced noise wall heights and lower haul and construction truck traffic.

The primary risk was the potential need to redesign much of the backbone drainage system in the affected areas.

This alternative received an overall performance rating of 1.0 and an estimated cost savings of $3.6 million. It was ultimately selected by all participants during the outbrief meeting.

During our workshop, I also prepared a risk assessment for determining the best procurement methodology for the project. I evaluated:

- Traditional Design-Bid-Build (DBB).

- Design Build (DB).

- Construction Manager/General Contractor (CM/GC).

- Construction Manager at Risk (CMAR).

I was provided names of MnDOT staff to interview. I spoke with each of them to understand MnDOT's experience, successes, and challenges with these procurement methods and drafted a report with my recommendations.

MnDOT had extensive experience and success with both DBB and DB. However, they had very limited experience with CM/GC and CMAR and expressed concerns about using those methods on the TH 252/I-95 project.

Based on my conversations, I recommended that MnDOT proceed with Design Build procurement for the project.

The VE efforts for the TH 252/I-94 project were highly successful and brought added value to stakeholders, decision-makers, and MnDOT designers. The combination of our procurement risk assessment and the involvement of certified VE specialist and facilitator Renee Hoekstra from RHA positively influenced outcomes and decision-making for the project.

I highly recommend including a certified VE specialist and an experienced facilitator for all team proposal efforts. VE (Value Engineering) is a unique, function-oriented, systematic team methodology that enhances customer value in programs, facilities, systems, or services. It focuses on improving performance and quality while optimizing initial and life-cycle-costs.

VE workshops are conducted according to the standards of SAVE International, the global value society, and follow a structured job plan—such as the one demonstrated in the case study above.

9. Development of Execution Strategy

You want to involve your entire team in developing a comprehensive execution strategy. The components will include production, design, construction, financial planning, permitting, stakeholder engagement, and so on. It all depends on the scope of work for your project—but this is where the rubber really meets the road.

What I like to do is go back and reference past projects. What have I done that's similar? Maybe I've used a successful execution strategy on a prior job. If so, I take that strategy and begin modifying it to fit the new project.

Don't try to reinvent the wheel on every job or proposal. It's not worth it. You're better off starting with something that worked well and adapting it to meet current requirements.

Once you've started modifying that plan, the next thing you'll want to do is make assignments:

- Get your whole team involved.

- Allocate tasks to all team leads and resource groups.

- Spread the work out—if you don't, the strategy won't be as impactful.

CASE STUDY: SOUND TRANSIT OMFE AND A TOD DE-SIGN BUILD IN BELLEVUE, WA

Let me share a case study related to developing an execution strategy. I worked on the Sound Transit Operations and Maintenance East (OMFE) and a Transit Oriented Development (TOD) project in Bellevue, Washington. We created an execution strategy during the proposal phase. This was a very complex project.

The owner had conceptually laid out a site plan that included the arrangement of all major site elements: the maintenance and administration building, employee and visitor parking, the rail yard, and potential TOD areas.

In addition to Sound Transit's requirements, the City of Bellevue had its own development standards and a strict schedule. They were not interested in adjusting to Sound Transit's timeline. They had their own priorities and were not very flexible. When a major third-party is involved, you have to incorporate that into your execution plan.

Mike Bell, the Senior Project Manager at Walsh, led the proposal efforts from September 2016 through January 2017—just seven months. My role as design director for proposal development was to support Mike. Ray Rojas, Program Manager for the Heavy Civil Group, and I brought my design build expertise to guide the team.

Challenges included:

- Poor soils and drainage conditions on the south end of the site.

- A 42-inch regional sanitary sewer line that bisected the site east to west.

- A compact project footprint.

Walsh used its Seattle office as the proposal base. The office had both heavy civil and architectural experience and was familiar with Bellevue.

The design team was led by David Borger, PE—Senior VP and transit lead at STV—who specialized in maintenance and operations facilities. He brought an architectural lead, track experts, and civil and traffic leads. We also brought in Richard Leiter from Trinity Real Estate, former mayor of Bellevue, who knew the city's leadership and processes well. Also, local architects, landscape architects, civil and geotechnical engineers with Sound Transit and Bellevue experience.

To develop an accurate bid, we needed a detailed execution strategy and schedule. The city's master plan approval and development process added complexity and uncertainty. I worked closely with Mike Bell and led the development of our execution strategy.

That included:

- A detailed outline of our organizational structure.

- An org chart and reporting structure—covering internal team, partners, subs, lead designers, consultants, vendors, and other key contributors.

- Using the org chart as a checklist for pricing.

- Updating our 30, 60, and 120 day startup plan with required resources.

- Working with the executive team to determine where those resources would come from.

We had to go beyond our existing resources and worked with Joe Lee, our West Region Senior VP, to develop a strategy and cost plan for obtaining additional resources and a tentative staffing plan over time. We had all team members go through the exercise and include all associated costs—recruiting, relocation, and travel.

Our execution strategy included:

- Production.

- Contractual and technical elements.

- Design and construction.

- Estimating and project controls.

- Major equipment needs.

- Scheduling.

- Environmental permitting.

- Community and political engagement.

- Public involvement and facilitation.

- Execution of ATCs.

- Traffic control strategies.

- Risk analysis and assessment.

- Value engineering and life-cycle-costs.

- Safety and quality.

- Bidding, meetings, Building Information Modeling (BIM).

- Revenue service, testing, and project close-out activities.

Since this was our first proposal and bid for Sound Transit, we didn't reference a previously completed project for the same owner. Instead, we used the Crenshaw LAX Southwest Maintenance Yard and Facility that Walsh bid in November 2016 for LA Metro. We also used input from our original estimator, Wes Lumpkin.

We reviewed all activities and strategies from that project and adjusted them based on the unique characteristics of the Sound Transit Operations and Maintenance East and TOD site. We accounted for:

- Sound Transit and City of Bellevue requirements, opportunities, and constraints.

- Utility and drainage needs.

- Poor soil conditions at the south end of the site.

- The location of the TOD.

We developed an ATC that allowed the 42-inch regional sewer line to remain in place, while still accommodating maintenance and operations. The ATC was approved by both Sound Transit and the regional facility that owned the sewer line.

We held six one-on-one meetings with Sound Transit to review our ideas, concepts, and ATCs, and to receive input and suggestions. We also discussed the unknowns surrounding the schedule with the City of Bellevue. We requested Sound Transit's support in engaging the city to clarify the schedule.

We met directly with the city as well. Richard Leiter helped arrange those meetings, and we shared our concerns and discussed challenges. While we received some guidance from Sound Transit, there was still uncertainty—so we added a cushion to our schedule and included additional costs to cover this item.

Our estimators and schedulers worked closely with our task groups throughout the proposal efforts to provide input and validate decisions. This helped them get up to speed on all aspects of the project, including phasing.

It was a requirement to use BIM during project execution. We worked closely with our BIM manager in the Seattle office to set up procedures and a framework for BIM use. Once awarded the project, BIM would assist with:

- Constructability reviews.

- Estimating.

- Scheduling.

- Implementation of ATCs.

10. Estimating and Bidding

CASE STUDY: SOUND TRANSIT OMFE AND A TOD DESIGN BUILD IN BELLEVUE, WA

We started our estimating and scheduling for the Sound Transit OMFE and a TOD project in Bellevue, Washington, as early as possible during the proposal phase. All items were included in the bid, and those within the risk register had defined mitigation strategies that were factored into the estimate. As part of our risk analysis, we conducted a Monte Carlo simulation and developed a contingency plan aligned with both the risk assessment and the simulation results. We also created a bidding strategy with our team, including requirements from Sound Transit, such as DBE participation. Our DBE strategy was considered well before selecting our teaming partners, major subcontractors, consultants, and other stakeholders.

We developed a detailed estimating and bid schedule that provided ample time for our team to review the estimate alongside our executive team. We worked closely with Wes Lumpkin, our Regional Chief Estimator, to ensure the process was well-defined and locked into our calendar—particularly for executive review. We also built in flexibility to accommodate any strategic changes during the bidding process, ensuring those changes could be reflected in both the technical proposal to Sound Transit and the required escrow documents. While we faced a few hiccups along the way, establishing our execution strategy and proposal schedule early allowed us to make timely adjustments and laid the foundation for a successful bid.

In the estimating process, it's essential to integrate your estimators and schedulers from the very beginning. This is not something to save for the end. If you think bringing them in at the last minute will work, you're setting yourself up for failure. They need to fully understand the complexity of what you're doing.

Let your schedulers and estimators:

- Start building the schedule as early as possible.

- Discuss production rates for different work items.

- Provide early cost insights.

The sooner you involve them, the more accurate and comprehensive your estimate will be—and the more time you'll have to refine a winning bid.

11.   Risk Strategy

Creating and maintaining a risk register is non-negotiable. I recommend starting it even before the RFQ phase. As you move through the RFQ process, continue refining it. Now that you've reviewed the RFP and possibly had one-on-one meetings with the owner, it's time to polish the risk register, elevate your mitigation strategies, and re-run your Monte Carlo analysis to determine the right contingency.

12.   Bidding Strategy and Owner Requirements

Develop your bidding strategy early. Incorporate owner requirements such as:

- MWDBE goals.

- Veteran participation programs.

- Local or small business engagement.

These elements should be addressed *before* the RFQ stage. Begin aligning your team early—identify your DBEs or Service Disabled Veterans Owned Small Businesses (SDVOSBs) and build the process from there.

During the proposal stage:

- Finalize your DBE/SDVOSB engagement strategy.

- Assign a team member experienced in DBE tracking and compliance.

- Break down scopes of work creatively for DBE participation.

Think outside the box. Consider farming out:

- Community engagement events (hospitality).

- Bonding and insurance support.

- Paperwork, reprographics, and admin tasks.

You'd be surprised how many subcontractors and subconsultants qualify. Don't underestimate your ability to meet or exceed DBE goals—especially when some owners, particularly on the East Coast, are now targeting up to 30% Women, Minority and Disadvantaged Business Enterprises (WMDBE) participation. That level of commitment requires creativity and early planning.

Bring in experts. I worked with Brian Ansari, a seasoned pro at crafting DBE strategies. He's helped me for years, and he's excellent at what he does. Bring in who you need—don't hesitate. Be bold.

The bolder you are, the more points you'll get.

13. Final Review and Adjustments

Allow plenty of time for final review and adjustments during the bidding phase. As mentioned in the Sound Transit example, issues *will* arise—unexpected changes, unforeseen challenges, or shifts in strategy that can alter your entire schedule or proposal approach. No matter how well you think you know the job or how aligned your team is, something will always require adjustment. Give yourself that cushion of time. It's critical.

CASE STUDY: PURPLE LINE SUBWAY EXTENSION SECTION 2 IN LA, CA FOR LA METRO

The Purple Line Subway Extension Section 2 was a proposal we worked on for LA Metro in Los Angeles, California, from January to June of 2016. I served as the design director and led proposal development for Walsh on this project.

Our team was composed of the Walsh–Strabag Joint Venture (JV), with Strabag acting as the design builder and bringing significant expertise in underground tunneling. Arup was our lead designer, and we engaged numerous subcontractors reporting directly to the JV, along with subconsultants reporting to Arup. This was a highly complex, three-mile-long tunnel segment with three massive underground stations running through Beverly Hills—an area known for its sensitivity and scrutiny.

The proposal manager, Matt Shepard, and regional manager, Bill Heathcutt, were fully engaged throughout the process. It's essential to have senior leadership actively involved in efforts of this magnitude. Our bid manager, Wes Lumpkin—who also led the bid on Walsh's successful Crenshaw/LAX project—coordinated closely with Strabag and executive teams from both firms to schedule estimating, bidding, and technical work groups. Since it was a JV, each company developed its own estimate, and then both estimates were reconciled—a common practice in joint ventures.

Technical work groups were formed for each major scope, including:

- Tunnels and underground stations.

- Architectural and civil elements.

- Other key technical areas.

These groups included designers, construction professionals, subject matter experts, estimators, and schedulers. It's critical to include estimators and schedulers in technical work groups from the beginning.

LA Metro required 18% DBE participation for the project and hosted two DBE open houses at their headquarters during the proposal phase. This meant we needed to allocate approximately $342 million of work to DBE firms. While LA Metro facilitated the events, we were responsible for:

- Hosting a booth.

- Developing logical work packages.

- Engaging directly with DBEs.

We began strategizing DBE participation even before the RFQ was released. Each designer and subcontractor was held accountable for meeting the 18% DBE requirement in their respective scopes. The Walsh–Strabag JV created a project website that included contract information and detailed work packages for various scopes, such as:

- Design.

- Community engagement.

- Environmental compliance.

- Construction and inspections.

- Materials and reproduction services.

- Hospitality.

We leveraged our database from the Crenshaw/LAX project—located just 8–10 miles away—to support the Purple Line effort. On the design side, Arup had several DBE subconsultants, and Walsh had DBE consultants supporting their portion of the proposal. In addition to the formal outreach, we hosted several one-on-one meetings with DBE firms and subcontractors.

Ultimately, the Walsh–Strabag JV met LA Metro's 18% DBE goal in our submitted proposal and bid. LA Metro's bid forms required detailed listings of each DBE firm, including:

- Roles and responsibilities.

- Contract amounts.

- A final tally confirming we met the DBE percentage.

The final bid and reconciliation sessions were held at Walsh's Chicago headquarters to ensure full executive participation. The risk register from the proposal was carried into the bidding phase. Per Walsh's philosophy, every item in the risk register—along with its mitigation strategy—was fully estimated and costed. We do not simply apply blanket contingencies.

Both teams collaborated on all aspects of the technical proposal, estimating, scheduling, and risk management. During the final reconciliation week, every work item was reviewed line-by-line by both parties. We also carefully reviewed:

- The organizational chart.

- Staffing plans.

- Schedules.

- Risk register.

- DBE plan.

- Project and support office logistics.

As this took place, subcontractor bids were received, vetted, and integrated into the master estimate. Any strategic changes were incorporated into the proposal before final submission. The two estimates were reconciled, agreed upon, and signed off by both Walsh and Strabag.

In the end, the Walsh–Strabag JV's detailed approach—particularly our proactive DBE strategy and commitment to estimating every risk line item—contributed to a competitive, compliant, and high-quality bid for the Purple Line Subway Extension Section 2.

14.   Negotiating your Agreement

Whether you're a major consultant, subcontractor, lead designer, design builder, or developer, you must negotiate and finalize the terms and conditions of your agreement with the client during the proposal phase. I recommend starting this as early as possible, as it can be time-consuming and may involve multiple parties, approvals, and legal reviews. This is not something you want to resolve after selection—these terms must be agreed upon before you submit your bid.

The client will typically use a standard boilerplate agreement and modify it based on the terms of the prime agreement. All parties involved must review the prime agreement, and your client's terms, as soon as possible. Have your legal team and business leads review and provide comments, edits, and concerns.

In a P3 (public-private partnership), developers must begin early, as their agreement with the owner will cascade down—what I refer to as a "flow-down." This means your own agreement must reflect those flow-down terms, your scope of work, and any exclusions, clarifications, or assumptions.

Just like the design builder builds their bid from the bottom up, you must build your estimate by fully understanding your scope and detailing every aspect required to accomplish the work.

CASE STUDIES:

SH 130 TURNPIKE EDA FOR TTA AND TXDOT

AECOM and LSI negotiated and finalized the design agreement during the proposal effort. AECOM had a detailed scope and a bottom-up estimate aimed at securing:

- A lump sum fee for basic design work.

- A time and materials contract for post-design services.

I was the principal in charge for AECOM, and Bruce Houghton worked closely with our subconsultants to refine the scope and estimate. During negotiations, LSI's Doug Fuller disagreed with the lump sum approach, citing that 95% of the design would be done in the project office and should use a field rate. LSI proposed a target price structure, which we ultimately agreed to after:

- Restructuring the estimate.

- Modifying the design agreement.

- Accepting LSI's requirement for approval on annual compensation adjustments.

- Agreeing to report weekly on labor and expenses per WBS.

Had we not started negotiations early, we would not have finalized the agreement before proposal submission. In hindsight, LSI's annual compensation approval process was time-consuming, requiring us to justify each staffing increase.

IH 635 MANAGED LANES P3 IN DALLAS FOR TXDOT

I was the proposal manager for AECOM and responsible for the design agreement, fee estimate, and scope. Dragados was the managing partner.

Midway through the proposal, Williams Brothers exited the JV. Bob Swanigan from AECOM worked with Dragados to bring in Kiewit, Granite, and Zachry.

While working with Dragados' proposal lead, Bernardo Palicio, I submitted our scope and fee. He responded by saying he had "thrown the fee in the freezer"—refusing to negotiate. With no progress, I reached out to Rob Anderson at Kiewit. After reviewing the materials, he approved the scope and fee on behalf of the JV, and we finalized the agreement within weeks.

I-595 CORRIDOR ROADWAY IMPROVEMENTS P3 FOR FDOT

I joined after the agreement, scope, fee, and schedule had already been signed with Dragados (Dec. 9, 2008). I began work on March 30, 2009, at which point the project was already in crisis. EarthTech had led the proposal, but by award, AECOM had acquired them—and the 2008 recession was in full swing. This $1.27 billion construction project required 465 designers over 14 months.

Despite internal warnings, AECOM signed an agreement that was $30 million below what former Earth Tech leadership deemed necessary. The agreement obligated AECOM to perform any work Dragados requested—an unsustainable and regrettable commitment.

PURPLE LINE SUBWAY EXTENSION SECTION 2 FOR LA METRO

As Executive Design Director for Walsh, I was fully engaged from January 25 to June 1, 2016, supporting proposal manager Matthew Shepard and regional manager Bill Heathcott. Arup, our lead designer, had performed well on prior work (e.g., Crenshaw/LAX), but contract negotiations were difficult and slow.

It took three months to finalize the design agreement. Richard Prust, Arup's LA-based infrastructure principal, delayed the final scope and fee proposal, delivering it just two weeks before the bid deadline—over a month later than promised. The proposal was excessively high. At that time, Bill Heathcott said that he had too much else to deal with and accepted their proposal. I felt Arup's tactic was poor and expressed this directly to Prust.

15. Negotiations with the Owner

So, I'm assuming we're now moving into negotiations with the owner, having been selected for the project. This is the time to sit down with the owner—possibly for the first in-depth meeting. You may have had some one-on-one sessions during the proposal phase where the owner gave you insight into what would be acceptable or preferred. On many of our projects, one-on-one meetings are now common practice. Learn as much as you can during those, but understand that you won't get all the answers there.

Formal negotiations with the owner are absolutely necessary for both parties. During these discussions, you'll want to revisit key areas:

- Bid and schedule – See if updates are needed based on new direction or feedback.

- ATC evaluations – Owners may introduce ideas from other proposers. Often, proposers who are not selected receive stipends, giving the owner the right to incorporate their ATCs. You may be asked to evaluate and potentially integrate these into your plan.

- Team strategy and staffing – Reassess your strategy, team composition, and schedules, especially in light of any newly proposed ATCs.

- Risk assessment – Update your risk register based on owner discussions and potential changes.

Don't be afraid to ask questions—this owner will be your partner for years. Use this opportunity to open meaningful dialogue. If you haven't had time to review the risk register together during earlier meetings, now is the time to address major items. Make sure you're aligned on key processes, especially regarding reviews, approvals, permitting, and third-party involvement. These are critical for successful execution.

Also, revisit your MWDBE and SDVOSB compliance:

- Confirm that you are fully compliant with the owner's participation goals.

- If not, use negotiations to adjust and ensure compliance.

- If a DBE or SDVOSB dropped from your team, disclose it and outline your plan to replace them.

Be open and transparent. Treat the owner like a partner—because if they're not, I guarantee your project will struggle.

CASE STUDY: SH 130 TURNPIKE EDA FOR TTA AND TX-DOT–INCORPORATING SELECTED ATCS

TTA and TxDOT asked if we could incorporate ATCs from other proposers into our project to help reduce costs. We evaluated three ATCs in total and ultimately decided to integrate two of them. Each ATC was assessed based on its impact on cost—whether positive or negative—as well as sequencing, schedule implications, resource availability, and overall risk.

We ran all three ATCs through our risk register and performed a detailed analysis. This included evaluating how each would affect our construction sequence, whether additional resources would be needed, and how responsibilities would be divided among LSI, AECOM, and the various subcontractors and subconsultants. We also examined potential adjustments to pricing, schedule, and staffing needs.

To help guide our decision-making, we developed a matrix-based evaluation that clearly laid out the pros and cons of each ATC. Once that analysis was complete, we met with TxDOT and TTA to present our findings. Our conclusion was that two of the ATCs were feasible and could be integrated without disrupting the project. The third, however, would significantly derail the schedule and jeopardize our timeline. TxDOT and TTA reviewed our recommendation and agreed that the third ATC should be dropped. They also supported our plan to update the risk register, schedule, and estimate accordingly.

TxDOT gave us the time we needed to finalize the changes, and once the adjustments were complete, we held another meeting to confirm pricing and scheduling. We also went back through the risk register to ensure that all necessary updates were made based on the new plan.

This process not only enhanced the overall quality of the project but also strengthened our relationship with the owner. If those relationships haven't been built yet, this is the perfect opportunity to establish them. It's a chance to show that your team operates with transparency, collaboration, and professionalism—qualities that lay the foundation for long-term success on any job.

16. Validate Original Assumptions

When going through this process, you'll be looking at four key things. The first is scope validation. Don't skip this step, and don't handle it superficially. This is where you sit down with the owner and strive for full transparency. Get everything out on the table.

1. Go through your initial scope assumptions with the owner.

2. Validate whether those assumptions are correct or need adjustment.

3. Don't leave this to just your project director. Involve your team in negotiations.

4. Let the owner see how your team works together—this builds trust.

Come prepared: develop a clear agenda, send it ahead of time, and walk the owner through it during the meeting.

Make sure the owner brings their key team members—whether that's a structural discipline lead, the general consultant, or others involved in oversight or reviews. If reviews are happening at the district level, ask when central office staff will be brought in. Understand who the stakeholders are, how community engagement will be handled, and who from the owner's side will lead those efforts. Clarify whether your assumptions around public engagement are accurate and what adjustments might be needed to align the scope.

CASE STUDY: SH 130 TURNPIKE EDA FOR TTA AND TX-DOT

On the SH 130 Turnpike project, we were actively negotiating the incorporation of selected ATCs from other proposers. During that process, we sat down with TxDOT and TTA to validate our scope assumptions and align on expectations. We confirmed the owner's approach to stakeholder involvement and community engagement, and agreed on the cadence and structure of meetings like task group sessions, progress updates, and director-level briefings.

This was the first time we were getting detailed input from the owner on these task group meetings. Up until that point, their involvement had been limited. We invited them to join these sessions going forward because they needed to be part of the decision-making process if the project was going to be successful.

We submitted detailed agendas to TxDOT in advance and documented all meeting notes. Where there were differences in assumptions, we evaluated them from multiple angles—cost, schedule impact, resource needs, sequencing, and risk. Fortunately, there were only minor differences. For example, we had assumed that TxDOT and third parties would participate in the task group meetings, and this aligned perfectly with their expectations.

We made a few minor adjustments to our scope and schedule based on invalid assumptions, communicated those changes to TTA, and were able to finalize negotiations and receive our first Notice to Proceed (NTP).

17. Stakeholder and Third-Party Involvement

CASE STUDY: SH 130 TURNPIKE EDA FOR TTA AND TX-DOT

Stakeholder and third-party involvement played a critical role in the success of SH 130. Our engagement started nearly two years before the RFQ was issued. By the time we submitted the proposal and bid, we had already attended most of the community meetings, met with key stakeholders, and participated in every TTA and TxDOT session related to the project. We also engaged with local and statewide political leaders and followed the full environmental review process.

Our connection with TxDOT's Strategic Projects Group, including Phil Russell, gave us an even deeper understanding of their expectations. AECOM's local strength in Austin—particularly through TCB—was invaluable. Bob Cuellar, a former 25-year veteran of TxDOT, helped us navigate both the politics and the processes. He was instrumental in helping us understand stakeholder engagement, public expectations, and what mattered most to TxDOT.

Although AECOM's official scope excluded utility coordination, ROW acquisition, environmental permitting, QA, and outreach, we were still responsible for communication and collaboration with the subcontractors performing those services. Subconsultants working under LSI and the design builder were fully engaged and informed throughout the process. Firms like Sanders Wingo and Galvin & Morton Advertising, Inc. led LSI's community engagement efforts.

That early and consistent engagement—with both the public and political stakeholders—significantly influenced the strength of our proposal and, ultimately, the success of the project.

Chapter 5
Project Execution

1. Transitioning from Proposal to Execution

We're going to start with the transition from proposal to execution—a very important step. Our objective is to carry forward all the documents developed during the proposal phase into project execution. This includes the negotiation session we just completed and any changes made along the way. We must ensure:

- We are using the most current and accurate versions of every document.

- Everyone on the team knows where all documents are stored and how to access them.

We'll need to create or refine several key documents:

- Refine and broaden the execution strategy developed during the proposal into a full execution plan

- Fully update and implement the 30, 60, and 120 day startup plan, including any modifications made during the proposal phase.

We'll also review and finalize the project org chart:

- Identify and fill any missing roles or responsibilities.

- Ensure a complete staffing plan is in place to match what was used to develop the proposal pricing.

Finally, we must ensure that all commitments made in the technical proposal are integrated into the execution plan. These represent the owner's expectations—and it's our responsibility to deliver on them.

CASE STUDY: SAN JOSE TERMINAL AREA IMPROVEMENT PROJECT (TAIP)

This project, delivered for the City of San Jose, involved Hensel Phelps and Granite as the design builder. Though not a joint venture, Granite was a subcontractor responsible for all civil work. AECOM was the lead civil designer, and Fentress served as lead architect. Fentress had a strong working history with Hensel Phelps, and AECOM had successfully partnered with Granite on several past design build efforts.

TAIP was one of the first progressive design build projects in the U.S. Initially, the city hired URS and Parsons as program managers, but every bid package they released came in about 20% over estimate. Frustrated, the city decided to engage a design builder who could collaborate with them on defining scope, schedule, and budget across the entire $750 million program, executed by task order.

The program included upgrades to Terminals A and B, improvements to Terminal C's baggage claim, and reconstruction of the terminal roadway network. Execution was scheduled for 2007 to 2009—just two years. However, our team began collaboration in 2006, even before the RFQ was issued. We worked closely with Hensel Phelps and Fentress early in the process. Mike Gasparro, VP and aviation lead for AECOM's western region, reached out to me, and we began developing the team.

We met with Hensel Phelps in San Jose, brought in Granite for roadway and bridge work, and Granite added Flatiron for additional bridge support. We conducted a SWOT analysis and created a risk register with mitigation strategies based on our due diligence. After submitting an SOQ, we were shortlisted and invited to interview.

Our proposal and interview focused on how we would collaboratively define work packages, develop schedules and estimates, and monitor the budget with the city. We updated our SWOT, risk register, and mitigation strategies and included aerial flyovers to present our approach to delivering the program within budget.

Although the city initially selected Bechtel and began negotiations, they were unable to reach an agreement. Two months later, the city contacted

Hensel Phelps, who successfully negotiated a contract within about three weeks.

During the proposal phase, our team had already developed a detailed staffing, mobilization, and startup plan, along with a packaging strategy. Mike Gasparro and I finalized AECOM's execution plan and mobilization readiness. The city provided a project office to house the design build core team and key staff. Once we received notice to proceed, mobilization began immediately.

The seamless transition from proposal to execution—grounded in pre-project planning, risk management, and team alignment—was critical to meeting early milestones and achieving overall project success.

CASE STUDY: I-595 CORRIDOR ROADWAY IMPROVEMENTS P3 IN BROWARD COUNTY FOR FDOT

This project highlights what can go wrong when the transition from proposal to execution is misaligned. I previously wrote about the challenges AECOM faced in negotiating its design agreement and fee with Dragados prior to my involvement.

As the team attempted to move into execution, they struggled with a lack of clear direction from Dragados. AECOM's fee and schedule were based on continuing the work as laid out in the proposal. However, Dragados had different plans that were never communicated during final scope and fee negotiations.

This disconnect between proposal assumptions and execution realities created major issues on the ground. It underscores the importance of fully aligning expectations, scope, and strategy during the transition phase. Any deviation from the agreed-upon plan needs to be discussed and incorporated before execution begins to avoid confusion and disruption.

Dragados was seeking significant construction cost savings on multiple major elements of the project and began pressing AECOM to revisit these elements. This was a $1.27 billion construction contract that required over 465 design staff to complete the design work. However, AECOM's schedule and fee never accounted for these major revisions.

- The agreed schedule included:

- Six months to obtain approval of the Corridor Master Plan (CMP) from FDOT.

- Fourteen months to complete most of the final design.

Introducing major changes to the work scope raised red flags with FDOT and their general consultant, as such revisions invited deeper scrutiny. The AECOM team tried to communicate these risks to Dragados, but our concerns were dismissed. As the design team began implementing cost-saving design changes at Dragados' request, FDOT and their GC began challenging nearly every modification submitted.

I joined the project in late March 2009 and was brought up to speed by Bruce Moulds, AECOM's project director. At the time, Palicio was leading the project on the Dragados side. Bruce had previously established an AECOM executive committee—comprising corporate risk, the EVP of America Infrastructure, regional leaders, accounting, corporate legal, and key project team members—to advise and support the project team.

In late April 2009, Dragados changed leadership. Juan Miguel Perez, EVP and project manager from Madrid, took over. Soon after, Dragados' legal counsel began attending all project meetings, and a steady flow of letters began between the two companies. We added a contract administrator, Mark Wistoff, to help manage all correspondence and contract modifications. Mark and I coordinated daily with Bruce and Chuck Juliana from corporate legal.

FDOT made it clear that no final design could proceed until the CMP was approved. As we continued to address comments from FDOT and their GC, we learned—six months into the process—that FDOT Central in Tallahassee had not yet been involved in any submittal reviews. Tallahassee was now being brought in, further complicating and delaying progress.

By September 2009, we were able to negotiate with FDOT to begin reviewing our final design. However, they stated they would not officially review 90% submittals until the CMP was approved. We were in the process of closing out CMP and bridge concept report comments and had started receiving feedback on our 90% design plans.

Throughout this period, Dragados consistently challenged our progress reports and invoices, delaying payments by two months per invoice. Every action taken by Dragados caused time losses, financial strain, and delays. In May 2010, Juan Miguel Perez sent me a letter asking me to remove myself from the project. I left the project office and transitioned AECOM's new project manager from AECOM's Sunrise office through June 2010.

Dragados negotiated a contract modification payout with one of AE-COM's EVPs—agreeing to pay only 23 cents on the dollar for all of AE-COM's submitted change orders. The project ultimately opened in 2014 as required by ACS's prime agreement.

In July 2019, I received a call from Ray Rivas, AECOM's former design manager, informing me that Dragados had filed a claim against AECOM and asked if I would be willing to serve as an expert witness. I worked with their attorneys, Smith, Currie & Hancock LLP, from February through my testimony on October 11, 2019. I was informed months later that Dragados had won the award.

This case study shows how a terrible transition from proposal documents to execution played a critical role in missing project milestones and ending up in legal arbitration. Not negotiating a reasonable agreement, and not having a good understanding of the culture of how exactly Dragados was going to approach the project, led to delays and significant problems.

2. Your Role as Principal-In-Charge and Leadership

Your role as principal in charge, project executive, or any senior leadership position is to support both the project and your people. If you're not physically on the ground with your team, you must develop a strategy to understand what's happening from the start—tracking real project progress so you can provide meaningful support when needed. Every AD Mega-Project comes with its own unique challenges, complexities, and opportunities. That's the nature of these large-scale efforts, where diverse personalities and high stakes are always in play.

CASE STUDY: SH 130 TURNPIKE EDA FOR TTA AND TX-DOT

A strong example of this is the SH 130 Turnpike EDA P3 project for TTA and TxDOT in Pflugerville, Texas. Lone Star Infrastructure (LSI) was selected by TTA on April 8, 2002, and as the lead designer, AECOM began mobilizing immediately. Bruce Houghton, who led the proposal efforts, worked closely with Doug Fuller, the project director from Fluor, on a day-to-day basis.

I was the principal in charge for AECOM. Bruce and I had developed our 30, 60, and 120 day startup checklist and plan during the proposal and began using them as operational tools from day one. At the time, I also served as the regional manager for AECOM's mountain region, overseeing eight offices across five states and 350 staff. My home office was in Phoenix, which was our largest and most profitable operation.

LSI had already set up a temporary project office in Austin during the proposal phase. Doug decided this would remain our base until the permanent office in Pflugerville was ready. My supervisor at the time, Doyle Wiste (West Group Infrastructure Leader), had just completed the successful T-REX project in Denver, where both DMJM Harris and TCB handled segments under Parsons and Kiewit. To support SH 130, Doyle brought in key team members from T-REX, including Chuck Jones—former U.S. Army Corps of Engineers and segment manager for DMJM Harris—to serve as our design director.

AECOM had a small team of 12–20 staff working in the temporary office in Austin, including Bruce Houghton, who kept our 30, 60, and 120 day startup plan updated. I held weekly calls with Bruce to track status updates and manage action items. Things were progressing well, and by October 2002, we transitioned to the permanent project office in Pflugerville.

Once the move was complete, I began visiting the project office every two weeks. During these visits, I:

- Held meetings with our internal project management team.

- Met with LSI leadership, TxDOT representatives, and HDR (the general consultant).

- Collected feedback on project progress, issues, and expectations.

- Shared updates with AECOM corporate and provided input on strategy and problem-solving.

Mary Terrell, my business unit manager, often accompanied me on these trips. During each visit, I also met with our project controls group and continued weekly calls with Bruce Houghton and the on-the-ground project team.

During my first formal site visit, I learned from LSI, TxDOT, HDR, and our team that we were about three weeks behind schedule. Several key issues were identified:

- QA/QC concerns.

- Delays in staffing and DBE onboarding.

- Problems with toll road architecture.

- Other execution-related issues.

Bruce also flagged a potential issue with Chuck Jones, our design director. Chuck was spending too much time in meetings and not enough on key responsibilities. I met with Chuck to address the concern, asking him to prioritize the meetings most critical to his role and to stay focused on his core project duties.

After my first formal visit to the SH 130 project office, I began working more closely with Chuck, trying to support him and offer help where I thought it was needed. One of the first issues I noticed was his difficulty in completing the staffing plan. I worked with him and Pam Hoebner to get it finalized. However, it quickly became apparent that Chuck was struggling in his role as the design director and didn't fully understand what was expected of him.

I explained the responsibilities of his position and expressed my concerns. I also spoke with Bruce about what I was observing, and we both agreed it would be best to begin planning for Chuck's replacement. I shared my concerns with Doyle Wiste and our corporate leadership and recommended that Chuck be removed from the project as soon as possible. Doyle mentioned that Mike Ofenstein might be available—Mike had been instrumental on DMJM Harris's segment of the T-REX project and came highly regarded.

Doyle and corporate leadership agreed with my observations and recommendation. During one of my visits to SH 130 on January 15, 2003, I met with Sharon Gookin, Deputy Director for LSI, to discuss staffing. I also met with Chuck and Bruce to address key project issues and the need to finalize a management recovery plan.

On January 18, I signed an executive search agreement with Bill Bielfeldt, a recruiter, to help us find a new project director. Around that same time, Bruce prepared a memo outlining critical items for success on SH 130, and we both began working on a formal transition plan.

On February 4, I met with Doug Fuller and Sharon Gookin from LSI to present the transition plan. We explained that we would be removing Chuck from the project and appointing Bruce Houghton as the interim design director until we secured a permanent replacement. I then met with the entire project management team to explain the situation and walk through our game plan. I also met with the segment and discipline managers to ensure alignment and followed up with a formal memo documenting the transition plan that same day.

By February 24, Bruce forwarded me the final draft of the SH 130 recovery and management plan—an eight-page document outlining strategies to recover from our current two-to-three-week delay in delivering roadway packages. The plan detailed:

- Roles and responsibilities of each major position.

- Meeting management expectations.

- Milestones and accountability structure.

I reviewed the document, provided feedback, and Bruce finalized it before sending it to the project team, Doug Fuller, and Sharon Gookin at LSI.

That same day, I sent Doug Fuller a memo titled SH 130 Project Accomplishments on Management Recovery Plan and Critical Items for Success, and I copied the project management team, Sharon Gookin, and Doyle. The memo reinforced the content of our earlier communication and laid out how we would course-correct and move forward.

Sometime in March, Bruce let me know he was having issues at home— his wife wanted him to return to Chandler, Arizona. I worked with him, LSI, Doyle Wiste, and my team in Phoenix to coordinate his transition back to the Phoenix office and officially change the interim design director role from Bruce to me for the SH 130 project. LSI approved the change, and I asked Steve O'Brien to take over responsibility for running day-to-day operations in the Phoenix office.

I immediately began weekly commuting to Austin from Phoenix to assume the interim design director role. Meanwhile, Bill Bielfeldt, our recruiter, had been actively searching for a permanent replacement. After a few candidates didn't work out, he sent me the resume of Glenn Sadulsky, based in Framingham, Massachusetts.

Glenn had over 25 years of engineering management experience in the transportation industry, including:

- Leading large-scale transportation Mega-Projects up to $1 billion in construction value and $100 million in design fees.

- Serving as project director and senior project manager.

- Managing operations for a 95-person, multidiscipline engineering office.

After thorough due diligence and negotiations, I sent Glenn an offer letter on July 22, 2003, with an agreed-upon start date of July 28. He joined the SH 130 project office on that date.

I worked closely with Glenn in the project office for the next three months to fully transition him into the design director role. Once the transition was complete, I returned to Phoenix to resume my previous responsibilities, but I remained engaged throughout the life of the project.

From 2003 through 2008, I continued to provide consistent support through:

- Weekly calls.

- Monthly site visits.

- Quarterly project reviews.

The project was extremely successful. AECOM and the entire team delivered SH 130 on time and within budget. I continued supporting Glenn and his successors—Mike Ofenstein, Brian Dodson, and Matt Anderson—through the project's completion on February 7, 2008.

3. Developing a Project Work Plan

I know we've touched on this topic before when discussing proposal efforts. Now, during execution, you're going to want to take everything developed in the proposal phase, update it, refine it, and transition it into your execution plan. You don't need to start from scratch on everything—but for some areas, you will, because those pieces were only developed to a certain point during the proposal.

You may have begun organizing for execution during the proposal phase, but now you need to fully develop and implement your execution documents. Here's where to start:

- Gather everything created during the proposal phase and organize it into a file or folder.

- Begin drafting your work plan using that material as a foundation.

- Leverage internal templates—many organizations, like AECOM, have detailed templates that can carry over directly into execution.

This isn't a solo job. Collaboration is key:

- Involve your project controls team and other key staff early

- Don't develop the work plan in a vacuum—it will fail if you do

- Even during early drafts, conduct team reviews to ensure alignment and ownership

Host a startup meeting with your key staff. During this, review:

- Roles and responsibilities.

- Expectations for team contributions to the work plan.

- How each person's responsibilities tie into project execution.

Once the draft is complete, obtain necessary approvals. This could be from:

- An executive committee.

- Your AD leadership team.

- The project's principal-in-charge.

Find out who the approval authorities are and work closely with them. Don't see this as a check-the-box exercise—this document is meant to guide you and your team through the life of the project. On AD Mega-Projects, this might be four, five, or even eight years. A good work plan should evolve over time.

Remember, the work plan is not static. Once it's published, you'll find things that need to be revised:

- You may have missed something.

- Something may no longer reflect how you're actually doing business.

- Changes must be updated, reviewed, and approved.

As the **project manager or director**, it's your responsibility to ensure the plan is usable, accurate, and reflects real project execution. It must:

- Work for you and your team.

- Work for the owner and the developer.

- Work for your subconsultants and subcontractors.

Treat it as the living, breathing implementation roadmap that it is.

CASE STUDY: I-595 CORRIDOR ROADWAY IMPROVEMENTS P3 FOR FDOT

The I-595 Corridor Roadway Improvements project in Broward County, Florida, was delivered as a public-private partnership (P3) for FDOT District 4. As part of project startup, FDOT required the creation of a formal Project Management Plan (PMP). Since this was a P3, the owner of record for the PMP was ACS Infrastructure, the developer.

FDOT required a very specific PMP format, which included eleven chapters. These covered areas like team organization, design and construction management concepts, interface with QA/QC, design–construction integration, cost and schedule management, environmental and life-cycle considerations, and interfaces between construction, operations, and maintenance teams. A series of appendices supported these chapters.

ACS, the developer, followed this format, and the PMP became a major collaborative effort among ACS, Dragados (the lead contractor), AECOM (the lead designer), and other partners like HNTB (CEI) and Jorgensen (O&M). As project manager for AECOM, I was responsible for several critical portions of the PMP. These included team organization, the design management concept, portions of the interrelationship between design and construction activities, approaches to environmental compliance, cost and schedule management, and interactions with FDOT District 4.

I also developed several appendices, including the AE organization chart, AE project work plan, and the design inputs to the DBE utilization plan. These documents were highly detailed. The organization chart outlined the internal structure of our design organization, reporting relationships to Dragados USA (DUSA), subconsultants, and all supporting AECOM offices, including their leads and roles.

The design team for this project included 465 team members, nine sub-consultants, and multiple AECOM offices across the country—all contributing to the success of the project.

The project was divided into eight construction zones, with clearly defined responsibilities for both design and construction in each zone. I also wanted to walk you through one of the attachments included in the Project Work Plan. This document was extremely detailed.

Section One outlined the purpose of the plan.

Section Two provided a description of the project, including a project overview, project history, confidentiality protocols, major phases of the I-595 project, and the scope of work.

Section Three addressed the project approach. It covered general project management strategies, including the overall design approach and coordination meetings. It also included information on design package submittals, work plans and design workbooks, the development and management of as-built plans, and the review and approval process for shop drawings.

Section Four focused on project organization. It described the project team structure and the layout of the project office. Interestingly, while the design team included 465 people, the project office itself was relatively small—about 35 people—highlighting the contrast between the scale of the team and the onsite operations.

Section Five detailed the roles and responsibilities of key team members, including the project manager, design manager, discipline leads, task leads, and task teams, and how those roles interacted.

Section Six outlined the codes, standards, permits, and licenses required for the project.

Section Seven addressed the safety, health, and environmental programs in place.

Section Eight covered the Procurement Management Plan, which outlined the administration of the prime contract and subcontracts and provided an overview of the overall procurement process.

Section Nine was not used.

Section Ten addressed Project Administration, detailing communication protocols (both incoming and outgoing), meeting structures, monthly reporting requirements, and personnel policies.

Section Eleven focused on Document Control, specifically the handling and management of deliverables.

Section Twelve covered Project Controls, which included three main areas: general controls, project task schedules, and project close-out procedures.

Section Thirteen was dedicated to Quality Control and Quality Assurance. It included subsections on general design reviews, maintaining quality records, oversight of subconsultant work, conducting internal quality audits, overall project audit activities, and collecting feedback from the team.

Section Fourteen covered Team Feedback.

Finally, the appendices of the work plan included several key components. These featured Exhibit A Organization Chart (also found in the PMP), Exhibit B Project Schedule (also part of the PMP), and Exhibit C, which was the component matrix submittal team flowchart. This flowchart visually illustrated how a project component moved through the design process, into approval, and ultimately became a construction document issued to the contractor and their team to begin work. Exhibit C1 Component Set Matrix and Exhibit C2 Bridge Group Matrix, which was essential given the scale of the project. There were over 500 bridges, supported by six or seven different offices, along with several subconsultants working on bridge-related design. It was certainly a very intense and complex coordination effort.

Figure 3.1 in the Project Controls Approach illustrated the project management flow and detailed our coordination responsibilities with FDOT, DUSA, O&M, and various external stakeholders. These responsibilities covered permitting, the master corridor plan, detailed design, construction documents, and post-design construction services. It took a few rounds of review to get everything approved by FDOT, but we moved through the process relatively quickly.

In fact, we had both the Project Management Plan (PMP) and the Project Work Plan (PWP) essentially completed within the first month and a half of project kickoff—which, in my view, was a strong accomplishment given the project's complexity.

The thoroughness of our PMP and PWP played a critical role in the success of the early execution phase. Their development emphasized collaboration with the project controls team and early buy-in from the owner.

This upfront alignment helped streamline internal processes and laid the groundwork for what would become a highly successful project.

4. Using a 30, 60, and 120 day Startup Plan

Let's talk about using the 30, 60, and 120 day startup plan. We covered the formation of this plan during the proposal phase. At that time, once we had reviewed the RFP and all the owner's requirements, we revised and refined the startup plan to align with what was being asked. Now that we're in the final phase, it's time to revisit that plan one more time to ensure it's executable.

We want to gather all the team members who will be involved in executing the startup plan. On this job, I believe we had close to 20 core team members engaged in the startup activities. In addition to that, we brought in what I call a "SWAT team," consisting of another 20 people who were not part of the main project office. These individuals had specific responsibilities for the startup and were brought in to give it the boost it needed. That's what it takes on AD Mega-Projects. When you're launching a $1.27 billion project, there's no room for faltering. You must be fully operational within the first 120 days and hit all your milestones.

I mentioned earlier that we had already incorporated the startup plan into the proposal schedule, and we finalized it as part of that process. Once execution begins, that startup plan becomes a key tool for tracking readiness and progress. It's critical to maintain engagement with your full team. Progress on startup activities needs to be tracked weekly—not monthly—like you might with some project control elements. You must keep up with it every week, and your project controls group should help ensure you're staying on course.

CASE STUDY: I-595 CORRIDOR ROADWAY IMPROVEMENTS P3 FOR FDOT

Now, let me share a bit more about how this played out on the I-595 Corridor Roadway Improvements P3 project. As you can imagine, we had a very intense 30, 60, and 120 day startup plan. Here's how I became involved.

I joined the team in our Doral, Florida office on March 30, 2009. Just a few days earlier—on the Friday before—I received a call from Bruce Moulds, AECOM's P3 Managing Director. He asked if I could join the team on the ground to help organize and lead the project startup efforts. I told him I was scheduled to attend a design build conference in Baltimore the following week and asked when he needed me. His answer: "Monday." That was a bit of a surprise, but I made it work and arrived on the ground that Monday afternoon.

When I arrived in Doral, I met with Bruce and the team: Jiri Filipovich, the project manager at the time; Ray Rivas, the design manager; Gorky Charpentier, the roadway discipline lead; and Saul Perez, the bridge lead. I was informed that the contract with Dragados USA (DUSA) had been signed back on December 19, 2008—over three months before I arrived. AECOM had recently acquired EarthTech, who had led the proposal and much of the negotiation process.

One major challenge was that none of the people on the ground had ever worked on a P3 project of this size—$1.27 billion. I also learned that the project director for DUSA was Bernardo Palicio, someone I had worked with previously on the $2.4 billion IH 635 Managed Lanes P3 proposal in Dallas. I had served as the proposal manager for that project for 19 months, so I had an excellent rapport and working relationship with him.

In fact, I had a meeting with the new executive VP the same week he arrived. I asked if we could set up a recurring monthly meeting to review progress and alignment. His response was short and dismissive—he said, in a few words, that I was "just the designer" and that he doesn't deal with designers. He said his people would deal with me. That set a tone that, frankly, was not productive—and it wasn't a good start.

To continue the case study: during that first meeting, I learned that the project was already in trouble with DUSA. They were directing our team to re-examine major parts of the design—parts that had already been agreed upon and scheduled for inclusion in the Corridor Master Plan (CMP) as outlined in our proposal. According to the original timeline, we had six months to get the CMP approved and fourteen months to get construction documents finalized and released to the field.

At that point, the team on the ground had mobilized, and most of our subconsultants—as well as our internal AECOM offices—were actively engaged in design work. This included survey, geotechnical, CMP components, and other design tasks. The structure of the design effort was straightforward: all discipline leads reported directly to the design manager, Ray Rivas, and all subconsultants did the same.

One of my first actions was to check if a startup plan was in place. I quickly found that while the team had been working on the Project Management Plan (PMP) and the Project Work Plan (PWP), they had no formal startup plan in place.

We had four people assigned to document control, project controls, and administration—but no one dedicated to leading quality assurance or a formal project controls group. That was a major gap. On a project of this size and complexity, that kind of oversight is critical from day one.

We had a submittal coordinator responsible for tracking and coordinating all submittal packages. Early on, I discovered that our discipline lead for bridges and structures, Saul Perez, was overwhelmed with the workload. We also had no one designated to coordinate with the system-wide design team, which meant interdisciplinary reviews were not being properly orchestrated or completed.

Bruce informed me that due to the project's complexity—being a design build, a P3, and the first of its kind for FDOT—and considering the contractual challenges we were facing with DUSA, the project would be classified as a C0 category. That meant it would fall under the highest level of internal scrutiny within AECOM. It also meant the project would be assigned an AECOM internal executive committee, and I would be required to report weekly to that committee, as well as monthly to the C0 review team. We would also need to produce a formal C0 review report, for which Bruce provided the template and requirements.

After reviewing the C0 review expectations, I began meeting with the executive committee weekly. I also started assisting Jiri with change order management, including letters and documentation to DUSA. At the same time, I began assembling a 30, 60, and 120 day startup checklist and plan, working closely with the team on the ground and with Bruce Moulds.

There was already a plan in place to co-locate the core design team in the project office with ACS, DUSA and FDOT, so we added those items to the checklist, though they weren't our primary focus at that point. Based on my review of the C0 requirements, monthly reporting to FDOT and DUSA, and the fact that we were already more than three months behind schedule, our focus shifted to the critical missing elements.

We urgently needed a project control lead, a QA manager and assistant, a deputy bridges and structures lead, and someone to take ownership of minor structures. We also needed an interdisciplinary coordinator, a deputy design manager, and a DBE reprographics firm to round out our resource plan.

We received approval from Bruce and the executive committee to move forward with hiring these roles. I began working with the office manager to advertise the positions both internally and externally. Fortunately, we were able to fill the QA manager and assistant roles internally with two outstanding team members from the Sunrise, Florida office. The remaining positions were filled through efforts led by Jiri, Ray, Saul, and myself. We brought the new hires on board within a month and worked closely to ensure they were fully onboarded and integrated into the team.

I personally led the effort to bring on the DBE reprographics firm and the project controls lead. We established systems to automate the weekly schedule updates, manage monthly progress reporting, handle invoicing to DUSA, and track all submittals. We also implemented tools and processes to support QA activities, change order management, and monthly C0 review requirements, including financials and contingency planning.

The original team on the ground had never worked on a P3 project of this magnitude—$1.27 billion—and they needed someone with the experience to lead and support them through it. I became that person.

5.   Finalizing Engagement Strategies

When I talk about engagement strategies, I'm referring to your MWD-BE or SDVOSB plan—defined earlier, which ensures your minority-, women-, and disadvantaged-owned business participation is confirmed, along with any veteran-owned business requirements the project may carry. On large projects, community and political engagement is also often required. At this stage, these efforts should already be developed, staffed, and moving into execution.

These are not strategies you cobble together at the last minute. Ideally, they were discussed long before the proposal phase and refined during it. Now, your team should be actively implementing them, with clearly assigned responsibilities and consultants or specialists in place. Whether you're coordinating facilitation, political strategy, risk management, or community outreach, your plans should already be budgeted and scheduled. Any startup activities associated with these should've been integrated into your 30, 60, and 120 day startup plan. By now, your consultants should have written scopes of work and should be ready to engage fully.

CASE STUDY: SH 130 TURNPIKE EDA FOR TTA AND TX-DOT – DBE ENGAGEMENT (AECOM)

Lone Star Infrastructure (LSI), the design builder, was fully committed to meeting the Texas Turnpike Authority's (TTA) DBE goal of 18%. In line with the RFP and Exhibit H of the EDA, LSI took proactive steps to ensure meaningful minority and female representation throughout the project. Their outreach efforts began more than six months prior to proposal submission and included mailings to over 500 DBE firms (with a 15% response rate), placing ads in local and state newspapers, attending business opportunity symposiums, and connecting with DBE associations. They also built a comprehensive database of DBE firms to support contract fulfillment.

LSI lead member Fluor Daniel had a strong reputation in DBE inclusion. On a previous $200 million design build contract in Chicago, they exceeded expectations by awarding $47 million to 94 disadvantaged firms—an effort recognized by the Governor of Illinois with a declaration of "Fluor Daniel Day."

For this project, TTA required 95% of the design work to be completed in the project office located in Pflugerville, Texas, where 168 full-time design staff were stationed. Before the proposal phase, AECOM brought on several local DBE firms, including PE Structural Consultants, a TxDOT-certified DBE, to support structure design efforts. AECOM mobilized 16 additional full-time design staff, both locally and nationally.

Pam Hoebner, AECOM's HR lead on the project, played a pivotal role in building out the team. She hired 100 new employees for the Pflugerville office, working with five highway-specialized recruiting firms. A staffing plan, drafted during the proposal phase, was finalized and executed during the 30, 60, and 120 day startup. Pam and senior staff wrote detailed job descriptions, reviewed resumes, conducted interviews, and managed relocations, using a dedicated relocation fund or TDY agreements.

Within three months, 100 staff were fully onboarded—nearly 20% of them placed within DBE firms, generating revenue for those firms. Pam and AECOM's senior leadership worked directly with subconsultants to ensure successful transitions. They also developed a de-staffing plan, making sure that all parties understood when personnel would roll off and where they would transition next, whether to the original firm or another location.

CASE STUDY: LAX CRENSHAW DESIGN BUILD FOR LA METRO

On the LAX Crenshaw project for LA Metro, the alignment included nine miles of light rail transit running through Los Angeles, mostly parallel to Crenshaw Boulevard. The project featured two underground stations, several at-grade stations, and several aerial structures—each with the potential to affect the surrounding community and political stakeholders. Along the alignment were businesses, traffic corridors, pedestrians, schools, churches, parks, and community centers.

During the proposal phase, we worked with Jamara Hayner from the Lee Andrews Group, who led the public affairs and communications strategy for community and political engagement. Prior to proposal submission, Jamara left Lee Andrews Group to launch her own MWDBE firm, JHK Consulting, which specialized in the same work. Because of the strong community and political relationships Jamara had built, we retained her and continued her involvement on the project. Walsh Shea, the joint venture contractor, brought her firm on board after the award to lead the community and political engagement strategy during execution.

As she had during the proposal phase, Jamara worked closely with Project Manager Jeff Mays and Senior VP Joe Lee to finalize and implement the community and political engagement plan. She also coordinated with counterparts at LA Metro, including Phil Washington, CEO, and Richard Clark, Chief Program Management Officer. Her first step during execution was to review the plan submitted with the proposal and align it with current expectations and upcoming construction activities.

Because the project had a nearly five-year timeline—from startup through testing, closeout, and revenue service—the engagement strategy needed to address all phases of construction: underground, at-grade, and aerial. The first step was introducing the project to the community and political leaders. Jamara and Jeff held one-on-one meetings with stakeholders, business owners, and elected officials to outline the project schedule and anticipated impacts such as traffic disruptions, noise, vibration, utility relocations, dust, and hauling.

They received a tremendous amount of feedback during these meetings, learning even more about the stakeholders' and community's concerns. These inputs were continuously integrated into the strategy. After these one-on-one conversations, Jamara launched broader community meetings along the corridor. These were initially hosted in an open-house format after work hours, with senior project team members available to answer questions. The meetings also included formal presentations from Jamara and Jeff, explaining the construction phasing, techniques to be used, and timelines for activities within each neighborhood.

As more input was received, the team adjusted construction techniques where possible to show the community and political leaders they were being heard. Ongoing communication was maintained through monthly newsletters, mailings, and electronic updates. Jamara developed a meeting schedule, tracked attendance, created contact lists, and built a stakeholder database to manage feedback and ensure the right information reached the project team in real time.

She established a virtual feedback loop between stakeholders, Jeff, and the construction team. She and Jeff met weekly to review developments, address concerns, and refine the strategy as needed. A monthly engagement report was also produced and included in Walsh Shea's monthly progress report to LA Metro.

As construction progressed and activities ramped up, new community meetings were scheduled to keep stakeholders informed, gather fresh input, and make ongoing improvements. As with any major construction project, incidents occurred. However, Jamara's work helped build trust with the community. One particularly successful initiative was a TBM naming contest for local elementary schools. The contest was announced in the newsletter and newspapers. Jamara and Jeff visited schools to educate students on how the tunnel boring machine worked and what role it would play in the project.

Hundreds of students submitted names. The winning student was recognized in a public announcement, and the selected name was placed on the TBM. The student received a framed photo and a small gift, and the event was covered by local media. The TBM became a source of community pride.

Throughout the project, additional events were hosted by Walsh Shea: holiday celebrations, charity gift-giving, and milestone lunches—bringing the community together and building goodwill. All of these efforts were led and coordinated by Jamara. Newsletters and local media covered these engagements extensively.

In the end, the trust between Walsh Shea, LA Metro, the political and business community, and the residents along the corridor was deeply rooted in the community and political engagement strategy. It played a vital role in minimizing disruptions and facilitating smoother project execution.

6. Finalizing Subcontractor Agreements

This is a really important part of the work. Hopefully, during the proposal phase, as you were collaborating with your major subcontractors, partners, lead designers, and their subconsultants, you were already starting to put together a contractual structure. We talked about this earlier in the proposal process—you're building the framework for those teaming agreements.

As a contractor, I don't even submit a bid unless I have firm pricing from my major subcontractors and lead designer. They must have already signed off on our teaming agreement and design agreement. Everything included in the bid should reflect exactly how you plan to execute the work.

Now, things may shift slightly after submission, but once you've been selected, you should be finalizing those subcontract agreements, getting everyone mobilized and ready to work. That's the critical piece—getting your team into action.

When finalizing contracts with your subcontractors or subconsultants, keep in mind:

- Each agreement must include a detailed scope of work, a compliant schedule aligned with the master project schedule, and the correct fee structure.

- These fees should've already been negotiated and agreed upon during the proposal phase. It's now about formalizing them in the final documentation.

- Subcontractors must be committed to supporting progress reporting, and that requirement should be clearly spelled out in their contract. This includes their role in:

  - Monthly invoicing

  - Earned value tracking

  - Regular schedule updates

Earned value reporting isn't difficult—but it does require time and consistency, especially on AD Mega-Project. Some subcontractors may have contracts worth hundreds of millions, while subconsultants might have $100,000 or more. Either way, expectations need to be clearly defined.

It's also important that you don't try to take all this on alone. I highly recommend bringing in a contract specialist. Finalizing these agreements is detailed work, and on large projects, you simply don't have enough arms to do it all yourself. Build a reliable team, delegate, and manage through collaboration.

CASE STUDY: I-595 CORRIDOR ROADWAY IMPROVEMENTS P3 FOR FDOT – FINALIZING SUBCONTRACT AGREEMENTS

When I joined the I-595 project, we still had four critical subcontractor agreements to finalize. As mentioned in the section on using the 30, 60, and 120 day startup plan, these included:

- DigiPlot, a DBE reprographics firm

- HBC Engineering, another DBE firm, responsible for interdisciplinary coordination

- MPS3D, specializing in subsurface utility engineering and radar (SUE/RT scanning)

- Stanley Consultants ADC, brought on for minor structures

Many of these were brought in after the proposal had been submitted and the project was awarded. Our management team on the ground consisted of Jiri, Ray, and Gorky, and I joined them to serve as the interview team for these firms. Together, we ensured that each selected firm met the project's technical, contractual, and DBE requirements, and that all agreements were brought to final execution quickly to maintain our start-up momentum.

We wrote a project position description and scope of work for the inter-disciplinary coordinator. Both Ray and Gorky knew Bayo Coker, who was a PE at HBC—and was actually the owner—and had worked with them on several FDOT projects in the past.

Ray and Gorky led the efforts to fill the interdisciplinary coordinator position. I worked with Kim Windloss, the office manager in Doral, to identify a local reprographics firm. I wrote up the project's reprographics needs, and Kim contacted several firms to submit proposals based on the scope of work we developed. Proposals came in quickly. Our submittal coordinator, Matt Gans, reviewed and commented on each. Since Matt would be the primary point of contact with the selected reprographics firm, his input was critical.

We shortlisted three firms, and Kim scheduled interviews with each. During the interviews, we met Hamid Sharif (President) and Richard Brockman (VP of Business Development) from Digiplot. After our initial meeting, we had a follow-up discussion with them to better understand the equipment they would install in the project office and how it would function practically. Based on their responses, we requested a final pro-posal, scope of work, and price sheet.

Meanwhile, Ray and Gorky also worked with Kim to evaluate the inter-disciplinary coordination role. They met with Bayo, explained the role and requirements, and received an updated resume and capability statement from HBC Engineering (Bayo's firm). These were shared with the rest of the team, who provided feedback and questions, which were then passed along through Ray. After meeting with Bayo in person, we were confident he was the right fit. Ray finalized the scope and fee structure with him. Bayo agreed to a full-time role during the design phase, with minor sup-port from his team at HBC.

For the SUE/RT scanning, we were encountering significant issues with utility identification in the field. Our current SUE provider, Greenhorn O'Mara Inc., used as-built plans and vacuum potholing, but we were fre-quently running into unmarked utilities. These unanticipated findings caused design delays and added redesign costs.

Ray and Gorky suggested exploring SUE/RT (Subsurface Utility Engineering and Radar Technology) with Greg Jeffries from MPS3D in Boca Raton. I asked Ray and Gorky to define the scope and locations for the scanning, and I sent this information to Greg before setting up a meeting. The four of us met with Greg, who walked us through the technology, its limitations, accuracy, and how the data could be seamlessly integrated into design plans using automation.

We checked Greg's references, which confirmed his reliability and expertise. Based on the meeting and reference feedback, we asked him for a detailed scope of work and fee proposal. After receiving and reviewing it individually, I compiled our feedback and sent it to Greg. He responded to our questions and sent a revised proposal.

Since we had already introduced the idea of SUE/RT scanning in our weekly executive committee meetings and had received tentative approval to use contingency funds for it, we brought the final proposal to the next meeting. After answering additional questions, we received full approval to proceed.

The final contract was for minor structures, awarded to Stanley Consultants ADC. Early on, we discussed how to handle the volume of minor structural work. Bruce Moulds and Saul Perez, our structures discipline lead, suggested engaging AECOM's Shenzhen office in China to perform this work at a significantly lower cost. The plan involved bringing a senior structural engineer from the Shenzhen office to work full-time in our Doral, Florida office and coordinate with Gary Walker, a senior engineer based locally.

The Shenzhen office would handle the design of minor structures—sign supports, bulkheads, and other similar elements. Bruce led this initiative and arranged a meet-and-greet with two VPs from the Shenzhen office in Miami to discuss logistics and establish commitments. Following the meeting, the Shenzhen team submitted a detailed scope of work and fee proposal based on the minor structure inventory we provided.

Our structures team—Ray, Saul, and I—reviewed the proposal from the Shenzhen office and provided comments and questions. The Shenzhen team responded promptly, addressed our concerns, and submitted a revised proposal. Throughout the process, we kept the executive committee informed during our weekly meetings and presented the updated proposal for their review and approval.

The committee had a few additional questions, which we answered, and they gave us the green light to move forward with an intercompany agreement. We used AECOM's standard intercompany agreement format, attaching the approved proposal, detailed scope of work, and an exhibit showing the location and types of minor structures. Bruce Moulds coordinated directly with the VPs in the Shenzhen office, and the agreement was fully executed.

Mobilization of the Shenzhen team began immediately. However, our team closely scrutinized their work and quickly realized they were struggling to meet the project's technical requirements, including those from FDOT, the American Association of State Highway and Transportation Officials (AASHTO), and other regulatory agencies. We kept the executive committee informed of these challenges and advised that we were preparing to seek a new solution. After a month of difficulties with the Shenzhen team, we recommended transitioning the work to Stanley Consultants ADC (Stanley).

The executive team approved our recommendation to terminate the Shenzhen office's involvement and bring Stanley on board. We requested a formal proposal from Stanley to take over the remainder of the minor structures scope. Their proposal included the full scope of work and schedule, which our team reviewed and deemed reasonable.

We executed the agreement using AECOM's standard subconsultant contract, which included:

- A detailed scope of work.

- Project schedule and deliverables.

- Fee structure.

Weekly and monthly participation requirements, including:

- Coordination meetings.

- Earned value tracking.

- Reporting on physical percent complete by activity.

- Invoicing protocols.

- Termination clauses and criteria.

I collaborated with our contract specialist, Mark Wistoff, to finalize and approve each subconsultant agreement. These clearly defined contracts—with embedded earned value tracking and performance expectations—helped us maintain cost control and ensure schedule adherence. Our project controls team tracked all progress and reporting metrics, ensuring alignment between scope, cost, and performance across all subcontracted work.

7.   Mobilizing Staffing and Resources

We have to take the staffing plan created during the proposal phase and update it to reflect specific roles, reporting structures, and start and end dates for each position. It's critical to know who is coming on board, when they start and finish, and how they fit into the overall project structure.

Ideally, you've already been working closely with your discipline leads and management team throughout this process—and that collaboration must continue as you finalize the staffing plan. This plan needs total buy-in.

From a logistics and coordination standpoint, it's smart to assign some-one—an HR or talent acquisition lead—to manage staffing on the ground. On AD Mega-Projects, especially if you're working out of a project office, it's a lot for one person to handle. If your team is geographically dispersed, responsibilities can be delegated across local offices. For subconsultants, their staff can be managed directly within their firms.

CASE STUDY: SH 130 TURNPIKE EDA FOR TTA AND TX-DOT–HAVING FULL-TIME HR ON-SITE LEAD

This brings me to a case study on the importance of having a dedicated HR lead on-site. It's unrealistic for a project manager to also handle HR for 168 staff members—it's just too much. We'll also touch on the importance of a recruitment plan. On most large-scale projects, you'll be fortunate if 20% of the staff can come from within your organization or local offices. Hiring is inevitable.

For our projects, I made sure that all management team members were seasoned AD professionals—people who understood that discipline leads are not only responsible for technical work but also for managing their teams. Discipline leads must be engaged in recruiting and vetting their own staff.

If you're planning to use recruiters, you should already have budgeted and strategized for this during the proposal and bidding process. This isn't the time to make new decisions—just to finalize and implement the plan.

A well-defined interview and vetting process is crucial. You want people who know how to perform in high-stakes environments. We didn't bring interns onto these AD projects; we hired professionals with real experience. If training was necessary, particularly for CAD systems, the CAD manager was responsible. Most public agencies have strict requirements—MicroStation, AutoCAD, or otherwise—and those specifications must be met.

CASE STUDY: SH 130 TURNPIKE EDA FOR TTA AND TX-DOT–STAFF MOBILIZATION

As mentioned earlier, TTA required 95% of design work to be performed in the Pflugerville project office. That meant 168 full-time design staff—including all firm members and subconsultants—were needed on-site.

We successfully mobilized 68 full-time staff from around the country, including subconsultants. Pam Hoebner served as our full-time HR lead for AECOM on the project and was instrumental in hiring an additional 100 employees for full-time work in Pflugerville.

Pam hired five recruiting firms, assigning each 10–15 roles to fill. A flat rate was paid per position, with compensation based on seniority, experience, and technical expertise. Both Pam's position and the recruiting firms were built into the project budget.

We had created a tentative staffing plan during the proposal phase. During the mobilization and 30, 60, and 120 day startup period, we finalized it. The plan included:

- Design and management positions.

- Start and end dates.

- Reporting structure.

- Job descriptions for each open position.

All senior staff and discipline leads worked with Pam to write job descriptions, review resumes, and conduct interviews. Pam coordinated all efforts, including relocation support for staff as needed. We had a relocation and TDY fund built into the budget.

Within three months, we had onboarded 100 staff. Approximately 50% were assigned to subconsultant teams, including 20% placed with DBE firms. This structure ensured that subconsultants and DBEs received revenue from the staff assigned to them—meeting inclusion goals while also building strong technical teams.

Pam and our senior leadership team worked closely with our subconsultants and new staff to successfully transition team members into both the project and their respective firms. A de-staffing plan was also developed as part of the broader staffing strategy. This plan ensured that all team members and partner firms were informed about when staff would need to be removed from the project. As we began the de-staffing process, firms were given the opportunity to either reintegrate the staff back into their organizations or support their relocation to other offices or projects.

Even after the initial mobilization of staff and resources, Pam continued to play a vital role on the project. As the go-to HR representative for all 168 employees in the project office, she became an essential point of contact for HR-related needs and concerns. I strongly recommend having a full-time HR person embedded on any project of this size and complexity.

Having Pam in this role meant that senior management was not the first point of contact for HR issues. This allowed our leadership to stay focused on technical delivery and project execution, without being consumed by day-to-day personnel matters. That's not to say senior management didn't get involved—but they did so at escalation points, not as frontline HR.

Mobilizing a large, technically specialized team on short notice presented numerous challenges. However, by having a staffing and resource plan developed during the proposal phase—and refined during execution—we ensured those challenges were met proactively. Not only were staffing needs fulfilled, but in many areas they were exceeded.

This approach also ensured that we adequately budgeted for recruiting, onboarding, relocation, and HR support—activities that are essential to project success but often overlooked in early planning stages.

8.   Establishing Project Controls

The next item we're going to talk about is establishing project controls. Most of the schedule should have been built during the proposal efforts.

However, as you know, a proposal-level schedule won't capture every activity. There's simply no way to incorporate that level of detail during the proposal stage.

Typically, a proposal schedule might contain around 3,000 activities. But once you're awarded the project and move into final execution, that number can easily expand tenfold—up to 30,000 activities or more. That's the level of detail required to properly manage and execute these AD Mega-Projects.

Building that kind of detail into the schedule takes time. That's why it's critical to get your scheduling team and project controls group engaged as early as possible.

You'll also need to resource-load your schedule. There's no effective way to assess earned value unless your schedule is properly resource-loaded at the activity level. I'll get into more detail on that when we get to the case study.

Another important consideration is your progress tracking and reporting requirements—both for internal purposes and for owner reporting. You should already have a general understanding of these requirements from the proposal phase. In fact, I don't know how you can even submit a bid without knowing how invoicing, reporting, and your broader project control systems are going to work.

Once in execution, you'll need to refine your invoicing and reporting templates. If you're the contractor, work directly with the owner to finalize these. Sit down with them and confirm what the templates will look like. Then, make sure your internal teams and subcontractors understand their responsibilities:

- What data they're expected to provide.

- When it's due.

- How their reports fit into your master reporting process.

You want everything to be consistent and streamlined—not a reinvention of the wheel each month.

You'll also need to determine what internal reports are required by your organization. Whether you're a contractor, lead designer, subconsultant, or subcontractor, you may have your own company's reporting standards. Make sure these align with what's required externally so you're not duplicating efforts.

CASE STUDY: ESTABLISHING PROJECT CONTROLS

Let's look at project controls more broadly, particularly for AD Mega-Projects. Every AD Mega-Project comes with its own set of challenges—management, coordination, tracking, long-lead items, third-party approvals, permitting, environmental compliance, and stakeholder engagement, just to name a few.

Designing a project control system that works for your specific circumstances is crucial. It must support:

- Your project structure.

- The owner's requirements.

- The needs of the developer or contractor.

- All partners, including subcontractors, subconsultants, and internal stakeholders.

Your project control structure will also depend on how the prime contract is structured. Is it a task order contract? I've had task order contracts. Is it a lump sum, or is it a time and materials contract? And how does the owner want you to report and what internal reporting needs to be done? Also, how will you use some of the data that you create for future work, if any? What you're creating today may be able to be used down the road. These questions should be asked before you get started—even as you're working on your proposal, final bid and escrow documents.

When creating a schedule, each project presents its own opportunities and constraints. Risks and mitigation strategies must be integrated into the schedule from the beginning. Defining those risks and developing mitigation plans should be a team-wide strategy that starts early in the procurement process and is finalized with the owner—continuing through execution, testing, close-out, and revenue service.

Project controls must be robust and adaptable. They need to track a wide range of variables and be flexible enough to support what-if scenarios and dynamic decision-making, including input from the owner.

CASE STUDY: I-595 CORRIDOR ROADWAY IMPROVE-MENTS P3 PROJECT FOR FDOT

Let's take a look at our I-595 Corridor Improvements P3 Project for FDOT as a case study. All external reporting was done through the developer, ACS, to FDOT. The reporting structure looked like this:

- DUSA (the design builder), the concessionaire, CEI, O&M teams, HNTB, and Jorgensen, all reported up through ACS.

- AECOM, as the lead designer, coordinated with its subconsultants, consultants, and vendors, who reported directly through AECOM to DUSA.

The schedule, invoicing, and reporting had to be structured in a way that allowed it to flow efficiently up through this chain to FDOT. DUSA worked with ACS and AECOM to finalize the detailed schedule and get it approved by FDOT. The schedule was extremely detailed and included:

- Startup activities, including mobilization of the core team into the project office with FDOT and our consultants.

- Design activities for CMP, 60%, 90%, and final construction document submittals by package.

- FDOT reviews (District and Central Office), third-party reviews, and permitting (drainage, streets, utilities, etc.).

- Long-lead items and detailed construction breakdowns for each package.

- Close-out for each construction element.

- ACS activities: financial close, stakeholder/political/community engagement, testing, and revenue service.

- ACS Milestone Payment dates.

All schedules were produced in Primavera P6, as required by FDOT, and complied with all their standards and constraints.

Initially, neither DUSA's nor AECOM's schedule accounted for DUSA's later desire to cut costs on major project elements. However, the schedule did include a value engineering activity, and AECOM had included some suggestions under that task item.

DUSA began demanding that AECOM reevaluate many major elements of work starting in the second month after signing the design agreement. As stated earlier, because of the complexity of this design build P3 project—the first of its kind for FDOT—and due to ongoing contractual challenges with DUSA, the project was designated as a C0 category project within AECOM. This meant it would be highly scrutinized at all levels of the organization.

An internal AECOM executive committee was established, and the project team was required to:

- Report to the committee weekly.

- Submit monthly C0 review reports.

- Provide weekly schedule updates.

- Submit monthly progress reports and invoices to DUSA.

- Maintain tracking systems for submittals, QA/QC efforts, change orders, and financials.

C0 Review Format Overview

Executive Summary

- Summary of project scope.

- Work status.

- Safety, profitability, schedule, staffing.

- Subconsultant performance.

- Changes, accounts receivable, contingency status.

- Client relationship assessment.

Project Status

- Narrative of current month's work.

- Pending issues and next month's work plan.

- Key issues for management attention or assistance.

Scope

- Fiscal percent complete.

- Percent complete by zone (project had 8 zones).

- Percent complete for over 500 bridges.

- Draft-to-final invoice comparison (noting delays and disputes with DUSA).

- Weekly (or daily) change request logs.

- Value engineering log.

- Project open issues list.

Scheduling

- Milestone status and critical path.

- Design forecast vs. baseline.

- Status of required permits affecting the critical path.

- Status of FDOT comments on non-permit design deliverables.

Budget and Financials

- Financial summary report.

- Receivables and cash flow.

- Earned value vs. revenue.

- Billing and unbilled status.

- Accounts receivable/payable reports.

- Budget allocations and explanations of significant metric changes.

Health and Safety

- Narrative on health and safety plan implementation.

- Report on any incidents.

Risk

- Narrative on maintaining the risk register.

- Report of major risk changes.

Quality

- Narrative on QA/QC plan implementation.

- Report of significant QA/QC issues.

Appendices Included

- Monthly progress report.

- Project execution plan.

- Four-week look ahead schedule.

- Project open issues list.

- Health and safety plan.

- Risk register.

- QA/QC plan.

- Drawing release log.

- Submittal log.

- Monthly estimate to complete.

- Work breakdown structure report.

- Deliverable release activities.

You can see how detailed the reporting was for the C0 review. Our monthly progress report was just as comprehensive. It included multiple task sections: Task 1000 covered design management, including geotechnical; Task 8000 focused on utilities; Task 10000 addressed SUE; We also had dedicated sections on drainage, roadway, structures, quality, and post-design services (Task 10600). Task 11000 on survey; Task 11001 on design surveys; Task 12000 on environmental permitting; Task 13000 on landscaping and aesthetics; and Task 14000 on traffic.

Additional tasks across zones two through eight included Task 15000 for lighting and Task 16000 for ITS infrastructure. The report concluded with sections on planned work for the next month, schedule variances from the previous month, and a list of open issues.

Based on the extensive tracking required in these reports and ongoing schedule changes, we formed a dedicated Project Controls Group (PCG) to automate reporting as much as possible. This group was led by Libertad Vargas, with Diana Rubio as the PC Administrator and two schedulers: Wilson Leon and Robert Van Gundy.

The FDOT-approved schedule became our baseline and was fully resource-loaded by activity and Work Breakdown Structure (WBS). This included labor for each position, other direct costs, and contingency, extending to subconsultants and vendors. The resource-loaded schedule equaled our design budget and generated a baseline cash flow curve, used to measure monthly earned value against actual expenditures.

Each month, the last Friday marked our cutoff date. From there, the PCG worked closely with all key project stakeholders—discipline leads, contract and design managers, quality and safety leads, and the submittal coordinator—to update the schedule and resolve any outstanding issues. Updates included progress via physical percent complete, revisions to the open issue list, health and safety plan, risk register, QA/QC, drawing release log, submittal log, and deliverable release activities.

Diana and Wilson prepared the first draft of the monthly progress report and C0 review, which was reviewed by Libertad and then by me. Any inconsistencies or unclear data were resolved collaboratively before final submission to DUSA and AECOM internal recipients.

Cheryl Lawson, our Southeast region finance manager, led the monthly Estimate to Completion (ETC) and Estimate at Completion (EAC) process using AECOM's Oracle-based project management system. Labor and cost worksheets were completed by each discipline lead, reviewed by me, and submitted for regional controller review by Cheryl and her supervisor, Hovi Gwin, VP Controller for the Southeast region. A summary of the ETC and EAC was included in the monthly C0 review and presented to the executive committee.

Libertad and Wilson also coordinated weekly and monthly with DUSA's scheduling lead to review updates and changes. FDOT required all schedule submissions in native P6 format, so we removed resource loading before submission to protect proprietary budget data.

Schedule updates compared progress and forecast dates against the approved revised baseline. We also developed "what-if" scenarios to explore recovery options or potential resource shifts—these were shared with DUSA leadership. Budget revisions were reflected in both the cost-loaded project schedules and the WBS as updates occurred.

Overall, our robust project controls system—with resource-loaded critical paths and WBS—provided effective tracking of project progress, variance management, and comprehensive monthly and weekly updates. These reports ensured full transparency and engagement between our team, DUSA, and FDOT, supporting the success of this highly complex P3 design build project.

9.   Establishing Invoicing Procedures

We want to ensure that whatever invoice template we submit is approved by the owner. The first thing the design builder should ask is, "Do you have a template you want us to use for reporting our invoice?" If not, we'll offer a suggested format. Often, it's easier to use a template that aligns with our internal reporting structure, but in many cases, owners have specific requirements and will insist their format is used. Whatever the case, this decision must be made early—because how we report is directly tied to how we control.

Reporting and project controls must be fully integrated. When we design our project control system, we evaluate every facet of reporting and invoicing that will be required for the job. There may be occasional changes or additions, but overall, your invoicing format should be embedded into your project control strategy from the beginning.

As mentioned earlier, every AD Mega-Project will come with its own challenges. The structure of your invoicing process will depend on how the prime contract is set up—whether it's a task order, lump sum, or time and materials (T&M) contract. It's essential to review all invoicing requirements during the proposal phase, especially since they vary significantly across clients and owners. Some owners treat invoicing as a major deliverable and require monthly project updates, schedule revisions, and detailed backup documentation.

My strong recommendation: leverage your Project Controls Group (PCG) and accounting department for all invoicing tasks. Don't try to handle invoicing alone on an AD Mega-Project—it's simply too much. You need support from your internal accounting and project controls teams. You also need a dedicated contract specialist. Managing one of these large-scale projects without that support system is unrealistic.

CASE STUDY: SH 130 TURNPIKE EDA FOR TTA AND TX-DOT

Let me go back to the SH 130 Turnpike project as a case study. AECOM negotiated a T&M not-to-exceed contract with Lone Star Infrastructure (LSI). Per the contract terms, if we underspent the budget, we retained 100% of the underrun. If we overspent, we were only reimbursed for labor and fringe on the overage—no markup.

The detailed design scope of work that was part of our contract served as our baseline. As required by TTA and TxDOT, 95% of the project had to be executed out of the project office in Pflugerville, Texas. All project office work was billed at a field rate—our contract with LSI set this rate at a 2.22 multiplier. In contrast, work done outside the project office used a home office rate, typically around 2.92 or 3.0. For most of the project, 2.92 was applied.

This field-rate arrangement worked well for both AECOM and the project overall, especially considering the lower overhead associated with field operations. Our contract with LSI specified that we had ten calendar days from the monthly cutoff date to submit our invoice. This deadline required tight coordination between our accounting team, project control staff, and field operations to ensure accurate and timely submissions.

We were also required to produce a weekly labor report within five days of each Friday cutoff. These reports had to detail, by individual, the specific WBS activity they were assigned to, what they worked on, the time period covered, and whether the individual was billed at a field rate or a home office rate. This process was extremely time-consuming and labor-intensive to manage on both a weekly and monthly basis.

LSI's monthly invoice to TTA required a comprehensive progress report, organized by work breakdown structure. This report outlined:

- What was accomplished during the month?
- Submittals made.

- New or continuing issues that required TTA's attention.

- Progress on task group activities.

- Any scope of work changes.

- QA/QC activities.

- Schedule updates.

- Any schedule variances or recovery plans, if necessary.

AECOM was responsible for contributing major portions of the progress report—specifically around activity tracking, schedule updates, and scope of work progress.

Our project controls group (PCG) on SH 130 included Robert Contos as the lead scheduler, Stephanie Belluomini as the lead accountant, and Kendra Heath-McMahons as the project administrator. They were supported by Mary Tirrell, our business unit manager for the Southwest region at AECOM.

LSI's overall project schedule was built in Primavera P6 and incorporated all requirements and constraints from TTA and TxDOT. AECOM's design schedule also used P6, aligned to the same WBS structure, and was broken down by:

- Management responsibilities.

- Startup activities.

- Schematics for each of the five Segments.

- Segment design activities by discipline.

- QA/QC responsibilities.

- Review and approval timelines.

The schedule was further broken down by construction phase within each segment and key work items. Design packages were structured based on right-of-way acquisition, environmental approvals, permitting, and milestone design phases—30%, 60%, 90%, and final 100% construction documents. Each of these phases also accounted for review periods from TTA, TxDOT and their general consultants, HDR and Bridgefarmer.

Each bridge and major structure was assigned its own WBS. With over 500 structures on the project and a total value of $1.38 billion, this level of detail was essential for project control.

Once the baseline schedule was approved by both LSI, TTA, and TxDOT, it was fully resource-loaded to align with labor and cost planning.

Stephanie Belluomini created a project timesheet for all design team members assigned to the project. It included a WBS pull-down for accurate activity coding. All timesheets were filled out daily and submitted to Stephanie by mid-afternoon every Friday. She automated this process, allowing all timesheets to be downloaded into a database and stored in any format required.

AECOM's Oracle project management and accounting system was also used and kept current by Stephanie. However, this system wasn't as detailed as the customized project timesheet, which was intentionally kept simpler in Oracle.

Each week, Stephanie produced a labor report by WBS that included:

- Individual time charges.

- Billing rates.

- Activity descriptions.

- Whether the employee used a field rate or home office rate.

The draft weekly report was reviewed by the design director. Any questionable entries were flagged, commented on, and corrected before Stephanie submitted the final version to the design director and LSI for review and approval.

Robert Contos tracked all submittals, reviews, and approvals. He and Kendra Heath-McMahons began compiling the monthly progress report immediately after each Friday cutoff. They gathered input from the design manager, segment managers, discipline leads, and the quality manager on monthly progress, including percent completion of scheduled activities.

Robert updated the schedule to reflect any changes, submittals, and approvals. He also documented related issues in the progress narrative and adjusted percent complete values based on input from the team. Using the baseline resource-loaded schedule, Robert:

- Produced a cash flow curve.

- Tracked earned value versus actual spend (provided by Stephanie).

- Monitored monthly performance.

Kendra compiled everyone's inputs into a draft progress report and sent it to the design director for review and feedback.

Stephanie and the design director created the monthly invoice template before the first billing cycle. After receiving approval from LSI, the template became the basis for ongoing invoicing. Stephanie's monthly invoice summary included:

- Labor hours and costs for the current month.

- Other direct costs.

- Cumulative billings.

- Outstanding unpaid invoices.

Weekly backups were attached to the invoice. The design director reviewed the draft invoice and the progress report, resolved any questions, and finalized both documents. They were then back-checked and submitted to LSI for review, approval, and payment.

During the project's design peak, AECOM billed approximately $3.5 million per month—making it one of the largest revenue generators in the AECOM system between 2003 and the project's closeout in 2010.

As principal-in-charge, it was my responsibility to ensure payments were received from LSI within 30 calendar days. The design director provided weekly updates on payment status. If issues arose and the design director had already spoken with Doug Fuller, LSI's project director, but payments were still delayed without a valid reason, I would speak to Doug directly. I would let him know that I was going to talk to his boss and put pressure on his boss to get Doug to release payments. Doug was never very happy when I did this.

However, my job as principal-in-charge was to ensure that we were receiving timely payments. Developing and implementing a detailed invoice template and finding processes for accurate and timely timesheet collection, progress reporting, schedule updates, invoicing, and collection allows us to have smooth financial tracking and timely payments.

10.   Non-Standard Administrative Procedures

It seems like today, people are using all sorts of Zoom- and Teams-like programs to work with large groups. But on several projects, you may have an owner requirement that the core team must be in the project office. And that's actually pretty common.

The core team could be the developer, the concessionaire, or the design builder. It could include the owner and their general consultant, lawyers, or a whole variety of stakeholders. You might also have several subconsultants taking on major roles. So, when everyone is sharing a common space like that, you'll want to make sure you have some kind of non-standard administrative procedures that govern how things are run—especially when you're responsible for a lot of people who are constantly working in that office.

I'll get to a case study that explains this in more detail, but what you're really trying to do is create consistency across the project team. Whether you call it "Project Office Procedures" or—as I do—"Non-Standard Administrative Office Procedures," it's important to have something in place for the project team. These procedures can cover a wide range of items, and we'll talk more about that shortly.

The first step is to assign someone to lead this effort—ideally, someone experienced in writing office procedures. If you've written something like this before, even better. Dust it off, adapt it, and make it work for this project. There are all sorts of ways to go about it.

CASE STUDY: SH 130 TURNPIKE EDA FOR TTA AND TX-DOT

The first time I did this was on State Highway 130, because we had a lot of people in the project office. Without office standards and administrative procedures, it would've been chaotic. So, you're going to want someone to lead and draft those procedures early—ideally during the 30, 60, and 120 day startup period. In fact, it really needs to get done within the first couple of weeks.

One of the first things you'll likely need to roll out—depending on how your project is set up—is a customized project timesheet. It's a good idea to get this launched as soon as possible, since people will start charging time immediately.

That's just one example. Others include:

- Travel arrangements.

- Temporary living accommodations.

- Hotel stays or apartment leases.

- Use of company or rental vehicles.

Some people might already live in the area—but many won't. Big projects require a lot of people, and even on the I-595 Corridor Roadway project in Broward County (I mentioned earlier), we had 35 people full-time in the project office. They came from all kinds of firms and backgrounds, so we had to create consistency.

Once the procedures are written, post them somewhere accessible. Then, hold a kickoff meeting to explain the procedures, why they're in place, and what their intent is.

Now, going back to SH 130, that was the first time I was responsible for leading a team in developing these kinds of non-standard administrative procedures. And it was definitely unique. We had 168 full-time design team members in the Pflugerville, Texas, project office—not all of whom were AECOM employees. Many were from our subconsultant firms.

But because we were all working under our prime contract with LSI, we needed to make sure that everyone followed the same rules, practices, and procedures during the project. This isn't typical practice, but it was absolutely necessary for consistency.

We had project vehicles, business trips, temporary living arrangements, and relocation expenses that had to be handled uniformly, based on what was agreed to with each team member. All of that needed to be administered clearly and fairly.

We appointed Brown Goodwin to lead the development of these procedures. He had a lot of experience with this kind of work, so he was the perfect candidate.

These may not have been standard to the company, but they were necessary for consistency across the team. Your company has to understand why these procedures are being created—and they have to support them. Otherwise, the procedures won't be effective.

Sometimes people might have to complete two timesheets—one for the project and one for their company. That's just how it is. And if that's how it has to be to make things work, then that's what you do.

So, as part of this effort, you need to develop a clear policy for completing a project timesheet—one that everyone can follow from day one.

On this job, timesheets were specifically broken out by Work Breakdown Structure (WBS) activities. The timesheet had to be filled out daily, with an explanation of the work performed. It also specified when it had to be submitted—mid-Friday afternoon—so our project control group could track the progress of the project team throughout the duration of the project, including those who were off-site.

While 95 percent of the staff was on-site, the remaining 5 percent still had to complete a project timesheet. That allowed us to collect all the necessary data and use it to keep the project moving forward each week.

For team members traveling to the project, we had a corporate agreement with Staybridge Suites, a hotel chain where we secured a guaranteed corporate rate. The rate was incredibly competitive—we had one-bedroom suites for $45 a night, which was almost unheard of.

We also had vehicles for traveling staff, with a project requirement that each vehicle had to be shared. However, one individual was assigned responsibility for each vehicle—handling its maintenance, fuel, washing, and general upkeep. We didn't want everyone to have their own rental, so instead, we arranged long-term leases. Some leases were for six months, while others extended for three or four years, depending on the role and duration of the assignment. For a long-term project like this, that made good financial and logistical sense.

Brown Goodwin drafted an outline and a full set of project administrative procedures, which he submitted to Bruce Houghton, our project advisor during startup. Bruce reviewed and approved Brown's work along with Pam Hoebner, our full-time HR lead on the project. Pam was also in charge of recruiting and handling all our project agreements.

She negotiated the hotel and vehicle agreements and was actively involved in reviewing the project procedure documentation. Brown also collaborated with Stephanie Belluomini, our project accountant, to establish all the policies around timesheet submission and compliance.

Internet and tech infrastructure on the project workstations were set up and coordinated by AECOM's IT, working through Ty Gardner, who led our design efforts. Ty also coordinated with LSI's IT lead to ensure everything ran smoothly.

Our non-standard administrative procedures were established early in the project, distributed to the entire design team, and clearly posted. Training sessions were held to walk everyone through the procedures.

Of course, when you start up a project, you're not going to have your full team on Day One. We started with about 35 people and, over the course of three months, grew to our full capacity of 168 team members in the project office.

Implementing non-standard administrative procedures—like tailored timesheets and shared vehicle protocols—played a key role in keeping things efficient, consistent, and on budget. Most importantly, it allowed everyone to understand the rules and operate within a structure that supported the success of the project.

11.   Developing CADD/BIM Manual and Procedures

I want to talk about developing CAD and BIM manuals and procedures. Not every project will require CAD or BIM, but some do—especially when it's mandated by the owner. Sometimes there's a clear requirement for creating manuals and procedures; other times, it's left up to the team.

Still, I highly recommend developing project-specific procedures, especially for BIM. CAD also benefits from defined standards, but BIM especially requires structure. When using BIM:

- Everyone involved—vendors, subconsultants, contractors—should be trained.

- The model should be consistently used and accessible to all project stakeholders.

CASE STUDY: SOUND TRANSIT O&M EAST AND TOD DESIGN BUILD IN BELLEVUE, WA

On this Sound Transit project, the use of BIM was required during execution. While I was with Walsh, we worked closely with the Seattle BIM manager and proposal team to set up the framework and procedures for project delivery.

We planned to use BIM for everything, but especially for:

- Constructability reviews.

- Estimating and scheduling.

- ATC implementation.

Our BIM manager would have developed a project-specific manual tailored to the owner's needs, distributing it to contractors, subcontractors, the design team, and vendors. Training would be provided across the board.

BIM was intended for use from schematic design through to project close-out, supporting:

- Clash detection.

- Schedule simulations.

- Photo documentation.

- Tagging parts, vendor items, manuals, warranties, and certifications.

- Walkthroughs and punch lists.

Our BIM manager would have remained actively involved to ensure compliance with the manual and support proper model use—all the way through handover to the owner and O&M staff.

CASE STUDY: SH 130 TURNPIKE EDA FOR TTA AND TX-DOT

On SH 130, we used MicroStation and GeoPak for CAD and modeling. Richard De La Hoya served as the plan production manager.

He was responsible for:

- Creating and enforcing CAD standards and the GeoPak/plans manual.

- Training production staff on MicroStation, GeoPak, and the manuals.

- Auditing CAD work throughout the design phase to ensure consistency.

LSI used our raw GeoPak files to perform all earthwork on the project. With 59 miles of right-of-way and a 200-foot swath, balancing earthwork accurately was critical. Our data saved time and improved build precision across the board.

12.   Continuation and Expansion of Task Groups

So, what is the purpose of the task groups? Why do we continue the task groups we developed during the proposal phase?

Well, during proposal work, the only time we met with the owner was maybe five or six times total—and those meetings were limited. They were never involved in the task group meetings. Those meetings were really internal team discussions. Depending on the project, the group might include the contractor, P3 partners, O&M personnel, construction staff, and finance teams—but not the owner.

Now, here's the beauty of continuing those task groups and involving owners, third-parties, and stakeholders during project execution: they're in the room with you as you're making decisions.

Benefits of Expanding Task Groups During Execution:

- Key decision-makers (owners, reviewers, third-parties) are aligned with your rationale and direction.

- They can see why certain design or construction decisions are made.

- They provide feedback in real time—this streamlines the review and approval process.

What we've found is that this can save a tremendous amount of time and reduce friction later in the project.

So what I recommend is to build on your original task groups from the proposal phase, and also create new ones for areas that weren't a focus before but become relevant during execution. These might include:

- MWDBE engagement.

- Value engineering.

- Life-cycle-cost analysis.

- Risk management.

- Financial planning.

- BIM coordination.

- Safety planning.

- Project close-out and post-design coordination.

You'll hear different names for these groups—some call them technical work groups (TWGs), and others call them task groups. I've used both. With Kiewit, we used "task groups." With LSI and others, we used "TWGs."

Either way, I highly recommend expanding these groups during execution. In the proposal phase, we only had limited access to the owner, but during project execution, these groups become a key opportunity to bring in collaboration from owners, third-parties, stakeholders, and SMEs.

CASE STUDY: SH 130 TURNPIKE EDA FOR TTA AND TX-DOT

On SH 130, LSI continued with the original TWGs that were formed during the proposal phase—and we expanded them.

TWGs included:

- Roadway: pavement, earthquake response, geotechnical, signing, guardrail, striping.

- Structures: bridges, interchanges, major culverts, major sign structures, retaining walls.

- Drainage.

- Aesthetics and landscape.

- Toll facilities.

- Environmental.

- Scheduling and estimating.

- Traffic management.

- Construction phasing.

- Pre-construction (added later): right-of-way acquisition, utility relocations, surveys.

- Public outreach (also added during execution).

To give you some context, SH 130 was designed as a turnpike and constructed as a toll facility. A major design constraint was the median, which had to be built with future capabilities for rail and other transit modes. That introduced some complexity—because the design standards for highways and railroads (like stopping distance and grades) are different. That constraint had to be considered across multiple TWGs.

We used the charrette process to mold SH 130 through active public participation into a functional, aesthetically pleasing roadway—one that would not only enhance the regional transportation network but also serve the communities along its path. The project passed through five or six different communities along the 59-mile route, each with its own needs and concerns.

We had to navigate a range of environmental and permitting requirements. That included 404 permitting, special protections for the Edwards Aquifer, mitigation for historic properties, and Section 401 water quality certifications. In total, we dealt with 265 acres of compensatory mitigation for waters of the U.S. On top of that, there were outstanding revisions to the schematic designs since the issuance of the Record of Decision, which had to be addressed. We also needed to ensure compatibility and uniformity between SH 130 and other toll facilities being developed throughout the state.

Because of all this, we had to design specific charrettes tailored to different topics and regulatory needs. Charrettes became a crucial tool for aligning all the stakeholders and managing the complex decision-making process.

The original project goal was to design and construct a 91-mile toll facility (Segments 1 through 6) for $1.38 billion. However, another developer came in and proposed taking over Segments 5 and 6, so we ended up building only 59 miles (Segments 1 through 4). That said, we completed all schematic designs for all six segments through what was known as an Early Development Agreement (EDA). We began the project in April 2002 and were expected to complete the design work by 2007.

Beyond design and construction, the proposal also included a proactive public outreach program that addressed:

- Public perception.

- Traffic management.

- Construction staging.

- Environmental concerns.

These commitments weren't just good ideas—they were contractual. TxDOT and TTA made it very clear: if it was in your proposal, it became part of your contract.

Additional project objectives included staying on schedule, meeting quality standards, and integrating the design into the local environmental and cultural context. Aesthetics were important. We also committed to keeping all construction within a defined 200-foot-wide SH 130 corridor. This approach was meant to optimize safety and productivity while providing a safer, faster, and more resilient route between Georgetown and Seguin.

One of the goals of SH 130 was to reduce congestion and pollution around Austin. IH 35, the primary corridor through the city, was overloaded. SH 130 was built two to three miles east of IH 35 to relieve some of that pressure. The new highway also served as a catalyst for economic development, rerouting hazardous and flammable materials away from city centers and other congested areas.

Importantly, this was the first public-private partnership (P3) of its kind in the state of Texas. Naturally, there was a lot riding on its success—not just for this project, but for future P3s in the state.

The project was organized into six segments and 20 design sections. These were laid out based on factors like earthwork balance points (identified by the LSI team), county line boundaries, CSJ sections, and interstate limits.

Technical Work Groups (TWGs) were a key part of the project management structure. Each TWG was led by either a construction or design lead. TTA (or TxDOT), HDR, third-party stakeholders, and subject matter experts (SMEs) were all invited to participate. The TWGs met weekly to ensure steady progress and alignment across disciplines.

A TWG coordinator—selected from the construction team—was responsible for organizing all TWG activities and schedules. This helped avoid scheduling conflicts and ensured smooth communication. The coordinator also:

- Provided a standard template for TWG leaders.

- Ensured timely meeting notes and their distribution.

- Scheduled interdisciplinary reviews.

- Compiled and submitted project reports to the project director, Doug Fuller.

Having all the major players—TTA, TxDOT, HDR, third-parties, stakeholders, and SMEs—at the TWG table dramatically expedited the review and approval process. Their input helped shape decisions in real time and eliminated the lag that often comes from siloed communications.

Once we reached 60 percent design, most of the TWGs were disbanded. But by that point, their job was done. They had already improved communication and alignment between all parties tremendously, and that momentum carried through the remainder of the project.

13. Establishing Tiger Team and Independent Technical Review Team or Peer Reviews

So what are some of the roles of a Tiger Team, or an Independent Technical Review Team (sometimes called a peer review team)? The truth is, their roles are virtually limitless, depending on the needs of the project. But at its core, the value comes from having someone outside of the project—independent from the day-to-day team—who can offer expert advice with a fresh perspective.

And this can't just be a one-time activity. These reviews should happen early and often, beginning as soon as possible during project startup and continuing through execution, and even into close-out. Peer reviews aren't meant to be a "check-the-box" event. They are most effective when integrated consistently across the entire project-life-cycle.

During my time with Walsh and AECOM—from 1996 through 2018—I personally performed peer reviews on 12 projects with a total construction value of about $7.54 billion. My roles ranged from Chief Operating Officer, to Principal-in-Charge, to Executive Design Director—each time bringing a different perspective to the table.

These Tiger Teams or review groups should be set up on every alternative delivery (AD), including Mega-Projects. And they should be budgeted for from the start—not pulled together only when something goes wrong. Schedule them early to review your 30, 60, and 120 day startup plans.

At AECOM and Walsh, we used a common checklist for every visit to evaluate consistently and thoroughly.

When planning a site visit, request the following from the project director or PM ahead of time:

- Project Management Plan (PMP) or Project Work Plan (PWP).

- Startup plan (30, 60, 120 day).

- Prime agreement.

- Project budget.

- Schedule.

- Execution plan.

- Most recent progress report or invoice.

These documents allow your team to come prepared and informed. You also want to ensure your executive committee or leadership team supports the review effort. Without that backing, it's hard to know whether your recommendations will be taken seriously. I've always had their support before stepping into a peer review, and it made a huge difference.

As a team member, your role is to lend your expertise, identify areas of performance—whether they're subpar, satisfactory, or exemplary—and provide objective, actionable feedback. Time is of the essence on AD projects, particularly during startup. So it's important for the team to be hands-on, using the checklist as a baseline while also engaging in real-time observation and interviews.

These site visits typically last three to four days. Attend task group meetings, sit in on owner meetings, observe the team dynamics. Visit the site and get a sense of the physical conditions and layout. Afterward, team members should compile their notes, discuss findings, and complete the checklist. Choose a team lead to guide this process.

In addition to the checklist, discuss observations that fall outside the scope of the template—anything important that needs to be addressed. Present your findings to the management team in a collaborative way. Don't dominate. Ask them to confirm or clarify if you've missed something. You may even adjust your recommendations based on their feedback. The goal is what's best for the project, not to prove what you know.

Personalities will always come into play. There will always be strong voices and big egos. Maybe the project director thinks he's the whole show. That's human nature. Treat everyone with respect and kindness, and keep the focus on the work.

Once your team finalizes the checklist and report, include follow-up actions, assign responsibilities, and set timeframes. Make it clear how the follow-up will be handled, and that the report will be shared with the executive team and the head of AD. Schedule a debrief with them as well.

The role of these teams is critical. Follow-up throughout the life of the project must happen. The frequency depends on how the management team is performing and how well they respond to recommendations. If your first visit happens within 30 days of NTP and the team isn't hitting the mark, get back there within the next 30 days. At a minimum, I recommend peer review visits every six months to reassess progress and offer new insights.

CASE STUDY: PENNDOT RAPID BRIDGE REPLACEMENT P3

I served on a Tiger Team for the Pennsylvania Department of Transportation's Rapid Bridge Replacement Design Build P3—a statewide project with a construction value of $850 million. I was the design director for Walsh at the time.

In early 2016, I received a call from my boss, Joe Lee—Senior Vice President and Business Group Leader for the Western Region heavy civil group. He asked if I'd be part of a five-person Tiger Team to work with the design build team. The issue? The first letting of 100 bridges (out of 560 total) was coming in nearly 20% over budget.

Walsh was the managing partner of the Walsh-Granite Design Build Joint Venture. We met quickly with the Tiger Team, the VP, and the project Principal in Charge at the project office. They walked us through the team structure, the problem at hand, and introduced us to key personnel. HDR was the lead designer.

Each of the 560 bridge sites was unique. The average cost per bridge was $1.5 million—modest on its own, but the total added up fast. Beyond general project constraints, each site had its own challenges, including:

- Roadway geometry.

- Hydrology & hydraulics.

- Permitting.

- Grading & erosion.

- Earthwork.

- Signing & striping.

- Guardrail.

- Construction phasing & staging.

We decided to start by interviewing the Project Manager, Design Coordinator from the Walsh-Granite JV, and the Design Director from HDR. From those interviews, we discovered a major gap: there was no formal process for evaluating structure types across the sites. A matrix had been created during the proposal phase, outlining the approach for each bridge, but the team wasn't using it to inform decisions.

That became one of our key recommendations—get back to the matrix, and use it as the foundation for decision-making.

During the proposal phase, technical task groups were formed that included all the necessary disciplines to assess the site-specific requirements for the various elements mentioned earlier. During the proposal phase, technical task groups were formed that included all the necessary disciplines to assess the site-specific requirements for the various elements mentioned earlier. However, a major oversight was that estimators were not included in these technical task groups. Instead, they worked independently. The designers used a matrix developed during the proposal to make assumptions about the requirements for each item of work, and based on that matrix, the estimators bid the project.

Although the bidding team had done their due diligence by lining up local and regional bridge contractors to ensure capacity for building 560 bridges across the state, none of these contractors were involved in the actual bidding or estimating process. That turned out to be a significant mistake.

The team had not developed a process to involve the estimators in the design analysis during the proposal. As a result, there was no coordination to ensure that each bridge design aligned with the estimates. Once design began, the designers took the lead, operating with very little input from the construction team or estimators.

The disconnect led to:

- Estimators working in isolation from design assumptions.

- Contractors left out of constructability review.

- No validation of design decisions against budget realities.

- A lack of process for feedback loops between design and estimating.

After our task team learned about this gap, we asked for a working group to help assess the overruns on the first 100 bridges that had already been bid. The next day, we sat down with the team and compared the proposal-phase matrix and assumptions with the actual results from the design and bidding phase.

We found that many of the original assumptions were not carried forward into design analysis or execution. Due to time and resource constraints, designers made broad, uniform decisions that didn't reflect the site-specific nature of each bridge. Too many designs relied on generic standards rather than tailoring the work to actual terrain and field conditions.

As a result, significant cost overruns occurred in:

- Erosion control.

- Guardrail.

- Pavement.

- Earthwork.

- Roadway geometry (designs did not match existing topography and went way beyond the limits used in the proposal matrix).

Rather than fitting bridges to real-world conditions, designs were attempting to resolve unrelated site issues such as rideability—issues that were never part of the original criteria requirements.

On the third day, our task team focused on what to do with the 100 bridges that had already been bid. We determined that each bridge needed to be individually evaluated to see whether redesign could bring it back within the original estimate. In some cases, a full redesign was necessary; in others, it made more sense to move forward with the existing bid as-is.

We also turned our attention to the next 200 bridges already in design. These needed immediate review to assess their status and apply course corrections before designs progressed too far. We discussed this approach with the principal-in-charge and the team on the ground. Based on our assessment, significant changes were made to the design workflow, review process, and estimating strategy.

As a result, many of the bridges were redesigned to better align with the original budget. The task team led training for the project team—including designers and project coordinators—on how to analyze each bridge in relation to its estimate. We focused on building strong coordination practices between design and estimating functions.

Moving forward, the team was trained to:

- Collaborate across disciplines and share assumptions early.

- Validate design solutions against cost impacts.

- Incorporate estimators and construction voices throughout design development.

Project managers and coordinators also received guidance on navigating complex design challenges and ensuring effective cross-functional collaboration. Thanks to these efforts, the project was ultimately brought back within budget.

This experience reinforced the importance of Tiger Teams, technical review teams, or peer review teams—not just as technical troubleshooters, but as critical problem solvers. These teams bring experience, perspective, and structure to help resolve challenges and improve delivery.

Their role should extend beyond technical feedback to include evaluation of:

- Team performance and structure.

- Collaboration between partners (owner, GC, design builder, consultants, MWDBEs).

- Communication and accountability throughout the delivery process.

A high-functioning team depends not only on technical ability but also on alignment, trust, and timely decision-making. The earlier these review teams are brought in—and the more embedded they are in project operations—the better the outcomes in cost, schedule, and team performance.

14. Finalizing and Launching the Project Execution Plan

During the proposal phase, we developed our execution strategy for estimating, bidding, and scheduling. We also created a detailed outline of our organizational structure, including the org chart and reporting hierarchy. This covered our internal organization, joint venture partners, major contractors, subcontractors, lead designers and their teams, consultants, vendors, and key project contributors.

We updated our 30, 60, and 120 day startup plan and identified the resources needed for each activity. Working closely with our executive team, we developed a resource strategy that included:

- Sourcing plan for staff and support.

- Cost estimates for recruiting, relocation, and travel.

- A phased staffing plan aligned with project milestones.

Every team member participated in this exercise to ensure ownership and clarity from the beginning.

We also developed a comprehensive execution strategy that addressed all critical functions, including:

- Design, construction, and project controls.

- Estimating, scheduling, financing, and permitting.

- Community and political engagement.

- ATC execution and financial risk management.

- Value engineering, safety, life-cycle-costing, and quality.

- BIM, testing, commissioning, and project close-out.

Our estimators and schedulers worked directly with task groups throughout the proposal process to provide input, validate assumptions, and understand project phasing. This collaboration helped bring them up to speed on the broader project context.

If BIM was to be used, we engaged our BIM manager early to set up procedures and frameworks. BIM supported constructability reviews, estimating and scheduling, and ATC evaluation—ensuring a smooth transition from proposal to execution.

As we moved into project execution, the focus shifted to refining and finalizing all the elements we had built during the proposal phase. This included:

- Developing the final project work plan and project management plan.

- Refining the 30, 60, and 120 day startup plan.

- Finalizing the CAD and BIM manuals and procedures.

- Establishing project controls and invoice procedures.

- Developing any non-standard administrative processes.

- Continuing and expanding task groups.

- Establishing Tiger Teams, peer reviews, or independent technical review teams.

All of this should feed into your execution plan, and it should directly tie back to your startup strategy. I recommend pulling everything together in the project work plan.

Once the execution plan is complete, have it reviewed by your internal management team. Then, bring the team together for a startup meeting.

At the startup meeting:

- Distribute your Project Work Plan or PMP.

- Ensure each team member receives a copy—redact sensitive financial info if necessary.

- Project controls, close collaborators, and leadership should have full access.

- Walk through the document together to align expectations and priorities.

Keep in mind, not all team members may be present on day one. If you can roll out the PMP and work plan within the first six weeks, that's a great window for building alignment. Hold a core team meeting with your designer, contractor designer, developer, financial team, and O&M leads. That's the best way to kick off a project.

As more key players join the team, make sure they're looped into the work plan and execution plan—and hold follow-up startup sessions to keep everyone aligned.

Everyone should be on the same page. That's the goal. You don't want the contractor working separately from the developer, who's siloed from the designer. This only leads to fragmentation. You want the full team aligned and functioning as a unit.

That includes the PMP. It might not need to include full budget details, but it should contain all key project information. And often, it'll need to be reviewed and approved by the owner.

This approach is one of the best ways to start a project strong.

15. Value Engineering, Life-Cycle-Cost Analysis, and Risk Management

Under strategy implementation, we're going to apply the analysis results from the proposal phase to optimize project delivery. Everything you did during the proposal doesn't get tossed—it transitions right into execution. So, if we completed value engineering during the proposal, along with life-cycle-cost analysis and risk management, all of that continues forward.

We need to decide during the proposal and bidding phases what the team will do for execution in these areas. That includes value engineering, life-cycle-cost analysis, and risk management. These are critical components, and the entire team should be involved in shaping those strategies. Everyone contributing to the bid needs to understand what's expected for these efforts during execution.

Finalize your strategy for:

- Value engineering.

- Life-cycle-cost analysis.

- Risk management.

Many owners—especially on P3 Mega-Projects—require formal value engineering that incorporates life-cycle-cost analysis and risk tracking. Make sure you're aware of this during the proposal phase and prepare both a budget and a schedule to carry these activities into execution. Ideally, much of this work has already been initiated during your proposal efforts. You should also bring on a certified value engineering specialist and a facilitator to support the process. I highly recommend using someone certified—there aren't a lot of them, but the good ones are worth it. I've worked with a few, and one in particular stands out. I'll talk more about her later on.

Facilitators can also play a crucial role. Some are specialists in value engineering; others are exceptional at guiding risk assessments. In fact, some of the best VE professionals I've worked with have also been expert facilitators. Whether they're partnered or working solo, find someone who can help guide the process and bring structure to both efforts.

Value engineering and life-cycle-cost analysis can generate enormous support from the owner, especially when you focus on developing real value for both sides. I've been in many VE workshops early in the project—around the 10% level of effort—and those sessions allowed us to validate the owner's goals, explore their early design work, and develop alternative scenarios with our SMEs. These sessions can also bring critical issues to light: sustainability, resiliency, phasing, constructability, life-cycle-costs, and financial strategies.

You don't need a month to do this. A solid VE effort can be completed in three to five days. But timing is everything. Don't wait until you've already started on schematics to begin VE—that's too late. You'll be wasting your time. Get it done up front. That early-stage VE sets the tone for everything else that follows.

Doing VE early also helps the owner feel included. In design build projects, owners can sometimes feel like decisions are being made without their input. Hosting a formal VE workshop that includes their design and maintenance staff gives them a chance to share their key performance goals and feel part of the process. I recommend scheduling a three- to five-day VE session that includes their team—early is best. The earlier the VE is done, the more opportunities there are for improvement. If you wait until design is already in progress, the pace of design build may limit your ability to adjust. Most of these projects are on fast-track schedules, so again—do it early.

When evaluating true value, don't just look at initial construction costs. Consider full life-cycle-costs, including O&M and, if it's a P3, the requirements for the handback. All of that must be factored in. Bring in SMEs with the technical and cost expertise to assess all aspects of the project—environmental, structural, financial, operational.

On the risk management side, risk analysis needs to be a continuous effort throughout pre-construction, design, construction, and revenue service. It's not a one-and-done activity. Use it to track, manage, and update your risks as the project progresses. Keep monitoring your high and moderate risks, your watch list, and identify new risks along the way. Implement positive, pre-planned mitigation strategies that address scope, cost, schedule, quality, and operations. This kind of active risk management strengthens delivery and builds trust with the owner.

Implement positive and pre-planned mitigation strategies to project scope, quality, cost, schedule, and operational certainties through the program delivery.

The owner should also be included in the risk analysis. Discuss risk and who should own each risk. The process includes the production of comprehensive risk registers and the development of quantitative top-down and bottom-up cost and schedule assessment models.

Contingency qualification, quantification, allocation, and management must be consistent with the perceived schedule in terms of flow and costs, in terms of contingency dollars at any point to provide a reasonable level of certainty in completing the project on time and within budget. The risk process should be supported by a comprehensive risk management plan and contingency management plan.

Your approach should establish a process for overall risk management, with the objective of encouraging proactive mitigation strategies, clear deliverables, and timelines aligned with program milestones.

During the pre-construction phase, lead your team—including the owner, developer, design builder, designer, and O&M team—in developing a comprehensive list of risk elements for the risk register. Each risk should include:

- A clear description.
- Potential consequences.
- Location.

- Likelihood of occurrence.

- Risk category.

- Source documents.

- Recommended mitigation actions.

The goal of the risk register is to support successful program completion by addressing risks related to public messaging, operational impacts, service disruptions, unforeseen conditions, cost overruns, procurement delays, decision-making disputes, and operational readiness and transition.

As you enter the design build phase, continue managing and updating the risk register. For each risk, identify the responsible parties, and determine who must be consulted or informed. Create and maintain a risk range model to quantify the cumulative effect of listed and emerging risks on overall program cost and schedule. This model should provide a realistic cost-benefit analysis and a range of potential outcomes.

Be sure to identify risk elements within the design build schedule and recommend adjustments to mitigate them. Pay close attention to the relationships between cost, schedule, and interface events, as these interdependencies can have a major impact.

Develop a unified list of mitigation activities, assign responsibilities, and hold weekly meetings to track progress and review open risks. Schedule monthly risk meetings with all key parties involved to ensure consistent alignment.

During the O&M phase, continue updating the risk register with a focus on maintenance and inspection. Provide risk analysis and assessments of work plans, update strategies and schedules, and ensure regular maintenance and inspection processes are in place. Also don't forget to pre-plan your handback requirements way before they must begin.

CASE STUDY: I-595 CORRIDOR ROADWAY IMPROVEMENTS P3 PROJECT FOR FDOT

Now let me share a case study about life-cycle-cost analysis. Success on AD Mega-Projects requires alignment across the entire team—including the owner, general consultant, developer, design builder, lead designer, subcontractors, subconsultants, stakeholders, and third-parties. Building trust and collaboration among these groups is essential, and just as importantly, it must be maintained.

AECOM

VALUE ENGINEERING LOG

Job No.: 111074 Project Title: I-595 Corridor Roadway Improvements

VE Option No.	Date Identified	Description	Date Approved by PM	Date Submitted to Client	Estimated Construction Savings	Date Approved by Client	Client Approved Amount	Comment
1		10 mph instead of 15 mph design to set stopping sight distance at the corners of bridges over the NNRC in Zone 5		4/9/2009	$ 307,386			1) DUSA directed to continue with Phase II on the VE proposal and to provide a cost analysis on 06/15/09 -2) VE Cost submitted to DUSA sent on 6/16/09
2		Increase in the cross slope for the right turn lanes along EB SR 84 from 2% to 3% in Zone 5		4/9/2009				1) DUSA directed to continue with Phase II on the VE proposal and to provide a cost analysis on 06/15/09 - 2) VE Cost submitted to DUSA sent on 6/16/09
3		Existing edges of pavement along the side streets and the Texas U-turns (i.e. Pine Island, etc.) to be maintained which will result in reductions on the construction of curve and gutter, pavement removal, drainage construction and potential utility conflicts.		4/9/2009	$ 19,996			DUSA did not expressed any interest in advancing this VE on communication dated - 6/15/09 -
4		Use of 2 drainage trunk lines along Eastbound and Westbound SR 84 instead of original proposal of 5 to 7 lines, one along each alignment for Zone 5.	6/16/2009	6/16/2009	$ 1,075,121			VE proposal and cost analysis sent to DUSA on 6/16/09
		Total Amounts To Date			$ 1,402,503		$ -	

156

The team dynamic on these projects can be fragile. Trust and collaboration can be lost quickly. As a project leader, it's important to show openness, honesty, transparency, and care. These qualities can go a long way in establishing a cooperative and effective team environment.

On our I-595 Roadway Corridor Improvement project—a P3 for FDOT—value engineering was contractually included between FDOT and ACS, and then between DUSA and AECOM. On April 1, 2009, AECOM submitted four VE options. (The following table outlines those in more detail.) VE cost estimates followed on June 15 and 16.

However, as of January 9, 2010, there had been no change in the status of AECOM's proposals. DUSA had not responded to written requests for direction, despite having verbally committed to resolve the items back in August 2009. The projected compensation for the VEs was 15%—about $210,375—pending actual construction costs and any FDOT claim offsets.

The contract language did not include a deadline for acceptance of the VE proposals, which may have been needed to preserve our right to claim the savings. In the end, the four VE options would only have saved $1.8 million in construction costs—and nothing was implemented.

The design builder was not on board, and this experience showed clearly that this was not a proper way to perform VE analysis. As mentioned earlier, VE should be done in a dedicated workshop, with an experienced VE facilitator guiding the process.

There's no need to go into the specific VE log here, but it included four items with proposed savings. The real takeaway is this: sometimes, your failures are your best lessons. This was one of those cases.

16.   Developing and Submitting the Quality Manual

In quality oversight, you'll prepare your review and submit the quality manual for approval. This happens right at project startup. Once your quality manual and procedures are drafted and approved, you'll meet with your quality management team to review the documents in detail.

Most owners have specific requirements for how the quality manual should be developed and submitted. These requirements may become apparent during the proposal period, and they must be reviewed during that time to ensure the effort is properly budgeted and resourced. This activity needs to begin immediately and should be a key part of your 30, 60, and

120 day startup plan. Your quality management team should be assembled right away to begin working on the document.

Typically, design cannot proceed until an approved design quality manual is in place. Some owners may allow work to begin with just the design quality manual, but at a minimum, you must have the full framework of the complete quality manual. If you've never worked with the owner before, be sure to confirm their expectations during the proposal phase.

While the design builder and lead designer may have experience writing quality manuals or using their own internal quality protocols for both design and construction, your team must meet the owner's requirements—including format.

CASE STUDY: TAPPAN ZEE BRIDGE CROSSING, NEW YORK STATE DOT AND THRUWAY AUTHORITY

I was on the program management team at AECOM for the $5.2 billion Tappan Zee Bridge Crossing project, a design build initiative led by the New York State DOT and Thruway Authority. I was responsible for all quality requirements on the project, including the development and authorship of Sections 111, 112, and 113 of the Design Management and QA/QC documentation:

- Section 111: Design Management and Design QA/QC.

- Section 112: Construction QA/QC.

- Section 113: Design Builder's Quality Plan.

From November 12, 2011, through February 13, 2012, I created a detailed outline and content for each of these sections. What follows is the table of contents for these plans to give you a sense of the depth and structure involved.

Section 111 – Design Management and Design QA/QC

1. General responsibilities of the design builder.

2. design builder's organization and obligations.

3. Design manager, responsible engineer/architect, QA/QC managers.

4. Design unit definition and development.

5. Relationship of early construction to design.

6. Schedule for checks, reviews, and submissions.

7. Design revisions and the design review plan.

8. Stages of design development and reviews.

9. Working plans, as-built plans, and certification.

10. Reviews: analytical, independent, as-built, and temporary works.

11. Design support during construction.

12. Quantity estimates and documentation.

13. CAD standards and project specs.

Section 112 – Construction QA/QC Manual

1. General procedures and definitions.

2. Inspections and testing of materials.

3. Quality assurance inspections.

4. Acceptance procedures and verification.

5. Referee laboratory protocols.

6. Contractor competence and process QA.

7. QA staffing, labs, and scheduling.

8. Documentation and electronic records.

9. Materials certification and final acceptance.

10. Appendices with inspection forms and sampling procedures.

Section 113 – Design Builder's Quality Plan

1. Quality plan submittal and coordination.

2. Management responsibility and authority.

3. Quality system procedures including:

    - Design input/output/review/verification/validation.

    - Control of documents and data.

    - Procurement evaluation and acceptance.

    - Traceability and process control.

    - Inspection and testing (incoming, in-process, final).

    - Control of non-conforming products.

    - Corrective and preventive actions.

    - Handling, storage, packaging, delivery.

    - Internal audits and record control.

4. Personnel requirements and training.

5. Statistical techniques and commissioning.

Each section of the quality manual must be formally approved by the owner. Once finalized, your quality management team should ensure the documents are posted in an accessible place for the entire team. In addition, schedule training sessions for both the design and construction teams so that everyone clearly understands the project's quality expectations and requirements.

As new members join the project, it's essential that the quality management team provides ongoing training to ensure alignment and compliance. Everyone—from subcontractors to senior managers—should understand how quality procedures apply to their role and responsibilities.

17. Performing Quality Controls

Moving into implementation, quality control measures defined in the Quality Manual must be applied across the board: designers, design builders, subcontractors, subconsultants, vendors, survey and staking crews, inspectors, and testing staff. These measures cover everything from material certifications to handling, storage, packaging, preservation, and delivery. They also include control of non-conforming products, QC processes, independent quality testing, and assigning originators and QC checkers for each design element.

Again, this all starts with a proper startup meeting. Your QC team should lead meetings focused on quality procedures specific to every project participant—from design teams to field staff, vendors, and inspectors.

Nothing will go perfectly on your project—or on any project—but having a well-developed Quality Manual, a strong management team, and sound procedures will go a long way in minimizing issues. Proper training, clear checks and certifications, and independent testing make a significant difference.

CASE STUDY: I-595 CORRIDOR ROADWAY IMPROVEMENTS P3 PROJECT FOR FDOT

Let me walk through a case I-595 Corridor Roadway Project in Broward County for FDOT.

FDOT had very specific requirements and formatting for the Quality Management Plan (QMP). Since this was a P3 project, the owner of the QMP was the developer, ACS. The QMP was a collaborative effort among ACS, the design builder (DUSA), lead designer (AECOM), concession CEI (HNTB), and O&M (Jorgensen).

Per FDOT guidelines, a Design Build Quality Plan must include procedures covering both design and construction phases, including:

1. **Compliance with FDOT Standards:** Design standards, construction specifications, and quality control procedures.

2. **Testing & Inspection Procedures:** Sampling plans, frequencies, and acceptance criteria for materials and workmanship.

3. **Quality Assurance Measures:** Internal audits, data analysis, and corrective action plans.

4. **Personnel Qualifications:** Certifications and experience requirements for all key design and construction staff.

5. **Design Review Process:** Review stages to catch potential issues early.

6. **Construction Change Management:** Systems to handle changes while preserving design integrity.

7. **Documentation & Reporting:** Tracking QC activities, test results, inspections, and NCRs.

8. **Communication Plan:** A clear stakeholder communication strategy.

9. **Project-Specific Needs:** Independent peer reviews for Category 2 bridges (led by Jose Ballista at APTESA, using Finley & Associates).

10. **Team Collaboration:** Involving all DB team members and FDOT in QMP development.

11. **Quality Audits:** FDOT retained the right to conduct regular audits—and did.

FDOT allowed a framework QMP for the initial submittal, which was broken down by phase: design, construction, revenue service, O&M, and handback. The design section was the first major portion submitted for review and approval.

Buddy Hudson, our Design Quality Manager, led the authoring of this section with input from Ray Rivas, PE, our Design Manager. Additional support came from AECOM's Regional Quality Manager. This DQMP section incorporated items 1 and 3 through 11 listed above. Fast turnaround was critical—it was submitted within three weeks and approved three weeks later.

For each design element:

- A qualified originator and QC checker were assigned.

- All deliverables (calculations, reports, plans) included documentation of methods, assumptions, and constraints.

- Plans were reviewed with a color-coded system:

- Yellow = checked.

- Red = corrections needed.

- Gray pencil = questions to resolve.

The originator reviewed all QC comments, made corrections, and addressed questions. Final documents were printed and re-checked. Any unresolved issues were clarified between the originator and checker before being finalized.

Each document had a cover sheet listing:

- Description of the work.

- Dates.

- Assigned originator and checker.

All QC documents were scanned, logged into the QA/QC system, and submitted to Buddy Hudson for QA. Buddy and Robert Burkhardt, the QA rep, reviewed the documents for conformance to the DQMP. If issues were found, they were flagged and returned for correction. Once approved, both signed off and logged the review in case of FDOT audits. If needed, non-conformance reports were issued.

For each submittal, Buddy issued a QA/QC report that documented:

- QA and QC steps.

- Issues resolved.

- Compliance with the DQMP.

These reports were shared with Ray Rivas and Deputy Design Manager Rick Rocktoff.

Interdisciplinary reviews were led by Bayo Cocker, who coordinated across disciplines and zone leads. Packages went through workshops to catch conflicts and gaps. Bayo documented the results and QA'd the work again.

Matt Ganz worked with Rick and the zone leads to finalize and submit packages. He:

- Verified all items in the QA/QC log.

- Coordinated missing pieces with Buddy or Robert.

- Collected all necessary signatures.

- Packaged and submitted to reprographics (DigiPlot).

- Worked with document control and project controls to track the final submission.

This robust quality system—complete with documentation, training, color-coded checks, and consistent interdisciplinary reviews—ensured that we met compliance and avoided costly rework.

A strong project management team, grounded in sound QA/QC processes, really is the foundation of any successful project.

18.   Developing and Submitting the Environmental Compliance Plan

Prior to the issuance of the RFQ, as stated in Chapter 2, attending preliminary planning, environmental, and community engagement meetings is an effective way to learn more about the project. It also provides greater visibility and helps expand your network of contacts related to the project.

If possible, engage with key players as much as practicable to show your interest and begin developing relationships if you don't already have them. When preparing your proposal, your environmental team must carefully review the RFP sections addressing environmental requirements and ask the owner for clarification on anything that's unclear.

As you work with the technical work groups (TWGs) during the proposal, provide input and expertise—especially regarding any proposed changes, including ATCs, that could impact previously approved environmental work. If the team decides to move forward with a proposed change, make sure to outline the mitigation measures required to gain environmental approval.

These changes may affect both cost and schedule.

During the proposal phase:

- Detail your scope of work and outline how you plan to meet all owner requirements for environmental work, including permitting.

- Provide input into the environmental schedule developed for each construction package.

During execution, continue collaborating with the TWGs to ensure that your environmental expertise is contributing to informed project decisions. Develop an environmental compliance plan that includes:

- Specific requirements for each construction package.

- A clear environmental schedule.

Review this plan with the full team, solicit their feedback, and, once finalized, submit it to the owner for review and approval. After the owner approves the plan, post it for the entire team and conduct a start-up meeting so everyone understands what the environmental team is doing and when.

Update your schedule with the project controls group at least monthly—and as soon as you learn of any significant changes in scope or requirements. Keep the project manager and contract specialist in the loop about these changes. Staying proactive in this area is critical to the project's success.

CASE STUDY: I-595 ROADWAY CORRIDOR IMPROVEMENTS P3 FOR FDOT

On the I-595 Roadway Corridor Improvements P3 project, the procedures above were successfully followed by our environmental team, which was led by Steve Dusa at AECOM and Wendy Cyriacks at Cecos, a trusted local environmental firm. During execution, they were assisted by Leslie Howard (AECOM) and Gail Stone (Cecos).

According to FDOT, design build projects must adhere to the environmental compliance standards outlined in their Project Development and Environmental (PD&E) Manual. This ensures alignment with NEPA and other regulatory frameworks. The design builder is responsible for:

- Identifying potential environmental impacts during design.

- Implementing mitigation measures throughout the project.

- Obtaining all necessary permits.

- Ensuring compliance with applicable environmental laws and regulations.

The FDOT Office of Environmental Management (OEM) is the lead agency for environmental reviews on highway projects, overseeing both compliance and permitting.

Design Builder Responsibilities:

- Obtain permits related to wetlands, endangered species, air and water quality.

- Monitor environmental impacts during construction.

- Submit regular environmental compliance reports to FDOT.

Key Compliance Focus Areas:

- Sensitive areas: Identify and protect wetlands, endangered species, and cultural resources.

- Waste management: Ensure proper disposal and recycling of construction debris.

- Stormwater management: Prevent runoff pollution using BMPs.

- Air quality: Implement measures to minimize emissions from construction equipment.

To provide context, I've pulled from the final RFP for the I-595 Corridor Improvements to illustrate what our environmental compliance team was responsible for. Section 1 of the environmental scope covered categorical exclusions and how they were updated.

On June 29, 2006, the Federal Highway Administration approved a Type 2 Categorical Exclusion for the I-595 PD&E study. However, FDOT later proposed changes to the previously approved elevated alignment for express lanes. These changes required a design change and a project re-evaluation to reflect new design elements and update existing commitments.

FDOT also completed updates to the traffic and revenue study to support the P3 delivery model. Any further changes proposed by the concessionaire that impacted the approved PD&E study or construction advertisement documents required additional re-evaluations.

It became the concessionaire's responsibility to complete all necessary work related to those re-evaluations, including coordination with FDOT's district planning and OEM for FHWA submissions.

According to NEPA and 23 CFR 1771, the department recently decided to change the previously approved elevated alignment for the express lanes and instead provide an accurate, ground-level alignment. To support this, the department completed a design change project re-evaluation of the original PD&E study to address the typical section modifications and document any updates to project commitments.

Environmental documentation and scope changes occurred after the issuance of the Type 2 categorical exclusion from FHWA. FDOT also completed variations of the traffic and revenue study to incorporate the P3 model and update various project commitments accordingly.

Any design proposal by the concessionaire that alters the approved PD&E study or the design change and construction advertisement re-evaluation documents may require further environmental re-evaluation. It is the concessionaire's responsibility to complete all related work, including coordination with the department's district planning team and EMO for FHWA submission and approval. All work must be carried out in accordance with established NEPA protocols.

During the development of the I-595 corridor improvements—through both the Corridor Master Plan (CMP) and PD&E phases—extensive coordination took place with:

- Government agencies.

- Municipalities.

- Public organizations.

- General public.

These discussions ultimately established the approved design concept and the project commitments that followed. The concessionaire was responsible for adhering to these commitments during design, construction, and O&M phases of the project. This included:

- Tracking the status of all project commitments.

- Coordinating and evaluating any changes to the original commitments.

- Establishing new commitments when necessary.

The proposed improvements required numerous permits across multiple jurisdictions. Agencies included:

- Broward County Environmental Protection Department (BCEDP).

- Central Broward Water Control District (CBWCD).

- Old Plantation Water Control District (OPWCD).

- Tidal Hammock Irrigation and Soil Conservation District (THISCD).

- Florida Department of Environmental Protection (FDEP).

- South Florida Water Management District (SFWMD).

- U.S. Army Corps of Engineers (USACE).

- U.S. Coast Guard (USCG).

To expedite the permitting process, FDOT initiated early efforts to secure the following permits:

- BCEPD Surface Water Management License.

- BCEPD Environmental General Resource License.

- CBWCD and OPWCD Surface Water Master Plan Permits.

- Joint FDEP/SFWMD/USACE Environmental Resource Permit, including Dredge and Fill.

- SFWMD Right-of-Way Occupancy Permit.

- THISCD Surface Water Master Plan Permit.

- USCG Bridge Permit.

Permit applications, Requests For Additional Information (RAIs), and responses were submitted by the department, but it remained the concessionaire's responsibility to:

- Comply with all existing permit conditions.

- Modify any permits, as needed, to match final design requirements.

- Report permit-related tasks and coordinate modifications.

In addition, the concessionaire was required to comply with minimum navigation clearance limits for the USCG and oversee stabilization of the North New River Canal as outlined in the SFWMD Right-of-Way Occupancy Permit.

Additional likely permit requirements included:

- FDEP National Pollution Discharge Elimination System (NPDES) (Stormwater Pollution Prevention Plan).

- SFWMD Water Use Permit.

- Toll Building Permit.

Our Environmental Compliance Plan spanned 35 pages; the key components are summarized below.

- Dewatering and Groundwater Management: Activities near the Turnpike Exchange and Florida Petroleum processes required careful groundwater modeling and treatment. We established modeling wells and adhered to FDEP/SFWMD rules for well abandonment.

- Turnpike Enterprise Permits: This included submitting design documentation for toll buildings to FTE and coordinating permit reviews with the state fire marshal and building code administrator.

- Water Quality and Runoff Management: We implemented strict erosion and sediment control using best management practices, especially in areas that discharged into golf course pond systems, such as:

  - Lagomar Golf Course.

  - Pine Island Ridge Golf Course.

  - Arrowhead Golf Course.

A Notice of Intent for NPDES permitting was filed prior to construction to address control device locations, inspections, and maintenance.

- Wetlands: Wetlands were identified, permitted, and protected per regulatory requirements.

- Noise and Vibration Monitoring: Given nearby schools, parks, and recreation areas, we developed a vibration monitoring plan to:

  - Document adjacent property conditions.

  - Monitor and record equipment-generated vibrations.

  - Identify and abate impacts where necessary.

Additional Elements Addressed

We also covered:

- Cultural and historical resources.

- Threatened and endangered species.

- Contaminated materials.

- Lighting and visual impacts.

- FAA and Fort Lauderdale Airport lighting coordination.

- Waste management.

- Air quality.

- Permit review processes.

The Environmental Compliance Plan was submitted to FDOT's OEM for review. After receiving their comments, we coordinated internally with DUSA, addressed feedback, and resubmitted for final approval. Once approved, the plan became our operational guideline for all environmental compliance work.

Our environmental compliance work was instrumental in addressing local concerns, meeting regulatory obligations, and maintaining strong community support throughout the life of the I-595 project.

19.   Finalizing and Submitting the Project Specific Safety Plan

Most state DOTs and transit authorities have their own guidelines for design build safety plans. These plans must include detailed strategies for managing work zone safety throughout the entire project-life-cycle, encompassing elements like traffic control, worker protection, hazard identification, safety training, incident response, and a robust monitoring system to ensure compliance with applicable safety standards.

These plans should be reviewed and updated regularly to reflect changing conditions, and they must prioritize a comprehensive approach to safety—strictly adhering to national and state mandates, industry best practices, and balancing cost efficiency without compromising safety during construction operations.

Key Elements of Design Build Safety Plans:

- Comprehensive Coverage: The plan should address all construction phases—site prep, demolition, excavation, new structure construction, interface with operational systems (e.g., active rail or pedestrian traffic), restoration, revenue service, O&M, and handback (if a P3).

- Hazard Identification: Include a thorough analysis of potential hazards specific to the project site (traffic patterns, pedestrian flows, equipment use, environmental factors).

- Traffic Control: Detail lane closures, detours, signage, temporary signals, and how traffic will be managed through the work zone.

- Worker Protection Measures: Define procedures to safeguard workers against traffic, falls, hazardous materials, etc. Include Personal Protection Equipment (PPE) requirements.

- Safety Training: Mandatory training for all personnel covering hazard recognition, incident reporting, work zone safety, and use of PPE. Include daily toolbox safety talks.

- Incident Response Plan: Outline communication procedures, emergency contacts, first aid protocols, and escalation pathways for emergencies or accidents.

- Monitoring and Enforcement: Implement regular inspections, monitor compliance with safety procedures, and outline corrective actions for deficiencies.

- Compliance with Regulations: Cover federal, state, and local safety standards, especially for transit-related construction activities.

- Risk Assessment and Mitigation: Conduct thorough risk assessments during design and construction to identify and mitigate potential safety hazards.

- Quality Control: Implement quality assurance checks to ensure materials, equipment, and construction methods meet safety specifications.

- System Safety Analysis: Identify operational safety risks and integrate preventive measures during both construction and long-term operations.

- Emergency Planning: Establish and regularly practice evacuation and emergency response procedures with staff and public awareness components.

- Continuous Improvement: Update the safety plan using lessons learned, industry best practices, and feedback from incident investigations.

Owner Priorities

- Life-cycle-cost Focus: Owners want cost-effective safety without compromising long-term operations and maintenance.

- Transparency: Clear communication of safety expectations to all contractors and team members is key.

- Stakeholder Engagement: Owners expect you to collaborate with communities, regulatory agencies, and technical experts.

Your project-specific safety plan should be part of your 30, 60, and 120 day design builders and lead designers already have safety plans from past projects—start by reviewing those and checking your RFP and prime agreement for project-specific requirements.

Have the safety management team review the scope with your project director, construction manager, and lead designer. Every project has its own unique complexities, so develop a safety hazard matrix that outlines those risks and how they'll be addressed.

Once your draft safety plan is complete:

1. Have your leadership team (PD, CM, LD, Quality Lead) review and comment.

2. Submit the revised plan to the owner or their rep for review, feedback, and approval.

3. Once approved, post the plan, so all team members can access and review it.

4. Schedule a startup safety meeting and follow-up meetings as needed.

Safety planning isn't "set it and forget it." As the project evolves, revise and improve the plan. If something isn't working, update it.

Keep holding your daily toolbox safety meetings. Conduct system safety analyses regularly. Have emergency response rehearsals. Maintain rigorous oversight with your safety team to ensure the plan is being implemented, followed, and enforced.

Make sure your safety plan is ready, approved, posted, monitored, and practiced. That's how you'll keep your people—and the public—safe.

20. Meeting Calendar and Agendas

From a scheduling standpoint, you want to establish a calendar for all key meetings—executive, owner, client, task groups, and others. It's critical to standardize your meeting agendas, develop templates for consistency, and include notes and action-item lists. An AD Mega-Project will have a tremendous number of meetings to keep things on track, support collaboration, keep stakeholders informed, and push the project forward.

CASE STUDY: I-595 ROADWAY CORRIDOR IMPROVEMENT P3 FOR FDOT

Let me walk you through a case study from the I-595 Roadway Corridor Improvement P3 Project.

We continued to work with our task groups and held weekly task group meetings throughout the project. Bayo Coker, our Interdisciplinary Lead, led the task groups for:

- Geotechnical.

- Pavement design.

- Utility coordination.

- Safety and fire.

- SUE.

- Environmental permitting.

- Drainage and hydraulics.

- Landscape and aesthetics.

- Lighting.

- Survey and mapping.

- Traffic and ITS.

Saul Perez, our Structures Discipline Lead, led the task groups for the Master Corridor Plan and advanced design packages for bridges and sound walls. Gorky Charpentier, our Roadway Discipline Lead, headed up the task group for the Corridor Master Plan and advanced design packages for roadways.

DUSA, FDOT, the general consultant, third-parties, and stakeholders were invited and attended all task group meetings. Ray Rivas, our Design Manager, created standardized templates for the agendas, meeting notes, and action-item lists. He also set up the groups, invited attendees, and coordinated these meetings through DUSA. Each task group lead was responsible for:

- Preparing the agenda.

- Taking meeting notes.

- Creating and tracking the action-item list.

In addition to task group meetings, we held:

- A weekly AECOM executive meeting.

- A monthly AECOM CO review meeting.

- A weekly owners' meeting with FDOT, ACS, DUSA, AECOM, and the general consultant.

- A weekly meeting with all AECOM discipline leads (led by Ray Rivas).

- A weekly AECOM internal design management meeting.

- A bi-weekly scheduling meeting between DUSA schedulers and AECOM's project control group.

- A monthly progress and invoicing meeting between DUSA and AECOM.

Yvette Guerrero, AECOM's Administrative Communication Lead, managed the master meeting calendar and tracked all scheduling logistics.

As AECOM's Project Manager, I tried to initiate a standing monthly one-on-one with Juan Miguel Perez, the Executive Vice President and Project Manager for DUSA (after he replaced Bernardo Palicio). We met once at his office, shortly after he arrived, and I proposed a recurring meeting to review progress and unresolved issues. He declined, saying he doesn't meet with his designers. That was the only project in my entire career where I didn't have direct communication with the client PM. The rest of our communication was done entirely by formal letters.

Despite that, I led several internal and external meetings, including:

- Weekly AECOM executive meetings.

- Monthly AECOM CO review meetings.

- Weekly internal design management meetings.

- Monthly progress and invoicing meetings with DUSA.

Ray Rivas, ACS, DUSA, and the general consultant took the lead on developing the weekly FDOT owners' meeting agenda. I was responsible for developing and distributing the meeting notes and action items for those.

Libertad Vargas managed the bi-weekly scheduler coordination between DUSA and AECOM's project controls.

All meeting agendas, notes, action-item lists, letters, and project correspondence were tracked and distributed by Yvette Guerrero. These meetings were fully established within the first month of the project.

Having a consistent meeting schedule with structured agendas, templated notes, tracked action items, and formal communications helped keep every party—internal team members, third-parties, and stakeholders—aligned and fully informed throughout the life of the project.

21. Quality Oversight and Reporting

The general approach is that the design builder holds overall responsibility for both quality control (QC) and quality assurance (QA) for both design and construction. The program management/construction management (PM/CM), acting as the agency's representative and under the direct supervision of the agency staff, will provide construction inspection oversight, materials verification, on-site observation, actual measurements, verification of sampling and testing, and quality audit functions.

If the project is a P3 with operations and maintenance (O&M) and handback requirements, the developer and agency will follow all quality oversight and reporting procedures throughout the O&M and handback phases as well.

In developing its quality plan, the design builder must establish appropriate controls across management, design, construction, installation, and documentation to ensure compliance with environmental mitigation, safety, and traffic maintenance requirements. The design builder designates a Quality Manager (QM)—a key personnel role—who is responsible for the overall quality plan and its implementation and updates. This QM must report to a senior level within the organization, not to the project manager, to maintain independence from construction and production operations.

This independence ensures the QM can speak freely about any issues without pressure from the production team. The QM receives copies of all relevant documents and communications but is not subordinate to the construction or project manager.

The design builder is solely responsible for producing design plans, project specifications, and working plans that meet contract requirements. Field dimensions must be verified prior to the development of any design documents.

A Design QC Manager will oversee all QC efforts by the design team. This individual will report to the overall QC Manager and supervise a staff responsible for conducting assessments, reviews, and certifications to ensure the design meets contract standards.

In addition, a Design QA Manager will be appointed to handle the assurance of all design-related activities. This person will report to the Quality Manager and ensure QA responsibilities throughout the design process and during design support in construction, including design changes and as-built documentation. The Design QA Manager evaluates the design QC work and certifies that it complies with the quality plan and contractual obligations.

Responsibilities include:

- Identifying and reporting non-conformities.

- Tracking and monitoring resolution of outstanding non-conformance reports.

- Submitting monthly reports and certificates for permanent and temporary components.

The design builder is responsible for QC inspections of all work and components provided by subcontractors, suppliers, fabricators, and vendors, both on- and off-site. This includes procurement, handling, fabrication, testing, repair, installation, and storage, ensuring all components conform to contract documents and function as intended.

Construction QC Inspectors will:

- Perform process control and acceptance sampling/testing.

- Use internal documentation for process control results.

- Provide test results to the PM, QC Manager, and agency's Construction Compliance Engineer (CCE).

- Complete forms and documentation for all observed deviations, corrective actions, and test outcomes.

Process control tests are internal to the design builder. These tests ensure source materials meet acceptable standards but are not shared with the agency unless used for acceptance.

Laboratory testing will be done by certified testing labs subcontracted by the QC Engineering Firm. All testing must meet agency certification requirements.

For P3 projects, these quality oversight processes must be carried through to the O&M and handback phases. Design acceptance will only occur once as-built plans are submitted, reviewed, corrected, and approved by the agency.

The CCE and Construction Compliance Monitors (CCMs) will observe testing performed by QC samplers and testers. If any deviation from procedure is found, it will be reported both verbally and through a written non-compliance report. The CCMs also conduct independent inspections to ensure accuracy and quality, per the agency's schedule.

Verification samples and witness samples will be taken from the same lot as QC samples. Failing verification tests will immediately trigger a non-compliance report. QA testers must be aware of failed test logs and coordinate with QC testers to attend reconciliation tests.

Independent Assurance (IA) testing, required under 23 CFR 637, helps reduce agency risk by verifying the accuracy and calibration of testing equipment and the proficiency of agency testers. IA testing will be performed by the agency.

A third-party certified laboratory will be retained by the agency as a referee lab for resolving disputes in sampling and testing. Its decisions are final and binding.

For O&M and handback in P3s, all the above quality oversight and reporting procedures continue through to final turnover.

22.   Tracking Submittals and Reviews

I'm going to look at a case study for submittals and reviews by revisiting our I-595 Corridor Roadway Improvement P3 Project for FDOT.

CASE STUDY: I-595 CORRIDOR ROADWAY IMPROVEMENT P3 FOR FDOT

On that job, Matt Gans served as our submittal coordinator. He worked closely with Rick Rocktoff, our deputy design manager, along with the other discipline and zone leads, whenever a package was ready for printing, packaging, and submittal. Matt ensured the QA/QC log was completed for the entire package. If anything was missing, he coordinated with Buddy Hudson, our design quality assurance manager, or Robert Burkhardt, our project quality representative, to determine the issue and resolve it.

Once the QA/QC log was complete and the documents were ready, Matt would contact all individuals required to sign off on the documentation. After the necessary signatures were obtained and the submittal log updated, Matt would then package everything and coordinate with our reprographic firm, DigiPlot. Together, they would assemble and submit the final packages.

Once a submittal went out, Matt notified everyone involved—Yvette Guerrero (our admin communications lead) and the project controls group included—so everyone knew what had been sent. Matt and Libertad Vargas, our project controls manager, would track all submittals and reviews. They worked closely with Matt and Rick to stay ahead of which packages were due for review and which submittals were scheduled for the coming week.

This system for tracking, packaging, QA/QC, submittals, and reviews minimized delays and significantly enhanced communication between the design team, DUSA, and FDOT.

23. Establishing Close-out Procedures and Responsibilities

From a responsibility assignment standpoint, the close-out manager is responsible for finalizing the framework and checklist for project close-out, as well as developing the final close-out plan and program. They are in charge of all close-out activities and must fully coordinate the close-out plan and its activities with the project and construction managers.

Closing out an AD Mega-Project is one of the most important pieces of the project and should never be overlooked. That's why I always include it in my 30, 60, and 120 day startup plan checklist. If you haven't considered close-out early in the project, you'll likely miss critical steps, schedules, and resource needs. That kind of delay can lead to holding onto staff, offices, equipment, and incurring overhead costs that ultimately eat into the project's profits.

I recommend identifying the close-out requirements and procedures during the proposal phase. That way, you can allocate the right time, resources, and budget in your schedule and bid. Assign a senior project manager—someone who has successfully closed out a similar project for that owner—as the close-out manager.

If it's a P3 or revenue service AD Mega-Project, don't forget to include operational connections and switchovers, operational testing, vehicle testing, revenue service, O&M close-out, and the handback phase. Be sure to include the developer and their O&M manager in developing the plan. Have your close-out manager review the RFP and owner's prime contract for all close-out requirements. Use that review—and your 30, 60, and 120 day startup list—as a foundation to create a comprehensive checklist.

Make sure the design builder can close out their phase once construction, operations, switchover, testing, and revenue service are complete. If requirements aren't clearly listed in the RFP or contract, ask the owner questions early. Budget the resources and schedule for close-out in your bid and escrow documents.

Below is a generic list of potential close-out activities—this is not project-specific, but a helpful guide:

- Finalize and archive the close-out project budget, tests, and sub-tests.

- Return or transfer hardware/software from the project office.

- Terminate the permanent project office.

- Close down and archive websites, file systems, and directories.

- Close out agreements for leased items (office space, vehicles, equipment).

- Finalize your de-staffing plan.

- Finalize and archive your resource-loaded close-out schedule.

- Close out and archive MWDBE participation, community and political engagement, and facilitation strategies.

- Close out subcontractor, intercompany, and vendor agreements.

- Demobilize staff and resources.

- Finalize and archive project controls and reporting.

- Close out and archive the project execution plan and hold a final owner/team meeting.

- Archive design deliverables, VE, life-cycle-cost assessments, and risk strategies.

- Archive the quality manual, safety plan, and environmental compliance plan.

- Submit final invoice, receive payment, and archive financial documents.

- Archive non-standard procedures, CAD/BIM manuals, and deliver digital models to the Owner, and O&M operator.

- Finalize and archive submittals, schedules, QA/QC documentation.

- Determine and document resources needed for close-out.

- Archive post-design procedures and controls.

- Finalize close-out checklist and plan, and archive it.

- Complete punch lists and submit for final approval.

- Return construction equipment and archive documentation.

- Ensure all manuals, certifications, and guarantees are tagged in BIM and delivered to the owner/O&M operator.

- Conduct and document lessons learned with the team.

- Solicit and archive owner feedback on performance.

- Close out bonding activities and archive.

Bring your close-out manager on board during execution. Have them work alongside the team to finalize the framework and close-out plan. Once developed, review it with your internal team. For P3s, include the developer and O&M manager in this review process. Once all comments are received and addressed, post the finalized documents to the team and hold a meeting to walk through the plan.

The close-out plan should be part of your baseline schedule and cost-loaded with resources. This lets the close-out manager track monthly progress and invoice consistently. I've seen too many cases where this wasn't done, and the team didn't get paid for close-out work until the end—that's a costly mistake.

The project manager and project controls group should provide the close-out manager with monthly reporting on cash flow, earned value, and expenditures to track progress and confirm whether they're on schedule. The close-out manager should begin closing out portions of the project as they reach substantial completion—don't wait until everything is done.

Delaying close-out until the end is where profits disappear and project wrap-up drags on. The close-out manager should meet regularly with the project and construction managers throughout to stay in sync. It's also critical that they're informed of any schedule changes, so adjustments can be made in real time.

Ultimately, continuous coordination between the close-out manager and project controls team is essential for a successful and timely project close-out.

24. Post-Design Services, Organization, Plan and Procedures

The framework setup for post-design services is essential to establishing an operational plan and procedures early—ideally during the proposal phase. It's possible to estimate the level of effort needed for shop drawing reviews, but this will depend on how the design builder and their subcontractors submit shop drawings.

Often, when the design builder uses subcontractors, they won't review the subcontractor submissions before forwarding them to you. These shop drawings are frequently incomplete and may require multiple review cycles to reach compliance. Reviewing the subcontractor's shop drawing packages for completeness should be the design builder's responsibility.

As the Engineer of Record (EOR), the designer's responsibility is to confirm that the shop drawings meet contract requirements and that the design intent is being correctly built. When negotiating your design agreement with the design builder, it's important to set expectations early for the submission and review process of shop drawings, RFIs, and other post-design services.

Too often, field staff working for the design builder haven't thoroughly reviewed construction documents before submitting RFIs. All RFIs should be routed through the design builder's design coordinator—not sent directly to the EOR. It's the design coordinator's job to support their field staff first, before forwarding requests. Without this control, design staff can become overwhelmed.

You should also clarify with the design builder their expectations for having designer personnel in the field to assist with inspections, observations, and guidance. Define a reasonable number of design staff per month that will be required for field support during construction. This must be clearly documented in the design agreement to avoid confusion later.

I strongly recommend structuring post-design services as a time-and-materials contract—not lump sum. This is because the designer has very little control over the volume or timing of field support needs, which are almost entirely dependent on the construction team.

Once both parties have agreed to the scope and structure of the post-design services, the designer can estimate the level of effort required. This helps both teams plan, schedule, and budget for the work appropriately and ensures the scope is reflected in the design builder's bid.

Here's what I recommend for developing and implementing post-design service procedures:

- Assign a qualified team member to draft the initial plan and procedures. Ideally, this person should have experience on several successful post-design service efforts for AD Mega-Projects.

- During the 30, 60, 120 day startup phase, finalize the draft plan. If possible, keep the same person who authored the initial version involved in the finalization.

- The plan should address all elements of post-design services including:

    - RFI tracking and documentation.

    - Shop drawing handling, reviews, and submittals.

    - Field services coordination.

    - QA/QC processes and controls.

    - Document control and standardized reporting.

Ensure the procedures are fully aligned with both the design agreement with the design builder and the prime agreement with the owner, including RFP requirements. Once the draft is complete, have it reviewed by the designer's management team. The lead author should incorporate feedback, finalize the procedures, and route them through your QA/QC process.

The QA manager and project manager should sign off on the final version, and the plan should be posted and submitted to document control. Following that, have the author hold a training session with the team to walk through the new plan and procedures. As new team members come on board to perform post-design services, make sure they're fully trained in these protocols.

I also recommend that the designer assign a separate, dedicated team to the field during construction. These individuals should be 100% committed to post-design services and not assigned to ongoing design work so they can stay focused. Include these personnel in your staffing plan, and bring them on board several months prior to active fieldwork. This allows them time to:

- Familiarize themselves with project documents, specifications, and expectations.

- Meet and build rapport with the design builder's field coordinator.

- Get aligned on coordination processes.

Finally, appoint a lead post-design field coordinator to oversee this effort. This person will manage reviews, coordinate reporting, serve as the main point of contact for the design builder's field team, and ensure all designer field staff are supported and held accountable.

With proper planning, experienced personnel, and a clear post-design services plan in place, your team will be positioned to support construction effectively and uphold the integrity of the original design throughout execution.

25.   Project Close-out Framework

Providing a comprehensive list to create a design framework and project close-out responsibilities and procedures, I'm going to walk through a case study for closing out a project—specifically the SH 130 Turnpike Project for TTA in Pflugerville, Texas.

CASE STUDY: SH 130 TURNPIKE EDA FOR TTA AND TX-DOT

I served as the principal-in-charge at AECOM for the design team. As we transitioned from design to post-design services, Brian Dodson moved from his role as structures lead to become the lead for post-design services. He led this group for four years.

At that time, the project underwent a significant de-staffing. Pamela Huebner, our HR representative in the project office, who had worked closely with the team on the de-staffing plan, demobilized the office. Approximately 148 staff members were demobilized, leaving only 20 staff in place.

Before those demobilization activities, Glenn Sadulsky, the project design director, worked with his management team and me to develop a transition and close-out plan checklist and program. This plan was reviewed internally, submitted to LSI (the design builder), and then to TTA and TxDOT for concurrence and approval.

Here was our close-out checklist for that project:

(Note: [*] Item to be archived at substantial completion. [**] Task completed by Pamela Huebner.)

- 1. Finalize close-out project budgets, tasks, and subtasks.

- 2. (**) Return or move purchased hardware/software to another job.

- 3. (**) Move out of the permanent project office – handled by Pam.

- 4. Close down and archive system directories.

- 5. Archive the project directory.

- 6. Close out agreements for leased items, vehicles, and equipment; archive.

- 7. Finalize the de-staffing plan.

- 8. Finalize and close out the resource and cost-loaded final project schedule; archive.

- 9. Close out DBE engagement participation, submit to LSI, and archive.

- 10. Close out subcontractor agreements and archive.

- 11. Close out intercompany agreements and archive.

- 12. (**) Close-out insurance certificates and archive.

- 13. (**) Demobilize staffing and resources; archive.

- 14. Finalize close-out controls: tracking, monitoring, analysis, and reporting; archive.

- 15. Close out the project execution plan. Hold a final meeting with TTA and TxDOT, LSI, and the team; archive.

- 16. Archive the quality manual.

- 17. Archive the project work plan.

- 18. Issue final invoice, submit for approval, receive payment, and archive.

- 19. (*) Archive non-standard administration procedures.

- 20. (*) Archive CAD manual, procedures, and files.

- 21. Archive the safety plan.

- 22. Finalize and archive schedules (milestones, submittals, reviews, etc.).

- 23. Finalize all QA/QC activities, submit to LSI, and archive.

- 24. Finalize and close out all submittals and reviews; archive.

- 25. Determine resources needed to close out the project.

- 26. Close out post-design organization procedures, resolve outstanding issues, and archive.

- 27. Establish and finalize the framework and checklist for close-out. Develop and archive the project close-out plan and program.

- 28. Develop and archive lessons learned with your team before staff departure.

- 29. Solicit and document feedback from LSI, TTA, and TxDOT on team performance; archive.

Glenn worked closely with Brian and Matt Anderson to oversee the transition and execute the close-out plan. As the project moved from post-design to full close-out, Brian handed over the closeout activities to Matt, who retained Pam, the project control group (PCG), and several staff to assist in closing the project.

Before Glenn departed the project, he collaborated with the team to compile a lessons learned report, broken out by:

- Procurement.

- Preliminary engineering and early design tasks.

- Program management oversight.

Each section included pros and cons. For example, under procurement, the team noted that using a formula-based evaluation of proposals and bids—considering technical scoring, cash flow, maintenance price, low bid schedule, and concrete vs. asphalt pavement—was a pro. It worked well and wasn't difficult to evaluate using present-day value formulas.

However, a **con** was that technical capabilities became more of a qualifier than a key scoring factor, and didn't heavily influence the final decision.

Lessons Learned on SH 130

PROCUREMENT	PROS	CONS
Use of formula for **evaluation of Proposal and Bids** by Technical, cash flow, maintenance price, low bid, schedule, and use of concrete vs. asphalt pavement	This went well and was not that difficult to evaluate by present day value and a formula.	A technical capability became a qualifier but was not a major influence in the scoring.
Complex **Request For Proposals** (RFP)	Gave TTA excellent control over what they received from the proposing Exclusive Development Agreement (EDA) Teams.	Major changes during the proposal process caused problems and time for the EDA Teams to keep track of the addendums.
Use of **Alternative Technical Concepts** (ATCs)	Allowed for innovation while keeping ATCs confidential to the competing teams. TTA was able to negotiate a final price by ATCs. This gave them ultimate flexibility.	Took a tremendous amount of resources for TTA in reviewing and approving ATCs. Twenty-five to 35 ATCs were submitted by each EDA Team.

Lessons Learned on SH 130

PROCUREMENT	PROS	CONS
Individual EDA Team Meetings with each EDA Team	Allowed each EDA team to meet independently with TTA during the proposal preparation to allow confidentiality of their ideas.	Could trigger losing EDA Teams to file a protest/appeals for giving a team an advantage.
Professional Liability Clauses	Provided professional liability insurance protection of $20 million for the EDA Team.	Language for professional liability insurance was deemed non-obtainable by the insurance companies.
Complexity of the EDA	Extremely tight and in favor of TTA. Major portions were written by a law firm.	Provided legal issues and not as much flexibility to TTA and the EDA Team during execution.
Required use of Independent Quality Assurance Firm (DQAF)	Guaranteed that quality measures were being performed by the EDA Team.	Allowed the DQAF to determine and establish their own role. Must have the right DQAF Team that understands Design Build processes. Problems with DQAF performing Quality Control instead of Quality Assurance. Led to DQAF using personal preference. They fell into the role of reviewers and CYA leading to schedule delays.

Lessons Learned on SH 130

PROCUREMENT	PROS	CONS
Right-of-Way certification process	Assures TTA that the necessary right-of-way is purchased on a given property once.	DQAF believed that they were also responsible for certifying the right-of-way along with the engineer and Right-of-Way Team for the EDA Team. This lengthened the certification process.
Definition of Design Review Procedures at 60%, 90% and 100%	Gave complete control to TTA of design elements.	Caused delays in allowing design to move quickly through the process and getting construction to start as early as practicable.
PRELIMINARY ENGINEERING AND EARLY DESIGN TASKS	**PROS**	**CONS**
Using Preliminary Traffic Volumes	Allows the Procurement Schedule to move quicker.	Causes potential claims and delays during the project to TTA by the EDA Team if volumes change significantly during the final update, requiring additional work and additional costs by the EDA Team.

Lessons Learned on SH 130		
PRELIMINARY EN-GINEERING AND EARLY DESIGN TASKS	PROS	CONS
Not Providing Geopak files to the EDA Teams	Allows the Procurement Schedule to move quicker.	Requires the EDA Teams to build their own models taking a tremendous amount of time and resources.
Have each EDA Team Develop Aesthetic Guidelines	Allows the Procurement Schedule to move quicker.	The EDA Teams could not work with the public in developing these guidelines and therefore did not know if all of their work would be acceptable to the public. This caused each team to spend a tremendous amount of time and money to develop these during the proposal preparation process.

Lessons Learned on SH 130

PROGRAM MANAGEMENT OVERSIGHT	PROS	CONS
Partnering	Allowed for a systematic approach and constant evaluation of performance by all parties.	Did not allow for common goals by each party to be established, issues of concerns by each party to be brought up in an open and non-threatening environment and to develop an action plan to work through these issues so that common goals were met.
Use of Technical Work Groups (TWGs) by discipline	Ensured that TTA and the EDA Team discussed design and construction concepts, materials and processes on a weekly basis, keeping TTA in the decision-making process. Ensured that TTA was getting what they wanted. Allowed for continuous value engineering.	Did not allow the EDA Team to work through cost saving issues and to monitor their bid costs versus actual costs in an open and non-threatening environment without TTA scrutiny.

Lessons Learned on SH 130		
PROGRAM MANAGEMENT OVERSIGHT	**PROS**	**CONS**
Development of Ultimate and Interim Schematics	Ensured that TTA was getting a facility that met their expectations now and in the future.	Was a time-consuming process that required the Ultimate Schematics to be approved prior to interim being approved. Required both Ultimate and Interim Schematics to be updated as changes were made during the final design process, causing the EDA Team to spend unanticipated resources and time delays.
Use of Owner Requested Changes (RCPs)	Gives TTA the flexibility to modify portions of the project to take into consideration unanticipated and unknown issues.	Can cost a significant amount of time and money to TTA and resources of the EDA Team to keep the project on its original schedule. Gives a reason for the CDA Team to file for a time extension.

So the lessons learned were shared with the AECOM, our management team, LSI, TTA, and TxDOT. The project was closed out successfully within a three-week period.

The development of the transition and close-out plan checklist and program ensured a smooth handover and satisfied all contractual obligations efficiently. The SH 130 Turnpike EDA project was extremely successful and profitable.

Chapter 6
Owner-Specific Processes and Case Studies

TOP HOW-TOS FOR OWNERS

As the owner, the way you structure your procurement, hire a general consultant and legal team, devise your diversity strategy, collaborate with the entire team, use value engineering, engage in partnering, implement risk management, incorporate Alternative Technical Concepts (ATCs) and Financial Technical Concepts (FTCs), get involved with the design builder's task group meetings, and assist in project close-out can have a significant impact on the success or failure of your alternative delivery (AD) Mega-Project.

I've worked on all sides of AD Mega-Projects over the last 32 years—since 1993. I've worked for both design builders and owners on 51 projects totaling $66 billion in construction value, including eight owner-side projects valued at $9 billion. Through this chapter, I'll share what I believe are best practices based on my successes and failures, supported by several case studies.

1. How-To: Hire and Provide Guidance to Your General Consultant

Your general consultant (GC) is a key member of your team. Make sure you hire one with a proven track record of delivering projects on schedule and within budget, and who knows how to collaborate effectively with the entire team—including the developer, design builders, stakeholders, key third parties, and the community.

When developing your RFQ and RFP for the GC:

- Score them based on your organization's and constituents' goals, objectives, and philosophy.

- Require a minimum of three similar projects (completed within the last 10 years) that demonstrate how they overcame specific project challenges.

- Ensure proposed key personnel are well-rounded in AD work and have held the same role on at least three similar owner-side projects.

- Each resume should clearly articulate the challenges faced and how they worked to resolve or exceed those challenges.

The key to success on these projects is cultivating trust, transparency, and collaboration across the entire team. That's what works in your best interest. Don't use your GC as a strongman. Be fair in your procurement documents and prime agreements. Allow developers and design builders to make a fair profit.

CASE STUDY: SH 130 TURNPIKE EDA FOR TTA AND TX-DOT

TTA hired HDR as their general consultant. I was the Principal-in-Charge for AECOM on the project. The requirement was that 95% of the project team had to be located in the project office in Pflugerville, Texas. Lone Star Infrastructure (LSI) was the design builder. We initially set up in a temporary office in Austin until the permanent office was ready. This allowed us to advance several aspects of the project without losing time.

Once LSI moved into the permanent office and brought in about 25 staff, HDR already had 50 staff on the ground and began demanding deliverables. LSI met with HDR and explained that all deliverables would be clearly detailed in our final baseline schedule, which would be submitted per the prime agreement. We asked them not to push us out of our planned sequence just to keep their people billable. At the time, we were still finalizing staffing and working on critical first-30-day submittals.

This wasn't a good way to start building trust. HDR wasn't collaborative with LSI and the design team. They treated us more like adversaries than partners—and that set a poor tone for the project.

2. How-To: Guidance for Your Legal Team

Your Legal Team Advisor (LT&A) is another critical player. Hire one with a strong success rate in advising teams through the development of RFQ and RFP documents, in alignment with your organization's values, goals, and the interests of your stakeholders. They should understand how to work collaboratively with the GC, developer, design builder, stakeholders, and community.

Key selection criteria:

- At least three similar projects in the last 10 years with a clear description of challenges and how they were addressed.

- Key personnel should have held similar roles on three AD Mega-Projects.

- Resumes should include the challenges faced and how they were met or exceeded.

Again, building trust, transparency, and collaboration is essential. Avoid using your LT&A as an enforcer. Several owners, under legal advice, have crafted overly one-sided procurement documents and prime agreements solely focused on protecting the owner. When developers and design builders propose modifications to share or better allocate risk, these suggestions are often denied. As a result, teams drop out post-shortlist or prequalification, leaving only one or two bidders. This leads to re-bids, budget overruns, extended negotiations, and ultimately, claims and disputes.

The recommendation was to prequalify 3–4 teams and maintain strong interest from them throughout the procurement process. Keep in mind, these teams are investing millions into their proposals.

CASE STUDY: TAPPAN ZEE HUDSON RIVER CROSSING DESIGN BUILD FOR NYSDOT AND TA

I was on the AECOM program management team for New York's first design build project—valued at $5.2 billion. Glenn Kartalis, our Program Director, brought in Nancy Smith (VP, Nossaman) to advise as LT&A. Her clear directive from the NY Thruway Authority and NYSDOT was to create fair, balanced documents that appropriately distributed risks and enabled design builders to earn a fair profit.

Arup, also on our team, facilitated multiple risk management workshops that included NYSDOT, NYS Thruway Authority, FHWA, Nossamon, and AECOM. The risks—technical, political, environmental, design, construction, utility, schedule, community, cost, and litigation—were categorized (low/medium/high), mitigation measures were proposed, and responsibility for each risk was assigned.

A final risk management plan was developed and reflected in the procurement documents and the design builder's prime agreement. This collaborative, transparent approach worked exceptionally well and serves as a strong model for this AD Mega-Project.

3. How-To: Bring More Diversity into Your Program (MWDBE)

Bringing more MWDBEs into your program requires thoughtful planning and skilled execution.

From March 2019 to July 2022, I was the co-founder of Construction and Transportation Solutions (C&TS). BrianAnsiri Associates (BAA), through its C & TS practice area, provided a full suite of construction-based support services, including program management, advisory services, and MWDBE strategy.

Our consortium included seven firms—either DBEs or SDVOSBs—with access to more than 200 staff. I led the program management side, while BAA offered public and private sector consulting to improve operations, efficiency, and MWDBE inclusion. With 31 years of MWDBE advisory experience, BAA brought a deep well of expertise in optimizing outcomes and promoting equity in infrastructure programs.

Although I already had a wealth of experience working with MWDBEs, my collaboration with Brian Ansari, CEO and President of BAA, gave me fresh insights into effective MWDBE strategies. One highlight I want to share is a panel discussion Brian and I co-led on MWDBE participation in AD Mega-Projects. We shared practical strategies, challenges, and success stories that are valuable to any owner looking to strengthen diversity in their infrastructure programs.

The synopsis and presentation was on the engagement in design build Mega-Projects, reconciling client goals and expectations. We gave that at the Design Build Institute of America (D) 2021 Transportation Aviation Conference on April 22, 2021.

Synopsis of Presentation/Panel Discussion for Engagement in Design-Build Mega-Projects Reconciling Client Goals and Expectations
DBIA 2021 Transportation/Aviation Conference
April 22, 2021

Moderator:

Michael Shapiro, PE

Owner of Michael S. Shapiro Consulting LLC and Co-Founder of Construction and Transportation Solutions

Panel members:

Michael J. Garner, MBA

Chief Diversity and Inclusion Officer, Metropolitan Transportation Authority, New York State

Brian Ansari

President, Brian Ansari and Associates, Inc. and Co-Founder of Construction and Transportation Solutions

Ural Yal, PE

Vice President of Alternative Delivery Projects, Flatiron Constructors

Jeff Gagné, PE, FDBIA

Vice President, SED Delivery Officer, HNTB Corporation

Presentation/Panel Discussion Summary:

Public sector agencies across the U.S. are embracing alternative delivery to get jobs done quicker and contain costs. MWDBE participation in alternative delivery can present significant challenges. MWDBE goals are increasing; the speed of the engagement is greater than many MWDBEs have experienced. The Biden Administration has signaled it intends to make MWDBE inclusion on federally funded projects a high priority.

- How do you design a strategy that successfully integrates MWDBEs into your project and delivers the expected goals?

- How do you accommodate your owner's expectations and keep the project on time, safely, and within the budget?

1.   Specific challenges that MWDBE participation in alternative delivery Mega-Projects present

Owner

- Creating an RFQ and RFP and evaluation system that rewards the responding teams for their past performance, creativity and planning for devising and executing a plan for achieving the Owner's goals and not a Good Faith Effort.

Strategic Advisor

- For all stakeholders not to look to the easy and perhaps obvious for what represents project and program success

- Easy program success equals achieving MWDBE goal versus what did we learn and how did it inform what is going to do differently in future projects?

- Have we been here before? Are we looking at the same problem we had on other projects or procurements? Have we grown accustomed to having this problem as the cause for our inability to scale or evolve?

- Are we growing enterprise MWDBE IQ across our organization that integrates our learnings into our communications and outcomes?

- How much are we relying on what we did last year? Are we encouraging innovation in how our franchise is growing? How is that being measured?

Prime Contractor

- Identifying firms with the necessary capacity to meet the goals (size of contracts, available pool of qualified firms, existing firms being overstretched)

- Timing and ability to receive appropriate and competitive bids and proposals

- Ensuring the success of MWDBE firms once selected for the project

  - Obtaining bonding and insurance, maintaining cash flow

  - Performance (safety, quality, schedule)

  - Paperwork (billing, compliance, etc.)

  - Changes and Disputes

Lead Designer

- Understanding actual scope required to develop our design team

- Understanding availability of MWDBE firms in marketplace

- Conflicted firms

- Prequalification list and process to add firms

- Past experience performing similar work

- What is the actual capacity that the MWDBE firm has to accomplish their work?

- How do I structure the overall design team to afford the maximum MWDBE engagement?

- Can the MWDBE firm meet the minimum requirements for insurance (professional liability, deductibles, special riders, etc.)?

2.   MWDBE goals are increasing; the speed of the engagement is greater than many MWDBE's have experienced. We must design a MWDBE engagement and execution strategy.

Owner

- Make provisions in working with banks to provide low-interest loans to equity firms

- Create an Owner Controlled Insurance Program or require Project Specific Insurance that can cover all of the MWDBEs within the project

- Message to the vendor community the value that the Owner is going to place on it

Strategic Advisor

- Insurance and bonding can be reimaged with a different risk share model

- Payment provisions for MWDBEs, creating escrows with the prime to ensure prompt payment to MWDBE primes and subcontractors

- Provide set asides within a design build project for MWDBEs make sense

- Create or foster MWDBE co-primes within specific trades

- Work with the design build team to specify capital equipment that have MWDBEs as part of their distribution installation and maintenance infrastructure

3.   Design a strategy that successfully integrates MWDBEs into your project and delivers the expected goals

Owner

- Determine when MWDBE consideration begins (make this sooner than later)

- Define your associated internal MWDBE quality assurance efforts (business process and workflows attached to this process)

- Put KPIs in place for program units and procurement and monitor and evaluate them

- Position your enterprise to embed inclusion because of these efforts

Prime Contractor

- Develop outreach and inclusion strategies that work effectively during project procurement and project execution

- Mentoring programs

- Set-aside procurements (design build)

- More targeted communication with project team rather than mass outreach events

Lead Designer

- Early engagement for mentoring MWDBEs

- Familiarization of your MWDBEs with Project Management Plan elements (document control, risk management, technology, change management, communications, etc.)

- Training & familiarization with an effective Quality Management System for your MWDBEs

- Development of Work Breakdown Structure and pricing process

- Familiarization with project controls process

- Review of reporting and invoicing

4.   Accommodate your owner's MWDBE expectations and keep the project on time, safely, and within the budget

Prime Contractor

- Supporting MWDBE firms to ensure they complete the project successfully (job-level contacts providing support on all aspects of contract management and execution)

- Use a collaborative approach to managing participation and support of the MWDBE firms during execution, point person from Owner and Design Builder meeting regularly, reviewing progress with transparent communication about challenges

Lead Designer

- Staff augmentation/co-location when appropriate (use this for mentoring and structure)

- Assignment of key discipline leads for alignment within the team, strong communication protocols

- Early development of templates, guides, design criteria

- Interactive review process, early and frequent (when not co-located)

- Early engagement for discussion of innovation

5. Owner to use procurement design to allow for greater and more meaningful MWDBE participation

Owner

Define MWDBE as a priority at the design build advisory level with technical advisors, invite them to contribute to the ideation of successful practices and processes (just as MWDBE scoring models pull from the technical score, invite technical resources to provide a certain value to the MWDBE process-ensure all resources, internally and externally are contributing to MWDBE outcomes)

- Define your intentions to incorporate MWDBEs at an Industry Forum

    - Stress the achievement of the MWDBE goals instead of a Good Faith Effort and the tools we are proposing to encourage those outcomes

- Articulate your MWDBE expectations at the RFQ level

    - Set the goals for all participants (Special Project Vehicle (SPV), Design Builder, Lead Designer, Operations and Maintenance, Manufacturers)

    - Make past performance on achieving MWDBE goals on similar past projects part of your scoring

    - Have a conceptual MWDBE Plan as a part of the submittal requirement and identify how it will be scored

    - Require a financial and operational model of how respondents will meet MWDBE goals to be evaluated in the RFQ

- Articulate your MWDBE expectations at the RFP level

    - Reinforce the goals and provide additional details in your contract documents, including any penalties or incentives

- Require a detailed MWDBE Plan which includes work during the proposal efforts and the execution phase and give this strong value in your scoring

- Use of compliance points

6. Define how the concessionaire (P3), prime contractor, and lead designer can develop a procurement methodology that can produce a greater MWDBE dividend

Strategic Advisor

- Develop tools that can be used to ensure MWDBEs can meaningfully participate in design build Mega-Projects.

  - Owners: encourage MWDBE innovation within design build proposals-Message the design build community innovation may be more costly but MWDBE engagement is important to the owner. Create weighted scoring for proposals that demonstrate how the design build team or SPV will facilitate MWDBE participation in these Mega-Projects over the entire life cycle and what they would do differently to produce these results. Disincentivize proposals that do not meet this threshold.

  - SPVs: Commit to a minimum MWDBE equity share and professional services commitment to democratize utilization opportunities across all areas of expenditure and encourage MWDBE innovation from all designers, contractors and operations and maintenance teams

  - Contractors and Designers: Adopt the Rooney Rule when forming teams to pursue Mega-Projects, they will interview at least one MWDBE for every major subcontracting category and be prepared to demonstrate this effort to the owner at the RFQ stage

Prime Contractor

- Mentoring programs that provide value to the overall equity program

- Equity set aside programs

- Use of Co-Primes concept

- Ensuring cashflow to equity firms

- Elimination of retainage

- Governance to ensure we are closing the MWDBE gap throughout the project

    - Use of technology to track progress as the contracts are procured (B2Gnow)

    - Develop ongoing relationships outside of the procurement cycles, so a reliable database is available when the procurement starts

- Expanding on traditional MWDBE utilization

    - Educating the MWDBE community about the types of opportunities in different types of projects and delivery methods – 1-on-1s with firms with the right people in the room

    - Engaging with industry stakeholders (other contractors, industry groups, owners, consultants) to expand capacity in the market

7.   Acquire skills to manage risks related to MWDBE participation in alternative delivery Mega-Projects for owners, concessionaires, prime contractors, and lead designers

Strategic Advisor

- Designate a leader with this specific expertise and make him a part of the executive team with specific operational controls to ensure MWDBE quality assurance leveraging all the project controls and tools available

- On a P3, this person should report directly to the SPV

- Each part of the organization must have a point person that will report to the lead

- Establish a culture throughout every part of the organization

- Develop a conceptual plan at the SOQ

- Develop a detailed plan for the proposal and for execution

- Include a financial plan on how MWDBEs will be paid within a 30-day period

4. How-To: Collaborating with Your Team (Including Internal Team)

I think you've heard me talk about trust and collaboration many, many times throughout this book. I'm going to talk about it again because it's that important. On every project I've worked where there was great team collaboration, we stayed on schedule, made money, and everyone genuinely enjoyed working on the job.

Let me reinforce: collaboration is the key to success on any AD Mega-Project. It takes understanding, transparency, and trust to build a successful working relationship and project team. When you start a project, assume that everyone involved wants it to succeed.

Even though the team may be made up of people from different organizations, every single member wants the project to meet its goals—quality, budget, and schedule.

CASE STUDY: I-17, BETWEEN THOMAS ROAD AND DUNLAP AVENUE DESIGN BUILD FOR ADOT IN DOWNTOWN PHOENIX

I want to share an early project example from I-17, between Thomas Road and Dunlap Avenue in downtown Phoenix. It was a design build for ADOT.

I was the principal-in-charge from AECOM, and we were the general consultant for ADOT. We had written the procurement documents and developed the preliminary design. Granite/Sundt was in a joint venture and had been selected as the design builder.

We assembled a small co-located team with ADOT and the design builder in a nearby project office. That small team worked really well—because it had the right people. You don't need a big team. You need a good one.

Terry Bourland was the PM for ADOT. Eric Crowe was our PM for AECOM. From the start, we had a very collaborative environment that carried over from the procurement process. This included respect, transparency, and trust—not just between our AECOM team and ADOT, but across nearly ten participating departments, FHWA, and key community stakeholders.

Before we finalized the procurement documents, Eric and Terry organized site visits to two active AD Mega-Projects—one in Southern California, the other in Salt Lake City. ADOT's procurement team and FHWA members went on the visits. We spent five days at each location learning from the teams—owners, design builders, and designers—what worked and what didn't.

Those visits helped build relationships and trust. We used what we learned to collaboratively develop procurement documents and the prime agreement based on how we believed the project would function best. We made the decision to collaborate with everyone—ADOT, FHWA, the City of Phoenix, utility companies, the design builder, stakeholders and the community.

As we identified project risks, we assigned them to whoever was best equipped to manage them. Sometimes it was ADOT. Sometimes it was the design builder. Sometimes the risk was shared. The prime agreement reflected this.

During execution, AECOM (as the GC) reviewed all design builder deliverables and provided comments. We also performed design reviews, QA audits for both design and construction activities—not to verify the technical accuracy (that was the responsibility of the design builder and designer), but to ensure work met the scope and specs.

Like any project, issues arose—in the office and out in the field. But we handled them quickly at the lowest level possible. The result? A project scheduled for 24 months was finished in 19.

At the ribbon-cutting, the president of Granite gave a speech thanking Terry and Eric for how they led the project, crediting the **collaborative spirit** of the team as the reason for the project's success.

5.   How-To: Using Value Engineering as a Tool

Value Engineering (VE), if done correctly and early in the project, can add value, save time, reduce haul, and cut costs.

I encourage owners to use VE early—even before selecting the procurement method.

CASE STUDY: GENERAL CONSULTANT FOR ADOT ON THE MAG REGIONAL FREEWAY SYSTEM

When I was principal-in-charge of the GC contract for ADOT on the MAG Regional Freeway System (to complete the $6.3 billion program) from 1995 to 2004, one of AECOM's responsibilities was developing 30% plans. Before reaching 10% design, we held VE workshops for every project.

Each workshop was led by a certified VE specialist. John Gerometta, PE—and also a certified VE specialist—participated in all of them for AECOM. SMEs and stakeholders from ADOT design and construction teams joined as well.

These workshops followed a structured five-day format:

- **Day 1:** Overview of the VE process, project goals, site visit, initial brainstorming.

- **Day 2–3:** Functional analysis, idea generation, evaluation.

- **Day 4:** Alternative development, cost estimates.

- **Day 5:** Final presentations and outbrief with decision-makers and stakeholders.

The results were outstanding. On the MAG freeway program alone—$6.3 billion in construction—we saved an estimated $600 to $900 million through VE. That's 10–15% savings just from structured collaboration and creative thinking.

If you're managing an AD program, I highly recommend implementing a VE workshop process like the one I've described.

6. How-To: Make a Success Out of Partnering

Partnering, when done right, is a powerful tool to build trust, align expectations, and deliver successful AD Mega-Projects. Since 1991, ADOT has led the way in formal partnering—bringing together agencies, municipalities, contractors, and stakeholders to agree on communication, goals, and dispute resolution up front.

John Halikowski, ADOT Director, put it best in 2016:

> *"Through partnering, we constantly get and give feedback. This helps us improve our next project, resulting in construction being on time and on budget, with a key amount of inconvenience for drivers."*

Here's how it works:

- Start with a **partnering workshop** including all major stakeholders—ADOT, city/county officials, utilities, contractors.

- Establish communication structures, team goals, and dispute resolution plans.

- Hold regular follow-up meetings and team-building exercises.

- Wrap up with lessons learned.

Before ADOT implemented partnering, the agency faced 60 legal actions in one year, costing $39.8 million. Today, disputes rarely escalate to that level. ADOT's legal team that once handled these issues no longer exists.

I've participated in ADOT partnering since 1993 on every project. Their approach is tested and effective.

On I-17 from Thomas to Dunlap Avenue—the same project I talked about earlier—we won the Malcolm Baldrige Award for partnering. It was a great success.

We also used partnering on the SH 130 Turnpike EDA in Pflugerville, Texas. But the partnering process there didn't live up to ADOT's standards, and we didn't see the same results. That's why I recommend you talk with ADOT's partnering group before starting your own program. They've perfected the process over 34 years.

7.   How-To: Using Risk Management Workshops Toward Your Success

It's extremely important when evaluating your risk management strategy on your AD Mega-Project that you consider not only the impacts on your own organization but on the entire team. Your success will ultimately be judged by your team's success. And your team includes everyone: the developer, design builder, board and committee members, agency partners, key stakeholders, third-parties, impacted communities, and politicians, and your MWDBE community.

I recommend you begin thinking about risk management early in the process—as you're doing your due diligence, talking internally, and formulating your project's goals and objectives. Every AD Mega-Project has its own unique challenges, constraints, and opportunities. Therefore, each will require a unique risk management profile and strategy.

If you don't have a risk management office or an in-house facilitator, I highly recommend hiring a consultant with proven experience in developing and implementing risk management strategies for AD Mega-Projects. Vet their qualifications and references thoroughly, and make them a key member of your team. Risk management is not a one-time event—it should be integrated throughout the life of the project, from procurement through execution to close-out.

As your project develops and due diligence advances, work with your risk team to:

- Define all project risks in detail.

- Establish a methodology for scoring risk levels (e.g., low, medium, high).

- Develop mitigation strategies.

- Assign responsibility for each risk to the party best positioned to manage it.

Bring in your technical, political, environmental, community, MWDBE, and agency experts to be part of this risk management effort. Their input is not just valuable—it's essential. Document everything in a risk register and keep it updated as the project evolves and new risks emerge.

As you move forward:

- Include your procurement methodology in the risk register to help define the most advantageous path.

- Define how risk management will be embedded in the RFQ, RFP, evaluation criteria, selection process, execution, and close-out phases.

- Clearly articulate expectations for collaboration and risk management in the prime agreement.

Collaboration, once again, is critical. It takes understanding, transparency, and trust to build a successful team. Make risk management part of your collaboration strategy. Talk about it in your industry reviews. Include it in your scoring for SOQs and technical proposals. Ask proposers about how they've handled risk and collaboration on past projects—and how they plan to do so on yours.

I recommend that you:

- Invite short-listed teams to discuss risk management and collaboration in one-on-one proposal meetings.

- Continue these discussions during negotiation meetings with the selected team.

- Kick off the project with a risk management workshop and follow through with monthly risk management meetings.

CASE STUDY: TAPPAN ZEE HUDSON RIVER CROSSING DESIGN BUILD FOR NYSDOT AND TA

As I mentioned earlier in the section on legal guidance, let me share a case study from the Tappan Zee Hudson River Bridge Project for the New York State Thruway and the New York State DOT. I was on AECOM's program management team and helped prepare portions of the procurement documents for New York's first design build project, with a construction value of $5.2 billion.

New York State Thruway and NYSDOT wanted fair documents that distributed risks to the parties best able to manage them, while also allowing the design builder to make a fair profit. Arup, who was also on our team, took the lead in developing the procurement documents and facilitating the risk management workshops.

Participants included:

- New York State Thruway.

- New York State DOT.

- FHWA.

- Nossaman.

- AECOM.

- Arup.

The workshops addressed technical, political, third-party, environmental, construction, design, right-of-way, utility, safety, quality, schedule, community, cost, potential litigation, and MWDBE strategy risks. The team scored risks by severity and identified mitigation measures and responsible parties.

The result? A final risk management document that was fully integrated into both the procurement documents and the prime agreement with the design builder. The process distributed risk fairly and gave the design builder the opportunity to succeed—both financially and operationally.

This collaborative, workshop-based approach was a key factor in the success of that project. And I strongly encourage you to make it a cornerstone of your risk management strategy for your AD Mega-Project.

8.   How-To: Using ATCs and AFCs (That's Alternative Technical Concepts and Alternative Financial Concepts.)

I've been responsible for the development of numerous ATCs and involved in two AFC efforts during proposal phases. Below is some guidance for owners on the use of ATCs and AFCs for your potential AD Mega-Projects.

Alternative Technical Concepts (ATCs)

ATCs in the context of transportation infrastructure projects refer to a process where potential contractors submit innovative design or construction solutions that differ from the standard project requirements—offering a potentially better or more efficient way to complete the project while still meeting overall goals. In short, ATCs allow bidders to propose alternative approaches that can improve outcomes beyond what's outlined in the RFP.

Key points about ATCs:

- **Innovation driver:** ATCs are meant to encourage creativity and technical innovation, allowing contractors to present unique solutions that might not have been considered by the owner or agency.

- **Design build synergy:** They are most effective in design build contracts, where the contractor is responsible for both design and construction and, therefore, can flexibly propose integrated alternatives.

- **Evaluation approach:** Owners must determine whether the proposed alternatives meet or exceed RFP requirements, factoring in cost savings, functionality, and risk.

- **Confidentiality is critical:** ATCs are usually submitted confidentially to protect the contractor's intellectual property. As an owner, you must safeguard this confidentiality throughout the process.

Here's an example: A contractor proposes a new bridge design using advanced materials, which could speed up construction and cut costs compared to the standard design in the RFP.

The Federal Highway Administration describes ATCs as suggested changes to the supplied project configuration, scope, design, or construction criteria—so long as they offer equal or improved solutions. If accepted, the ATC may be incorporated into the proposer's technical and price submission.

ATCs have proven especially cost-effective on large design build projects where the owner is looking for innovation that could impact technical performance and cost. Many state DOTs have successfully implemented ATCs, including California, Florida, Texas, Maryland, and Washington, as well as local agencies like the Port of Long Beach and the Riverside County Transportation Commission.

Use of ATCs on design build federal aid projects is permitted under 23 CFR 636.209(b). That's an important regulation to be aware of if your agency receives federal funding.

I reviewed the National Academy Press findings on ATC implementation in highway projects. Here are a few of the conclusions and recommendations I think are worth highlighting:

- **Confidentiality is essential.** It encourages bidders to develop innovative ideas and protects both industry and agency during discussions before the contract award. It also helps agencies assess the perceived risk from the proposer's perspective.

- **Resource requirements:** Evaluating ATCs takes significant agency resources. Owners must assess whether the potential cost and time savings (typically 10–15%) are worth the time and staffing needed to process the ATCs.

- **Cost-benefit evaluation:** If projected savings are minimal— say, 5%—it may not justify the resources required for evaluation. However, many teams are capable of delivering significant value through innovative proposals, so be open to the potential.

- **Limiting ATCs:** Some agencies limit the number of ATCs a team can submit or require that each one demonstrate a minimum estimated savings to justify the evaluation effort.

- **Terminology varies:** Different agencies use different terms for ATCs. For example:

- "Innovative Technical Concepts" (Army Corps of Engineers)

- "Pre-Approved Elements" or "PAEs" (Minnesota DOT)

- "Conceptual ATCs" or "CATCs" (Missouri DOT)

- "Alternative Financial Concepts" (Puerto Rico P3 Authority)

Evaluating ATCs: Panel Strategy

There are two schools of thought on how to staff the ATC evaluation panel:

- Some DOTs use a different panel from the one scoring the technical proposals to avoid conflicts of interest and improve confidentiality.

- Others use the same team due to resource limitations.

Both approaches have been successful. There are no legal challenges on record related to this issue, so it ultimately comes down to your agency's resources and comfort level.

As an owner, think about whether the structure and complexity of your project warrants the effort of incorporating ATCs or AFCs. If done right, they can unlock tremendous value. But it's not just about savings—ATCs also provide insights into how contractors interpret and plan to manage project risk. That alone can make the process worthwhile.

There are also two schools of thought regarding the inclusion of estimated cost savings information in ATC proposals. One side argues that cost data should not be included because the "equal to or better than" determination is a purely technical decision. Including pricing could pressure the review team to compromise standards in an effort to save money. The other side believes cost data is essential to evaluate why a deviation from the baseline design is warranted if the ATC is technically equivalent.

Additionally, including estimated savings provides a valuable performance measurement dataset for the ATC program itself. It helps DOTs make a stronger business case for continuing the program, especially when faced with industry skepticism. Again, the research concludes that this is a business decision that should be made by the agency. Some further research may help determine whether excluding cost data ultimately adds or detracts from the ATC evaluation process.

The third divergence in ATC practices involves whether clarifications to the RFP scope can be sought during one-on-one meetings. Practices vary widely. Caltrans, for example, specifically asked competing design builders to use these meetings to clarify their understanding of the RFP scope—citing this as one of the objectives of the confidential meeting. On the opposite end, some DOTs explicitly prohibit any discussion of non-ATC topics during these confidential sessions.

There is no case law directly related to this issue, which suggests it remains a matter of local interpretation. However, if you view ATCs as a risk management tool—as many do—then allowing clarifications in one-on-one meetings can help mitigate misinterpretation of the RFP's intent during procurement. The business decision here should weigh the impact on project risk. Legal research may help confirm whether permitting the discussion of non-ATC clarifications aligns with current procurement law.

Let me give you an example from TxDOT. This one comes from their Comprehensive Development Agreement (CDA) for a design, construct, finance, operate, and maintain (DCFOM) project. The ATC guidance was included in their Instructions to Proposers (ITP), which is essentially part of the RFP.

TxDOT defines ATCs as concepts that conflict with or require modification of the technical provisions for design, construction, operation, or maintenance—but that still meet or exceed the project performance and quality requirements. This process is designed to incorporate innovation and creativity early in the proposal stage, avoid delays or conflicts post-award, and ultimately deliver the best value to the public.

ATCs are only eligible if they do not reduce project scope, performance, or reliability. For instance, expanding the project to include new roadways or increasing time to substantial completion would not qualify. ATCs that require additional environmental evaluations may be permitted, but only if the proposer assumes all associated schedule and cost risks. If approvals aren't obtained, the developer must proceed per the original RFP requirements—at no additional cost or time extension. In short, the environmental risk lies squarely with the developer.

If a proposer isn't sure whether their idea is an ATC, TxDOT encourages submission for review anyway. Pre-proposal submissions must clearly be marked as ATCs and follow a detailed format:

- Sequential ATC numbering identifying the proposer.

- Separate submissions for multi-option ATCs.

- A description and conceptual drawing, including traffic operations analysis if applicable.

- A list of affected locations and how the ATC will be implemented.

- Impacts on operations, maintenance, handback, and life-cycle-costs.

- Any expected reductions in design or construction time.

- References to conflicting RFP requirements and a request for approval of deviations.

- A justification analysis, including impacts on traffic, community, permitting, safety, life cycle, maintenance, revenue, and more.

- If additional ROW is required, the proposer assumes full cost and risk.

- A history of the ATC's use on other projects, including owner references.

- Identification of added risk to the owner or third-parties.

- Cost implications for the owner, developer, and third-parties, as well as estimated savings.

- A final comparison to demonstrate how the ATC equals or exceeds RFP standards.

Owners may request additional information and are expected to respond by a set deadline, often within two to three weeks. Their responses generally fall into five categories:

1. ATC is acceptable for inclusion.

2. ATC is not acceptable.

3. ATC is conditionally acceptable—if modifications are made.

4. The submission isn't an ATC but may be included in the proposal.

5. The submission is not acceptable and cannot be included.

I've worked through many of these ATC processes. If the ATC is complex, it might take two or three rounds of back-and-forth to reach approval.

Once an ATC is approved, it constitutes a change to the CDA for that specific proposer. All proposers, by submitting a proposal, acknowledge that the opportunity to submit ATCs was open to everyone and waive any right to object to the owner's determination of ATC acceptability.

Pre-approved ATCs incorporated into the successful proposer's submittal will be reflected in the final CDA. Any conditions tied to ATC approval become part of the agreement. If a developer fails to meet any condition or gain a necessary third-party approval, the fallback is always compliance with the original RFP requirements—with no added cost or schedule impact.

In some cases, ATCs submitted by unsuccessful proposers may be shared at the owner's discretion with the winning developer—either during negotiations or later as a potential owner change request.

Alternative Financial Concepts (AFCs)

So the next section is really focused on Alternative Financial Concepts (AFCs). This was also part of the ITP for the proposal. TxDOT, on these P3 projects—what I refer to as P3s and what they call CDAs—tends to allow for both ATCs and AFCs. These AFCs can get pretty complicated, so I'm going to walk through this slowly so you get a better feel for how they work.

The process for pre-proposal review of AFCs is intended to allow proposers to incorporate innovation and creativity into their proposals. In turn, this enables owners to consider alternative financial concepts as part of the selection decision, helps avoid delays and potential conflicts in the commercial terms that could arise if AFCs were deferred until the post-award period, and allows for the best value to the public.

AFCs are proposed changes to the terms of the CDA documents—excluding those provisions specifically marked off-limits—that allow a different financial structure. These may include financial structures for the developer or for project management and operations, and they fall under what's called "structured AFCs." These are concepts that would otherwise be prohibited or impracticable under the terms of the as-issued CDA documents.

The owner has full discretion to allow or reject any AFC submitted. Proposers are advised that owners will allow an AFC only if they determine that the revised CDA terms provide the owner with substantially the same or better value for money, rights, and remedies.

Exclusions to AFCs include any concept that:

- Reduces the owner's value for money or contractual rights and remedies.

- Increases the term of the contract.

- Modifies provisions related to tolling systems, rates, pricing, speed requirements, user classifications, exempt vehicles, or post-termination tolling.

- Increases the owner's liability for project debt.

- Reduces owner compensation, including revenue payments, financial gain payments, or tolling method gain payments.

- Increases the amount of public funds or alters draw requirements adversely.

- Increases developer compensation in the event of termination.

- Changes conditions or procedures for substantial completion, service commitments, or final acceptance.

- Alters the allocation of responsibilities between the owner and developer related to design, permitting, ROW, utilities, construction, O&M, handback, or safety.

- Modifies provisions related to compensation or relief events to shift more risk to the owner.

- Changes the role or scope of the independent engineer or revenue-impacting facilities.

- Alters remedies, defaults, lender rights, dispute resolution, or any security or insurance provisions in a way that is less favorable to the owner.

If the proposer wishes to include AFCs in its proposal, the proposer must first submit each AFC for initial review by the owner. Submissions must be made in writing with a cover letter identifying the proposer, project, and marked "Confidential AFC for Initial Review." The AFC itself must be a concise description—no more than two single-spaced pages, not including the cover sheet.

After review, the owner will notify the proposer whether it may proceed with a formal pre-proposal AFC submission. Only invited AFCs will be considered for inclusion in the proposal.

Each formal AFC submission must include:

- A sequential AFC number and proposer ID.

- A detailed narrative description, including whether it is a financial or structured AFC.

- An explanation of the value to the owner.

- A markup of each CDA provision proposed to be changed.

- Justification for the AFC, including how it preserves or improves owner rights and remedies.

- An estimate of any potential savings to the owner.

If an AFC is pre-approved, it may be included in the proposal, subject to any stated conditions.

If the owner determines that the RFP contains an error or ambiguity as a result of the AFC review—or independently—they reserve the right to issue a modification to correct it, regardless of the implications for any proposed AFC.

Furthermore, the owner may modify the RFP documents to incorporate changes proposed by an AFC, provided the owner will not advise other proposers that the modification is associated with an AFC. The owner will also not make any such modification if they determine it would compromise the proposer's intellectual property.

The owner may request additional information regarding proposed AFCs at any time and, in each case, will respond to the proposer, provided all requested information has been received. The owner's responses will be limited to one of the following:

- The AFC is acceptable for inclusion in the proposal.

- The submittal is not acceptable for inclusion in the proposal.

- The AFC is not acceptable in its present form but may be acceptable upon satisfaction—at the owner's discretion—of specific conditions, clarifications, or modifications.

- The concept in the submittal is already permitted under the RFP documents.

Approval of an AFC will constitute a change in the specific requirements of the CDA documents associated with the approved AFC for that specific proposer. Each proposer, by submitting a proposal, acknowledges that the opportunity to submit AFCs was offered equally to all proposers and waives any rights to object to the owner's determination regarding the acceptability of AFCs.

The owner anticipates that its comments to the proposer will be sufficient to enable any necessary revisions to the AFCs. However, if the proposer needs further clarification, they may submit a written request to the owner.

Following the conditional award of the CDA, the AFCs that were pre-approved and incorporated into the successful proposer's proposal will be included in the final CDA documents in the form previously approved. If the owner responded to any AFC by stating that it would be acceptable upon certain conditions, clarifications, or modifications, then those identified terms will become part of the CDA documents as well.

The CDA documents will be finalized after award but before execution to reflect all approved AFCs. In some cases, following the conditional award, AFCs from unsuccessful proposers may, at the owner's discretion, be presented to the selected developer for potential incorporation through a change order, in accordance with the CDA.

Subject to applicable law and governing rules, all communications regarding ATCs, AFCs, and the concepts themselves will remain confidential until a proposer is selected or the procurement is canceled. At that point, any confidentiality rights will cease, except as otherwise allowed under the law. This provision does not prevent the owner from modifying the RFP or CDA documents as necessary to comply with applicable legal requirements or to incorporate information obtained outside the ATC or AFC process.

By submitting a proposal, each proposer agrees that, if not selected, they will disclose their AFC-related work product to the successful proposer. This is a key point, especially in cases where a stipend is paid by the owner for a responsive proposal. If a proposer refuses to share pre-approved AFC concepts with the successful proposer, they may forfeit the stipend.

That's an important takeaway. It ensures transparency and continuity in innovation while protecting the owner's ability to achieve best value—another example of why it's critical to read the fine print in your ITP and CDA documents.

The Financial Proposal Evaluation Subcommittee (FPES) will evaluate each financial proposal to determine the concession payment for both the base scope and the initial configuration, as well as the proposer's termination-for-convenience amount. The financial score will be determined based on two components: the price score and the termination-for-convenience score. No consideration will be given to any other revenue payments in evaluating the financial offer.

The price score for each proposer shall be based on a concession payment—payable by the proposer to the owner—greater than or equal to $0. This will include both the nominal amount and the net present value. The owner will not offset the concession payment by any public funds made available to the TMC Connector.

Additionally, each proposer shall offer a concession payment payable from the proposer to the owner that is greater than or equal to $0, again considering both the nominal and net present values.

A schedule of public fund payments and the net present value of such payments will also be provided. Prior to the proposal due date, the owner will determine a strike price.

If one or more Proposers offers a Net Price equal to or greater than the Strike Price, Owner will evaluate all Proposals based on the Initial Configuration Work. In that case, Owner shall award the full Price Score (76 points) to the Proposer or Proposers that offer the highest Net Price. Each remaining Proposer's Price Score shall be calculated as follows:

$$\text{Price Score} = 76 * \left(\frac{Pl}{PBest} \right)$$

Where:

Pl = the greater of (a) $0 or (b) the sum of (i) such Proposer's Net Price *plus* (ii) $100,000,000

PBest = (a) the highest Net Price offered by the Proposers *plus* (b) $100,000,000

If no Proposer offers a Net Price equal to or greater than the Strike Price, the Owner will evaluate all Proposals based on the Base Scope only (without the Work). In that case, Owner shall award the full Price Score (76 points) to the Proposer or Proposers that offer the highest Concession Payment. Each remaining Proposer's Price Score shall be calculated as follows:

$$\text{Price Score} = 76 * \left(\frac{Pl}{PBest} \right)$$

Where:

Pl = (a) the net present value of such Proposer's Concession Payment *plus* (b) $100,000,000

PBest = (a) the net present value of the highest Concession Payment offered by the Proposers *plus* (b) $100,000,000

Termination for Convenience Fee Score

As required each Proposer shall offer a schedule of Termination for Convenience Amounts. Owner shall award the full Termination for Convenience Fee Score (4 points) to the Proposer or Proposers that offer the lowest Termination for Convenience Amount. Each remaining Proposer's Termination for Convenience Fee Score shall be calculated as follows:

Termination for Convenience Fee Score = 4 * (1 − (Pl-PBest))

PBest

Where:

Pl = the net present value of such Proposer's Termination for Convenience Amount

PBest = the net present value of the lowest Termination for Convenience Amount offered by the Proposers

ESRC Evaluation of Technical and Financial Proposals

Before reviewing the FPES evaluation results, the ESRC will review the Project Development Plans and the ratings and points recommendations provided by the DPES with respect to each Project Development Plan. The ESRC may accept the recommendations provided by the DPES, may request that the DPES reconsider the DPES's recommendations, or may develop the ESRC's own recommendations.

After determining each Proposal's Technical Score, the ESRC will review the Financial Proposal and FPES evaluation results and determine each Proposal's Financial Score. The ESRC may accept the evaluation results provided by the FPES, may request the FPES to re-perform the evaluation, or may perform the evaluation itself.

Finally, the ESRC will determine the Total Proposal Score for each Proposal based on the formula and determine the rankings and the apparent best value.

9.　How-To: Getting Involved in Your Design Builders' Task Group Meetings

As you've heard me say several times in this book, collaboration is the key to success on any AD Mega-Project. It takes understanding, transparency, and trust to build a successful working relationship and project team. One of the most important members of that team is the design builder. As the owner, you have the opportunity to establish the framework for how you want to work with the design builder and their team.

You need to make a conscious decision on how you're going to structure this in your RFQ and how you want to promote the use of task groups—or technical work groups (TWGs)—during project execution. Most design builders use task groups or TWGs during the proposal efforts, and many of them believe in continuing these through execution.

As I discussed in Chapter 5, Item 12, I strongly recommend taking the task groups developed during the proposal phase and expanding them in execution. During the proposal phase, the design builder was limited to meeting with the owner only during one-on-one meetings. In contrast, task groups during execution should serve as collaborative working sessions that include input from the owner, third-parties, stakeholders, and SMEs. These groups are critical to streamlining the design and approval process and ensuring that all disciplines and SMEs are engaged in decision-making.

Expansion of these groups during execution can include topics such as:

- MWDBE engagement.

- Facilitation.

- Value engineering.

- Life-cycle-cost analysis.

- Risk assessment.

- Financial strategy.

- BIM coordination.

- Safety.

- Close-out.

- Post-design services.

I highly recommend getting involved in your design builders' task groups during project execution. Promote this approach in your RFP by asking the proposers what their strategy is for continuing these groups and make it a part of your scoring system. Let them know that you, as the owner, are willing to commit resources and staff to actively participate. This commitment reinforces the idea that the owner will work side-by-side with the design builder to support decision-making and expedite the process.

CASE STUDY: SH 130 TURNPIKE EDA FOR TTA AND TX-DOT

I also referenced a case study on the SH 130 Turnpike project, where the design builder, Lone Star Infrastructure (LSI), continued and expanded the original TWGs initiated during the proposal phase. These groups included:

- **Roadway**: pavement, earthwork, geotechnical, signing, guardrail, and striping.

- **Structures**: bridges, interchanges, major culverts, major sign structures, retaining walls, drainage, aesthetics, and landscaping.

- **Toll Facilities.**

- **Environmental.**

- **Scheduling.**

- **Traffic Management.**

- **Construction Phasing.**

- **Pre-Construction**: right-of-way, acquisitions, utility relocations, and surveys.

- **Public Outreach.**

Each TWG was led by either a design or construction lead. Representatives from TTA, TxDOT, HDR, third parties, stakeholders, and SMEs were invited to attend. These groups met weekly and had strong internal coordination:

- A TWG coordinator from the construction team oversaw all group activities.

- Meeting schedules were carefully managed to avoid conflicts.

- A standard meeting template was used.

- Meeting notes were distributed in a timely fashion.

- Interdisciplinary reviews were scheduled as needed.

- Progress was regularly reported to the project director, Doug Fuller.

Involving TTA, TxDOT, HDR, and other stakeholders in the TWGs significantly expedited the review and approval process by ensuring that all decision-makers were at the table early and often. Once we reached the 60% design milestone, most of the TWGs were disbanded, having already served their purpose effectively.

The TWGs had a measurable and positive impact on communication across the board. This success on SH 130 is a strong indicator that the same approach can be equally successful on your AD Mega-Project.

Work closely with your staff and the GC to make sure they understand the mission of these task or technical work groups: to streamline and expedite review and approvals—not to expand the design builder's scope. Done right, this approach will save you time, build team trust, and improve project outcomes.

10. How-To: Assisting with Project Close-out

In establishing close-out procedures and responsibilities (Chapter 5, Item 22), I laid out my recommendations to the developer and design builder on the importance of closing out the project on time. I recommended several key steps, including bringing on a close-out manager at the start of project execution. This person should work alongside the team to finalize the framework and checklist for project close-out, while also developing the close-out plan and program. Once that plan is developed, it should be reviewed by their internal management team.

If the project is a P3, make sure the developer and O&M manager are included in the review process. After all parties provide comments, the close-out manager should finalize the documents and plan. These should then be submitted to the owner for review and feedback. Once the owner's comments are incorporated, the finalized document should be returned to the owner, posted for the team, and followed by a management meeting to walk through the close-out plan in detail.

The close-out manager should begin closing out portions of the project as they reach substantial completion. This role must work closely with the project manager and construction manager throughout the process. Waiting until the entire project is substantially complete or finished to begin close-out is a common mistake—it causes unnecessary delays and added costs.

The owner also has a critical role to play in supporting close-out. It's essential that the owner work collaboratively with the developer and design builder to ensure that close-out is streamlined and efficient. This may involve assigning a dedicated close-out manager from the owner's side to work hand-in-hand with the design builder's close-out manager. That person becomes the single point of contact for all owner-side close-out issues.

The owner's close-out manager should have the authority and responsibility to:

- Review and comment on the design builder's close-out planning and program.

- Agree to allow the design builder to close out portions of the project as they reach substantial completion.

- Assist the design builder's close-out manager in resolving issues that arise on the owner's side, such as design agreement issues, political obstacles, community concerns, rolling stock delays, operational matters, and scheduling conflicts.

- Coordinate and schedule all owner-led close-out activities and necessary resources.

- Develop, approve, and manage punch lists.

CASE STUDY: CRENSHAW LAX LIGHT RAIL TRANSIT FOR LA METRO

Let me share an example. On our Crenshaw LAX Light Rail Transit (LRT) design build project for LA Metro, I served as executive design director for Walsh on this $1.3 billion project. I worked out of Walsh's LAX regional office from January 2016 through November 2018 and collaborated closely with Darrell Waters, VP and business group leader for Southern California.

We encountered multiple issues that held up project close-out—everything from delayed system equipment selection by LA Metro (some decisions were three years late) to coordination challenges around operations and testing. Darrell and project manager Jeffrey Mays worked hard to resolve the issues with their LA Metro counterparts, including reaching out to Rick Clarke, Metro's chief program management officer. But unfortunately, progress was slow and limited.

The lesson here is simple: it is absolutely critical that all parties—including the owner work together to close-out an AD Mega-Project. Ownership, communication, and shared commitment to closing out the job are what bring it to a successful end.

11.   How-To: Honor the Requirements Set Up in Your RFP and Validate What the Proposers Have Submitted

I've added this item towards the end of the chapter because if you don't honor the requirements set up in the RFP and fairly evaluate the proposals submitted, it can stain your organization and cause irreparable damage to your credibility. This can be one of the most damaging things that can happen and may take years to recover from.

The AD community is small. And when word gets out about decisions that are viewed as incorrect, it sows doubt across the entire AD community. This can lead to a loss of interest in your projects by formidable proposers—many of whom may decide not to do business with you now or in the future. It has happened before and continues to happen today.

The best thing you can do as an owner is guard against allowing proposers to violate the requirements in your RFP, especially if it's being done to accept a bid with significant cost savings. Once you've set the boundaries for your RFP, do not allow them to be violated. Stick to your guns. Every proposer will understand what just happened—and that will spread like wildfire.

If a proposer makes a statement in the technical or financial proposal that seems too good to be true or is not consistent with the other bids, question it. Have your internal or external experts analyze the proposer's claims, validate the accuracy, and determine how they could reasonably achieve those results.

If your team identifies an error, a missed item, or is simply uncomfortable with the proposal, send a clarification letter asking the proposer to respond to your concerns. If their response doesn't resolve the issue, discuss a path forward with your legal advisors that's consistent with your RFP and internal policies. You also want to make sure you don't violate the proposer's rights.

If needed, invite the proposer to a one-on-one meeting with your technical experts and legal team to lay out concerns in more detail. If the issue still isn't resolved after that meeting, and no agreement is reached on how to proceed, you may need to caucus internally and determine the best course of action. But whatever you do—don't give in if it compromises your RFP.

Let me give you two case studies to show what can happen.

CASE STUDY: US 60 FROM I-10 TO GILBERT ROAD DESIGN BUILD FOR ADOT

On the US 60 from I-10 to Gilbert Road Project for ADOT, the proposal process took place from 2000 to 2001. This was a $185 million design build widening and reconstruction project. The RFP stated that a retaining wall must be constructed from the Mesa city limits eastward. At that time, ADOT didn't use ATCs.

Our team—Flatiron/FNF JV and AECOM—noted during review that an earth berm could serve the same purpose as the retaining wall, but we decided not to challenge the RFP or violate its terms. At bid opening, the Granite/Sundt JV team was selected as best value, and their bid was significantly lower than the others. It soon came out that ADOT had allowed them to replace the retaining wall with a berm—directly violating the RFP.

Other proposers protested, but ADOT awarded the job to Granite/Sundt JV anyway. That decision left a lasting stain on ADOT's reputation and took them years to recover from. It was the first of several missteps that eroded their credibility on design build procurements and projects for ADOT.

CASE STUDY: IH 635 MANAGED LANES P3 IN DALLAS FOR TXDOT

Now for the IH 635 Managed Lanes P3 Project for TxDOT in Dallas. The short-list included only two teams. I served as proposal lead for AECOM, with ACS as the developer and Dragados-Kiewit JV as the design builder. The other team was Cintra as developer and Ferrovial as design builder.

Proposals were submitted in January 2009. Our team bid $2.4 billion in construction costs; Cintra-Ferrovial bid $1.1 billion—a difference of $1.3 billion. The AD community was stunned.

TxDOT selected the Cintra-Ferrovial team and spent more than six months negotiating the agreement. When results were released, the final agreed construction value had ballooned to $2.6 billion—$1.5 billion over their original bid and $200 million more than ours.

That caused shockwaves throughout the AD and P3 communities. TxDOT was scrutinized intensely. For years afterward, there was a noticeable reluctance by the industry to bid on their AD Mega-Projects with TxDOT.

12.   How-To: Develop Your Design Build Legal Documents and Procedures

If your organization has never done a design build but has experience with design-bid-build, you can convert your documents accordingly—but you'll need the help of a seasoned design build expert. Make sure the expert you hire has specific experience with AD Mega-Projects. Your internal legal team can help with the document modifications, but outside expertise is essential.

CASE STUDY: TERMINAL DEVELOPMENT PROGRAM AT SAN DIEGO INTERNATIONAL AIRPORT

Let me give you an example. At the San Diego Regional Airport Authority, for the Terminal Development Program at San Diego International Airport, AECOM was the program manager. Steve McCabe, AECOM's program manager, brought me in to provide design build advisory services.

The authority planned to procure two design build teams: one for the Terminal 2 West Building and Airside Expansion, and one for the Terminal 2 Parking Garage and Landside Projects—each valued at roughly $600 million. This was the authority's first time with design build.

I worked out of their offices for six months—from September 2008 through March 2009—reviewing and editing the draft agreements, converting their procedures manual from design-bid-build to design build, and coordinating reviews through the internal committee and airport director, Steve Cornell.

First, I prepared a full risk analysis of their proposed design build contracts. That risk analysis outlined potential exposures, the provisions in the current contracts that might create issues, and proposed alternate approaches. The team reviewed these risks and made decisions on how to proceed.

From there, we modified the front-end agreements: summary of work, time (including incentives), liquidated damages, compensation, escrow of bid documents, and Exhibits A through K. We also revised the general conditions: general provisions, responsibilities of the authority and contractor, control of work, subcontractors, safety, airport security, insurance, bonds, changes in work, schedule, payments, completion, partnering, dispute resolution, and termination.

Once those were finalized, we developed design build Contract No. 1 for Turner and Contract No. 2 for Kiewit, each with detailed scopes and compensation.

At the same time, we revised and finalized the Project Procedures Manual, including:

- 9 procedures for FAA correspondence to easements.
- 9 pre-design phase procedures.
- 12 design phase procedures.
- 8 bid phase procedures.
- 8 pre-construction procedures.
- 4 construction-phase legal procedures.
- 5 legal review procedures.
- 24 construction administration procedures.
- 9 closeout procedures.

That's 88 procedures in total. The staff was trained and began using the new design build procedures to administer the contracts. Both projects were delivered with minimal disputes and very few change orders.

13.   How-To: Make a Difference in Your Developer and Design Builder Selection and Execution Processes

Many of us have established policies, procedures, and programs over the last 10 to 30 years that now need to be updated to keep pace with the ever-changing demands of AD projects—especially AD Mega-Projects. We've seen these projects grow from $1 billion to $5 billion-plus in size. At the same time, we've seen major developers and design builders drop out of P3 and traditional design build projects. Profit margins are shrinking for developers, contractors, lead designers, and others in the delivery chain, while the cost to win and execute these projects has risen exponentially.

It's in the best interest of everyone involved in AD Mega-Projects to make some changes. Owners must take responsibility for refreshing their policies, procedures, and programs. It's a lot of work, yes—but if you want to continue to use P3s and traditional design build on Mega-Projects, it's necessary.

I challenge all owners to look inward and ask yourselves the hard questions:

1. Are we getting the best teams and personnel on our projects?

2. Are our agreements fair to all parties?

3. Are we providing enough time and early information for teams to assemble?

4. Does our scoring system reflect our project's actual goals, objectives, and needs?

5. Are we realizing the full benefits of using P3 and design build?

6. How do we handle significant changes to scope from outside influences?

7. How do we engage with proposers throughout the project?

8. Is our staff adequately trained for AD Mega-Projects?

9. How are we managing risk?

Let's take these one at a time.

1. Are we getting the best teams and personnel?

To do that, we must be the client of choice. It's not just about having a lot of work in the pipeline—it's about your reputation. Are you easy to work with? Do you support and collaborate with your developer and design builder? How quickly do you pay invoices? These things matter. Are you shortlisting or prequalifying too many teams? Most proposers are willing to compete in a field of four, but their odds and interest drop when the field gets too large.

2. Are your agreements fair?

Are you assigning risk to the party best equipped to manage it? What happens when something unforeseeable occurs? Do you fairly compensate for change orders, including administrative support and profit? How are you handling unforeseen site conditions? Do your requirements make sense—and are they clearly stated? Do you include partnering?

3. Are you giving teams enough time and early information to assemble?

As I mentioned earlier in the book, I recommend proposers begin their due diligence on an AD Mega-Project up to two years before the RFQ is issued. Most teams are formed at least six months prior. I suggest holding industry reviews to share key information with prospective teams—especially items like the prime agreement, scoring criteria, key personnel requirements, and MWDBE goals. Waiting to release these as part of the RFP—or worse, in an addendum—is a missed opportunity. Giving teams that information earlier helps them make better teaming and personnel decisions.

4. Does your scoring reflect your actual goals and needs?

Take a close look at how each section of your RFQ and RFP is scored. For example, if your MWDBE goal is 30% but it's only weighted at 5% in your evaluation, that sends the wrong message. On a $2 billion project, 30% is $600 million. That level of commitment needs to be backed by proper scoring and should warrant bringing in a specialized MWDBE advisor to help develop a strategy and culture to support success. Without that, you're likely to just get lip service.

5. Are you getting the full benefits of using P3 and design build?

This is a great question to explore with your team. Try this: create a matrix. On the left, list all the benefits you expect to achieve from P3 or design build. Across the top, list all your past projects. Go through each project and check off the benefits that were achieved. In a column on the right, explain why certain benefits were or weren't realized. This kind of exercise can give you real insight into what's working—and what isn't.

6. How do you handle significant scope changes from external forces?

If your prime agreement doesn't address this, or if you've made it the sole responsibility of the developer or design builder, you might need to revise it. Consider developing a partnering strategy that brings in key stakeholders, third-parties, community leaders, and elected officials at the beginning of the project—and keep them engaged through follow-up meetings. If a major issue arises, there should be a mechanism in place that allows for adjustments to scope, schedule, and compensation. These issues shouldn't automatically fall on the developer or design builder.

7. How do you engage with proposers throughout the project?

Think about how your RFQ, RFP, and prime agreement reflect your approach to collaboration. As I've said many times, collaboration, transparency, respect, and trust are critical to success. That spirit should carry from industry reviews all the way through to execution.

If a proposer has concerns about the prime agreement during the RFQ or RFP phase, how can they raise them? If you don't allow for clarification at the RFQ stage, you risk losing strong teams. One-on-one meetings during RFQ may not be appropriate, but a formal Q&A process could be the right tool.

Do you allow one-on-one meetings during the RFP phase—and if so, how often? These meetings are powerful tools for relationship building. I highly recommend them. Once the project moves into execution, I suggest weekly leadership meetings with the developer, design builder, and owner leadership team. Use task groups or technical work groups through 60% design to ensure decisions are made collaboratively and with input from all stakeholders.

8. Is your staff trained to work on AD Mega-Projects?

I cover this more extensively in Chapter 8, but I strongly recommend developing a best practices manual and a training program tailored specifically to AD Mega-Projects. Your staff and GC will benefit from these resources, and so will the project.

9. How are you handling risk management?

As I noted in Item 7 of this chapter, it's critical to consider not just how risk affects your agency but how it impacts the entire project team. Your success will be judged based on the success of your team—which includes the developer, design builder, board and committee members, agency partners, stakeholders, third-parties, MWDBE firms, and community and political leaders.

You should start evaluating your risk management strategy early, during internal conversations and due diligence. Every AD Mega-Project has its own unique profile—its own challenges, constraints, and opportunities. Make sure your risk strategy reflects that.

Chapter 7
Developer-Specific Process and Case Studies

TOP HOW-TOS FOR DEVELOPERS

In this chapter, we're going to discuss the top how-tos for developers. As the developer, you're the leader of any P3 project. The way you get to know and understand the owner, how you conduct your due diligence before getting started, your participation in soundings with the owner, how you develop your team, your involvement in risk assessments, how and when you make your go/no-go decision, your role in QA/QC, how early you mobilize prior to the issuance of the RFQ, your collaboration with the design build team, your engagement with ATCs and AFCs, and your partnering with the owner and MWDBEs—all of these can have a significant impact on the success or failure of your alternative delivery (AD) mega-project.

I've worked on all sides of AD Mega-Projects over the last 32 years—since 1993. I've worked for developers, design builders, and owners on 51 projects with a total construction value of $66 billion, 12 of which were P3s with a combined construction value of $28 billion. My overall win rate on AD projects has been 25 percent. Through this chapter, I'll share what I believe are best practices, along with my personal successes and failures on P3 projects, supported by case studies.

1. How-To: Getting to Know and Understand the Owner

As the developer—the lead on any P3 project—you need to have a deep understanding of the owner's team. This includes their experience and track record with P3 Mega-Projects, how they structure their P3 contracts, and their overall reputation in the industry. If you haven't worked with that particular owner before, see if anyone on your team has. Institutional knowledge—whether internal or external—is incredibly valuable.

If you don't have this intelligence or a subscription service that tracks owners, developers, and procurement details, you may want to explore that. Getting access to these tools can give you an edge in understanding what to expect, and how best to engage with the owner from the outset. Strong P3 developers make it their business to know who they're doing business with.

Inframation has news and databases for all P3 work around the world. If you go to their website and you call them, you can discuss their databases.

We touched a bit on due diligence in the previous item, but let's go a little deeper. One of the tools I've used before is a P3 intelligence platform is Inframation. I have no affiliation with them, but I've used their services, and they offer helpful reports and articles on the P3 business. They usually offer a 30-day free trial, which is a great way to get started.

By defining the types of projects you're interested in, you can pull up a list of agencies with past, current, or upcoming projects in the pipeline. These platforms often have hundreds of articles that provide insight into agency reputations and specific projects. If there's a particular project you're interested in, you can look it up and see who's leading it and how the agency is structured.

Many of these agencies have a dedicated P3 office. Reach out and schedule a Zoom call. You'll be surprised how much you can learn by having a candid conversation with key staff. You can also check the agency's website to see if they list their P3 contacts and organizational structure. That alone will help you figure out where decisions are made and who the influencers are.

P3 conferences are another good way to meet agency staff, though keep in mind most agencies won't have booths. Still, I recommend your company set up a booth—it puts you out there. You can meet a lot of the right people by being visible. It's all about getting to know each agency personally.

When I was with AECOM, I had my own corporate account with one of these P3 intel platforms. Every year, they held a conference in New York City that brought together many of the top folks in the P3 space—but it was still small enough to make meaningful connections. Other groups like DBIA, ARTBA, and P3 Bulletin also host great conferences. Joining a working committee with one of these organizations is a smart move, especially if you're looking to get more involved and meet agency decision-makers.

Hopefully, your organization already has staff who are members of these groups and can help with introductions. Over the last 32 years, I've worked in 36 states and in Canada, and I've pursued or worked on many P3 Mega-Projects with these agencies. Through that, I've built a wide network of contacts.

Most of the agencies that deliver P3 Mega-Projects are large, bureaucratic organizations with layered corporate structures. Visit their websites and try to download their org charts. Take the time to understand their structure. Most have multiple silos, and your goal is to figure out which silos you'll need to work with. Then, start building relationships with the key players. Be transparent. Be consistent. And earn their trust.

2. How-To: Do Due Diligence Before You Start

This step is foundational. Before you decide to pursue a P3 project, you need to thoroughly understand the owner's team, their experience and reputation with P3 Mega-Projects, and what one of their P3 prime agreements typically looks like.

Ask yourself: How is the owner's team structured? How will their prime agreement be structured—will it be fair to all parties? How is risk distributed? What happens if an event takes place that requires the scope of the project to be adjusted—how will compensation and time extensions be handled?

Who will serve as the owner's project manager, and have they administered a P3 Mega-Project before? If so, how did it go? Does the owner demonstrate a real belief in collaboration, transparency, and partnering—or is that just lip service? Is this philosophy reflected in their prime agreement?

How will disputes be adjudicated? Will the owner conduct soundings with potential teams, and will you be invited? How will the RFP be structured and scored? Will the owner short-list teams or only pre-qualify them? And when will they inform you about the requirements in the prime agreement—at the RFQ stage, or not until the RFP is issued (or even later)?

Will the owner allow ATCs and AFCs during the proposal? Do they understand and value, net present value appropriately—or is everything just about lowest cost? Who will be leading the general consultant, financial and legal efforts, and what's their reputation? Are the financial and legal advisors sophisticated and experienced in complex P3s?

Will the owner hold industry reviews prior to the RFP? Will one-on-one meetings be allowed prior to the RFQ? Will they let you know which other teams they've been speaking with? How will they conduct themselves during the proposal phase, and do they have a good reputation for maintaining confidentiality during those one-on-ones?

Will the owner give teams enough time to put together a strong, competitive proposal and bid? Are they sophisticated enough—and do they have the right advisors in place—to evaluate ATCs, AFCs, and the financial components of your proposal appropriately?

What is the owner's track record when it comes to proposal selection? Do they run a fair and transparent process? Who is your competition—and what is their reputation with this owner? Most importantly, do you have a fair shot at winning?

All of this must be evaluated—and answered—before you make the decision to move forward and submit a proposal and bid. Just doing this due diligence will require a tremendous amount of effort, especially if you've never worked with this owner on a P3 project before.

3.   How-To: Participate in Soundings with the Owner

If your owner is sophisticated enough, they'll likely hold soundings for their P3 Mega-Projects and invite prospective proposers. If you're fortunate—or skilled—enough to get invited, it's absolutely worth participating in.

CASE STUDY: SOUNDING FOR WEST SANTA ANA TRANSIT CORRIDOR PROJECT FOR LA METRO

When I was Executive Design Director at Walsh, we were invited to a market sounding for the West Santa Ana Transit Corridor Project in November of 2018. We signed a non-disclosure and confidentiality agreement with LA Metro and were provided with a project information packet, a list of market sounding questions, and the Project Labor Agreement—prepared by T. Brian Jenkins, Principal at Sperry Capital, Inc.

Before the meeting, we received 22 questions spread over five pages. They covered labor, schedule, project risks, design level, funding/minimum operating segments, commercial structure, and procurement. We were also given a 21-page project information packet titled *P3 Market Sounding*, which included "project at a glance," background and definition, potential delivery models, schedule and phasing, funding strategy, TOD strategic implementation, status of current activities, and timing. Appendix A covered the DEIS/DEIR with two alignments under consideration (Alternatives E and G) in plan and profile. Appendix B provided a detailed table of design refinements and justification by jurisdiction (including Los Angeles, South Gate, Paramount, Bellflower, Artesia, and Cerritos). Appendix C featured capital and O&M funding profiles from 2018–2057.

After reviewing all the documents, we prepped internally with our Walsh team, which included our legal lead, our head of P3 (Greg Ciabrone), Daniel Walsh Jr., three others, and myself. The sounding call with LA Metro lasted two hours. We learned a tremendous amount—probably more about their internal thinking than we would have gotten in any other meeting. We answered all 22 questions candidly, and both sides gained valuable insight into each other's concerns and priorities. It was an excellent meeting.

4. How-To: Develop Your Team

As the lead in any P3 pursuit, the development of your team is essential to your success. Who and when you bring on your design builder, legal advisor, financial advisor, investors, independent QA/QC, MWDBE advisor, O&M firm, political advisor, community engagement specialist, and others can make or break your pursuit.

There are several factors in making these decisions. Are you well-connected with the owner, or do you need local strength and support? If you've worked with this owner before and have internal capacity, great. But if you're unfamiliar with the owner, their politics, or the local landscape—and you don't have all the internal capabilities—you'll need to bring in a team that fills those gaps.

I recommend creating a teaming matrix for your specific AD Mega-Project and owner. List your strengths and weaknesses and identify the needs your team must fulfill. For each position, define the qualities you're seeking. Have you worked with them before? Was that experience successful? Have they worked with the owner before—and were they successful in that role? Is local presence important?

Once you've done that for every role, identify potential candidates and score them against your criteria. Hold brainstorming sessions with your internal team to validate the matrix, fill in missing information, and help refine the evaluation.

Make sure your team is aligned on the owner's hot buttons, requirements, and issues for this specific AD Mega-Project. If they're not, bring them up to speed. Then, identify the top two or three candidates for each role and assess the gaps. Strategize how and when each position needs to be filled, and assign responsibilities. Follow up regularly to evaluate your progress and adjust the strategy as needed.

Even if you don't need every role active immediately, it's important to fill them early. Once your team is assembled, you can start holding regular meetings to hone your due diligence and refine your win strategy.

5.   How-To: Participate in Risk Assessments

Conduct an internal risk assessment as early as possible with your core team. This first round should be a high-level pass. Categories might include:

- Your knowledge of the owner.

- Your knowledge of the project.

- The time you have to learn and prepare.

- Your current teaming and staffing strategy.

- Your potential return on investment and timeline.

This initial assessment helps you map out where your gaps are and what strategies you need to put in place. If you haven't already developed an action plan, now's the time to do it.

Once you've made progress and gained a clearer picture of the project, schedule a second risk assessment. Now, you can dig deeper. Evaluate specific categories such as:

- Owner.

- Political.

- Community.

- Technical.

- Financial.

- Investors.

- Environmental.

- Revenue.

- O&M.

- Contractual.

List your risks and sub-risks under each category, based on your research and due diligence. For each, develop a mitigation strategy and score it as low, medium, or high. Identify any remaining information gaps and update your strategy accordingly. Assign responsibilities and keep moving.

As you continue to gather insights and learn more about the owner, the project, and your competition, conduct a third risk assessment. Use the second assessment as your baseline, and go through each category with your team. Add new items, update existing ones, and identify outstanding gaps.

The goal is to assess your progress, determine whether you should still be pursuing the project, and—if the answer is yes—refine your strategy, tighten your execution plan, and fill in any remaining gaps.

6.   How-To: Making a Go/No-Go Decision

There are many opportunities out there, and limited resources to chase all of them. We cannot—and should not—go after every project. That's why it's so important to develop a Go/No-Go Worksheet and process to help guide decision-making. I recommend that a small group within your company create a standardized Go/No-Go Worksheet that can be completed by the Project Sponsor and approved by the Executive Team.

One of the best Go/No-Go Worksheets I've worked with was developed by Walsh. The worksheet included the project name, estimated value, and submission date in the top left corner, and the approval level and score in the top right. They used Approval Levels 1–5 based on the project value and monthly liquidated damages (LDs), with Level 5 reserved for the highest-value, highest-risk projects. The maximum score was 75, and any project scoring 30 or lower was considered a no-go.

Your team should agree on criteria and scoring that reflect your firm's values, strategy, and goals. Walsh's version required inputs in the following areas:

- **Project Description.**

- **Type of Pursuit** – Net present value, best value, or other.

The worksheet then scored 15 categories, each from 1 to 5, with 5 being the most favorable:

1. **Project Duration & Phasing** – Is the schedule realistic?

2. **Market Segment** – What's your current and past experience in this market? Have you worked successfully with this client before?

3. **Project Complexity** – What's the most complex feature? What are the design builder, workforce, and MWDBE requirements?

4. **Client and Design Builder Relationship** – Have you worked with them? What have you learned from the marketplace about them?

5. **Project Contracts** – What type of contract is it? Can the SPV and DB meet bonding requirements? Are there clauses for damages, unforeseen conditions, or unexpected events? Do you have a trusted O&M partner?

6. **Project Funding** – Is funding secured? Will federal dollars, PABs, or revenue funding be used? Can you be competitive?

Do you need new investors—and have you worked with them before?

7. **Competition** – Who are the other SPVs/DBs? What are their strengths or market advantages?

8. **Joint Venture or Partnering** – Should you consider a JV partner?

9. **Award Criteria** – Will the selection be based on net present value, schedule, or other factors?

10. **Technical Submission Requirements** – Can your team meet the technical bar? Do you have competitive advantages?

11. **Pursuit Cost** – Are there stipends or outside consultant fees? What staff will you need?

12. **Project Team** – Who will lead the proposal, manage the program, and support the pursuit?

13. **Project Strategy** – What is your win strategy?

14. **Self-Performed Work** – Are there scopes others won't pursue that you can self-perform? What risks or opportunities exist?

15. **Financial Health of the Business Group** – What's the group's cash flow, underbilled position, experience in the project type and geography? Are there active projects with claims, losses, or risks?

It's important to update your Go/No-Go Worksheet if project conditions change. Typical update points include before bringing on a major partner, after receiving and reviewing the RFQ, after being shortlisted, and again after receiving the RFP and Prime Agreement.

Customize your worksheet to fit your organization's specific needs. This is an invaluable tool to help you control and limit the number of pursuits and focus only on those with the greatest likelihood of success.

7.   How-To: Your Role in QA/QC

As the leader of a P3 project, your role in QA/QC is critical—and you should sit at the top of the chain. It's not something that can be pushed down to the design builder or another party. The design builder is only responsible for constructing and designing what's laid out in the design build agreement. Their QA/QC responsibilities end there.

But the prime agreement with the owner sits with the developer, which means the developer is ultimately accountable for all contract obligations—including QA/QC. While responsibilities may be delegated, the liability in the eyes of the owner and legal framework still rests with you.

That's why I strongly recommend assigning someone within your organization to serve as the overall quality manager for the project. The design builder's quality manager should report to this person. Your quality manager should also have oversight over any QA/QC processes conducted internally or by entities directly under contract with the developer.

This structure ensures that you, as the developer, retain full control of QA/QC across the project. Similar to how independent QA/QC is conducted during the proposal stage to protect investors and financiers, the same diligence must continue throughout execution. Your QA/QC team must oversee and audit all phases of the project:

- Pre-construction.

- Design and post-design.

- Construction and post-construction.

- Operations and maintenance.

- Handover.

- Warranty period.

- Finance, reporting, and invoicing.

- Contract management and controls.

Your quality team should also ensure that all parties reporting to the developer include a QA/QC section in their monthly reports. These reports must be reviewed and verified by your quality manager, who will also contribute insights from audits, non-compliance events, and corrective actions.

This level of oversight sends a clear message—to the owner, the investment community, and your internal team—that quality is a top priority. You'll cut down on errors, streamline compliance, and instill confidence in every stakeholder involved.

8. How-To: How Early Do You Need to Start Prior to the Issuance of the RFQ?

Doing your due diligence, meeting with the owner's team, learning everything about the project, forming your team, and positioning that team for a successful win and execution—much of this work needs to happen before the RFQ is even issued. Once the RFQ is out, your ability to have informal conversations with the owner disappears.

In my experience, to do this well and ultimately be successful, you should give yourself at least two years to prepare.

Chapter Two of this book outlines all the steps you should take before the issuance of the RFQ. As the developer and lead for the project, you need to be two to three steps ahead of your design builder and lead designer. You will also need those partners to begin their own prep work early so that when the RFQ is released, they are ready to hit the ground running.

The key to success is starting early. That means establishing a Memorandum of Understanding (MOU) between you and your design builder, and making sure the design builder has one with the lead designer. Without those MOUs in place, effective collaboration can't begin—and collaboration is what sets winning teams apart.

9. How-To: Collaboration with Your Design Build Team

As with any successful team, collaboration is the foundation. As the leader of a P3 or design build project, your team will look to you for leadership, communication, and alignment. Your collaboration efforts don't just matter during execution—they matter before the RFQ is released, through the SOQ phase, after shortlist selection, during the proposal, at negotiations, after award, during execution, through close-out, the warranty period, O&M, and possibly even through handback.

How you collaborate and lead sets the tone. It directly influences your team's performance and the overall project outcome.

To foster strong collaboration, you must lead with openness, transparency, consistency, and respect. Building trust across your team is vital. Here are some ways to support that culture:

- Hold weekly and monthly webinar meetings.

- Schedule key face-to-face meetings at critical milestones.

- Celebrate wins: go out for meals, host larger team sessions, or acknowledge individual efforts.

- Recognize success with awards or small gestures—certificates, handshakes, or simply expressing appreciation can go a long way.

These actions help keep people engaged and committed. Regularly scheduled leadership meetings give your team clarity on priorities and give others a space to voice concerns and share feedback. When problems arise, document them and create an action item list. Follow-up meetings should include that list as part of the agenda.

Using a set meeting format with recurring categories—old items, new items, and critical issues—will keep your collaboration organized and forward-moving.

On a P3 Mega-Project, your design builder's monthly cost can be one of your largest financial obligations, especially during initial construction. Their ability to stay on schedule and meet milestones directly affects your milestone payments from the owner. That's why understanding their schedule, challenges, and needs is essential. You must stay engaged with both the design builder and their lead designer through every phase of the project.

I recommend that your team meet with the owner weekly during both design and construction. Everyone should be aligned on key issues, timelines, and concerns. Remember: you hold the prime agreement with the owner. If a problem arises between the owner and the design build team that cannot be resolved at the working level, it's up to you to step in.

You might find that issues raised in your internal team meetings need to be addressed directly with the owner—and your leadership in those moments can make the difference.

At the end of the day, collaboration with your design build team is one of the most important keys to success on an AD Mega-Project.

10.   How-To: Involvement in ATCs and AFCs

I've discussed ATCs (Alternative Technical Concepts) and AFCs (Alternative Financial Concepts) in various places throughout the previous chapters—both in general discussion and through case studies. The developer's involvement in these is critical to their success, particularly in when and how they are developed and implemented—before the RFQ is issued, during the proposal, throughout the bidding process, during negotiations with the owner, and into project execution.

Although the team may begin exploring potential ATCs and AFCs early to get ahead of the curve—and to line up partners and SMEs who will be involved in developing and implementing them—it's not until the RFP is issued and reviewed that these can be fully developed and evaluated. You need to understand the specific requirements of the project, including ATC and AFC parameters, phasing of construction, testing and revenue service, O&M, and handback obligations.

Once the RFP has been reviewed by the full team—including developer, financier, O&M firm, design builder, and designer—I recommend conducting a three- to five-day workshop focused on VE, ATC, and AFC strategy, analysis, and evaluation. Assemble SMEs with the right technical and financial expertise across all project elements, including environmental and life-cycle-cost modeling.

A representative from each key party—developer, financier, O&M, design builder, and designer—should work with a VE and ATC/AFC facilitator to structure the workshop for maximum strategic benefit. I've previously discussed the use of VE and risk facilitators in Chapters 4 and 5; the same principles apply here and can be highly effective for ATC/AFC development and implementation during proposal and bid phases.

Before the workshop:

- The facilitator should request that team members and SMEs submit a brief memo summarizing initial observations, issues, and risk items.

- A baseline life-cycle-cost model should be developed to establish the framework for comparison.

During the workshop:

- **Day One:** The facilitator opens with an overview of the VE and ATC/AFC process. This includes a site visit, project background, a review of goals, workshop objectives, performance indicators, constraints, and the baseline cost model.

- **Day Two:** The team performs a functional analysis of the project and brainstorms ideas for ATCs and AFCs.

- **Day Three:** The facilitator recaps Day Two, adds additional ideas from the group, and leads the evaluation using a two-step screening process. Promising ideas are identified for further development.

- **Days Four and Five:** The team finalizes the evaluation of selected ATCs and AFCs, developing the detailed life-cycle-cost model and identifying potential cost savings. The focus is not just on initial construction costs but on total life—cycle costs, including O&M, handback, phasing, revenue potential, and capacity.

At the end of the workshop, the team should prepare a presentation that documents the value and benefit of each ATC and AFC, and submit these to the Executive Team for review and approval. Once approved, the ATCs and AFCs can be incorporated into the proposal and bid package.

When your team is selected for the project, the owner may ask your team to evaluate ATCs and AFCs submitted by other, unsuccessful proposers. This is common during negotiation and project refinement. The developer should lead these discussions.

After negotiating with the owner, the developer should bring the full team together to assess the external ATCs and AFCs, identifying pros, cons, and risks. A detailed evaluation should follow, looking at impacts on phasing, schedule, O&M, handback, life-cycle-cost, revenue, investor concerns, financing, and risk. You may want to re-engage your facilitator to help with this final review.

Once you've analyzed and discussed these with your internal team, determine your team's position. Agree on next steps and prepare for the next negotiation meeting with the owner. When agreement is reached, work with the owner to ensure that your ATCs and AFCs are reflected in the final prime agreement—and subsequently in the design build agreement and other relevant contracts.

As the project moves into execution, ATC and AFC implementation should continue to be a standing topic in weekly meetings. Track their progress and integration.

The developer should lead and stay involved throughout the entire process—from concept through final approval, from negotiation through execution.

11. How-To: Partnering with the Owner

In the previous chapter, I stated that partnering on an AD Mega-Project—if done correctly—is a valuable tool that can serve as the first step toward building understanding, transparency, and trust among project teams and stakeholders. It lays the foundation for successful working relationships.

Since 1991, ADOT has launched projects by engaging partners—ranging from contractors to municipalities and other agencies—in a structured process of aligning on goals, establishing communication protocols, and agreeing on how to resolve disputes. This approach has helped deliver projects on time and with far fewer conflicts, avoiding costly mediation, arbitration, or litigation—saving both the parties involved and the taxpayers.

I've used partnering on several AD projects, including the I-17 from Thomas Road to Dunlap Avenue design build project for ADOT in downtown Phoenix. That project earned the Malcolm Baldrige Award for partnering and was extremely successful. I also used partnering on the SH 130 Turnpike EDA in Pflugerville, Texas. However, in that case, the partnering workshops and follow-up activities were not conducted as effectively as ADOT's, and as a result, we didn't achieve the same level of success.

If designed and executed correctly, partnering can be an excellent tool. Here's what I recommend based on best practices and lessons learned:

If the owner includes partnering in their RFP and prime agreement, review it closely to ensure it contains the following:

- **Clearly define who will pay for partnering.** This cost should be split between the owner and the developer.

- **Agree upon a facilitator experienced in P3 mega-project partnering.** This should also be jointly selected and funded.

- **Define who attends the partnering sessions.** The owner and developer should work with the facilitator to structure the first workshop and follow-up meetings.

Usually, the first workshop includes an overview of the project from both the owner and the developer. Partnering is a formal, defined process that begins with this workshop and includes participation from the owner, developer, design builder, designer, key stakeholders, third-party agencies, utility companies, community leaders, consultants, and subcontractors.

The facilitator leads the group in establishing a communication structure and in creating project goals and objectives. They also help develop a dispute resolution process, which typically includes resolving issues at the lowest level possible and establishing an escalation ladder with clear timeframes. This environment allows attendees to express concerns openly while the facilitator emphasizes the value of working together as a unified team focused on overall project success—not on individual gain.

Once the project is underway, partnering continues through regular meetings led by the facilitator and attended by all relevant parties. These sessions serve to identify issues early and develop action plans. Team-building exercises are often included to strengthen collaboration. As the project progresses and wraps up, attendees evaluate the effectiveness of the partnering process, identifying what worked well and what could be improved. This feedback loop supports continuous improvement and mid-course corrections when necessary.

The facilitator should document and share the results of each meeting with all attendees. If problems arise, the facilitator must notify the owner and developer and recommend actions to resolve the issues. The owner and developer must then work collaboratively with the facilitator to agree on a resolution and act promptly.

If the RFP and prime agreement don't include the partnering process described above, I recommend that you share this approach with the owner and encourage them to make the necessary modifications. If partnering is not included at all, request that the owner add it—along with the recommended structure and expectations—to help set the project up for long-term success.

12. How-To: Participation with MWDBEs

Many owners today are setting requirements of 25 to 30 percent participation for MWDBEs on their P3 Mega-Projects. Let's take an example to understand what that means. Suppose your P3 Mega-Project includes:

- A construction value of $2 billion.

- O&M responsibilities for 50 years at $20 million per year (totaling $1 billion).

- A handback requirement valued at $400 million.

That's a total of $3.4 billion over the life of the project. A 25 percent MWDBE requirement on that value would equate to $850 million directed toward MWDBE participation over the full 50-year life-cycle. That's an enormous commitment. And it won't be achieved with a simple MWDBE engagement program. It will take a comprehensive, well-integrated approach.

As the leader of your P3 Mega-Project pursuit and execution, you must take the lead in ensuring that you—and all members of your team—meet these requirements. This cannot be an afterthought. It has to be part of your strategy from the beginning.

I recommend bringing on an MWDBE specialist or team prior to the issuance of the RFQ. This team should work directly with you and your leadership to develop a well-thought-out, skillfully crafted program that's embedded into your pursuit strategy and carried through the entire procurement and execution phases of the project. The right team can help you build and sustain an MWDBE culture across your organization and project partners.

From March 2019 through July 2022, I served as co-founder of Construction and Transportation Solutions (C&TS), a consortium that provided platform-based construction management and comprehensive support services tailored to the construction environment. Through C&TS, in partnership with BrianAnsari Associates, Inc. (BAA), we offered a full suite of project and construction-based support services, including MWDBE advisory services.

Our consortium included seven other firms, each certified as either a DBE or an SDVOSB. Collectively, we had access to over 200 staff members—providing a unique collection of talent, resources, and expertise under a single structure. This allowed us to offer a strategic and holistic approach to meeting MWDBE goals and building inclusive teams.

Brian Ansari and Michael Shapiro co-founded C&TS, with Michael leading the program management side of the business. I stepped away from the consortium in July 2022. Today, BAA continues as a management consulting firm providing public and private sector advisory services.

Their service portfolio includes program management, MWDBE advisory services designed to optimize MWDBE outcomes, and equity placement for capital infrastructure.

Brian Ansari has been working in the MWDBE space for 31 years, developing advisory services specifically designed to optimize program results. One example of the work we did is the presentation that we delivered to Accelerate Maryland Partners (AMP) on July 6, 2020, for the I-495 and I-270 Phase One P3. AMP was made up of Transurban and Macquarie.

Use the QR code below to get to my website and go into *Attachments To My Book* to find the AMP MWDBE Program Presentation from July 6, 2020.

SCAN THE QR CODE:

This is the kind of robust, strategic MWDBE program that can help you meet and exceed your MWDBE goals on your alternative delivery Mega-Project. If your team doesn't already have this level of expertise in-house, make it a priority to bring it in early. Doing so will position you for success from day one.

Chapter 8
Importance of Developing Best Practices Manual and Training

1.   Introduction

This chapter will discuss the importance of developing a best practices manual and training programs for your firm and project teams. I'll cover both topics broadly and present two case studies to illustrate their implementation. AD Mega-Projects are large and very complex. As I've been stating throughout the book—while sharing my expertise, lessons learned, and best practices—success on these projects often hinges on experience.

Many staff members on your team may be talented, but most will not have worked on an AD Mega-Project before. In my experience, only about 5 to 10 percent of your team will have prior experience on these types of projects. When I assemble teams for an AD Mega-Project, I make sure that almost every person in a management position has relevant AD Mega-Project experience. That significantly increases the chances of success. However, even those with experience may not be familiar with established best practices.

That means 90 to 95 percent of your team will be unfamiliar with the nuances of AD Mega-Project delivery—and even those who've done it before may not be following the best practices. No matter how strong your management team is, project success ultimately depends on the performance of the entire team. Without the right tools and training, the likelihood of success is greatly reduced.

If your organization already has an AD Mega-Projects manual and rigorous training programs in place for both regional offices and project teams, congratulations. It's likely that your regions and teams are functioning well, your profit margins are healthy, and your market share and industry reputation are growing.

2. Developing a Best Practices Manual

Creating a best practices manual for AD projects requires a meaningful commitment of time and resources. You'll need participation from some of your most experienced project directors, project managers, senior estimators, project controls managers, proposal managers, and a few of your executives. Their involvement ensures that the manual will be both useful and taken seriously by the rest of the organization.

Your best practices manual should reflect not only your firm's internal practices, but also how those practices align with and support the overall AD project team. It must fit into the larger context of collaboration with partners like the developer, design builder, owner, third-parties, and other stakeholders.

CASE STUDY: DMJM HARRIS' FIRST DESIGN CONSTRUCT GROUP PROCEDURES MANUAL

Let me share a case study from AECOM. Bruce Houghton, a senior project manager, and I, were the Deputy Director and COO of AECOM's Alternative Delivery Group at the time. Bruce led the development of AECOM's—then known as DMJM Harris—first design-construct group procedures manual, between March 16, 2005 and February 24, 2006.

The manual outlined the following intent:

> *"The design build business is significantly different from the traditional design-bid-build business. To that end, we created this procedures manual to provide guidance to those involved in the design construct business or those interested in learning more about how DMJM Harris conducts its work in this space. The goal of the manual and the design construct group is to minimize the risk of doing business within design construct and maximize our profits. This manual was created as a living document, meant to be updated as the design construct business model evolves and as we learn more from our experiences."*

The manual was organized into eight key sections:

1. Introduction.

2. Marketing and teaming.

3. Design build statement of qualifications.

4. Design build proposal.

5. Mobilization.

6. Project execution.

7. Demobilization.

8. Project close-out and appendices.

Within each section, the manual explained the group's philosophy, including the rationale behind specific decisions and practices. It covered everything from how to align with the right team to win a project, how to successfully negotiate teaming agreements and design contracts, how to implement and manage the project, and how to close it out.

In the appendix, they included sample agreements, go/no-go worksheets, risk analyses, proposal scopes and budgets, resource-loaded schedules, and a range of other tools and checklists designed to help teams execute successfully.

The Table of Contents is shown below.

TABLE OF CONTENTS

I. Introduction.

    A. Intent of This Procedures Manual

    B. How to Use This Procedures Manual

    C. Design Build Background Information

    D. Types of Design Build Design Contracts

        1. Lump Sum

        2. Time and Materials with a Target Price (Incentives/Disincentives)

3. Time and Materials with a Target Price (Incentives/No Risk)

E. Key Design Contract Issues and Risk

1. Design Build Prime Contract Terms and Conditions Flow-Down

2. Professional Liability Insurance Additional Insured Requirements

3. Retention Clauses

II. Marketing/Teaming

A. Identify Design Build Projects

1. Make Contact with Other People in the Design Build Industry (Networking)

2. Attending Conferences and Seminars Related to Design Build

3. Review Trade Journals and Magazines for Project Leads

B. Contact Design Build Project Owners

1. Follow-Up on Project Leads From Networking/Conferences/Magazines

2. Identify New Project Leads From The Owners.

C. Identify Potential Design Build Teams

1. Contact Potential Design Build Contractors Relative to Potential Projects

2. Contact Project Owners Relative to Potential Contractor Interest

3. Contact Project Owners Relative to Potential Teams Formed For The Project

4. Contact Potential Concessionaires Relative to Potential Projects

D. Select a Design Build Contractor

    1. Identify Contractor Previous Design Build Experience

    2. Identify Other Contractor Design Build Team Members

    3. Identify Teaming Relationship of Contractor Design Build Team

    4. Identify Contractor Project Manager Design Build Experience

E. Conduct a Go/No Go Decision With a Risk Analysis

F. Negotiate SOQ/RFP Teaming Agreement

    1. Scope of Engineering Services

    2. Scope of Preparation Services

    3. Scope of Production Services

    4. Terms of Labor Reimbursement

    5. Terms of Expenses Reimbursement

    6. Proposal Office Requirements

    7. Success Fee

    8. Design Contract Terms and Conditions For The Project

    9. Define Computer Needs For The Proposal

G. Establish a Business Development Charge Number for the Project

H. Assemble the Design Team (Lead Designer Position)

    1. Prepare A Design Organization Chart

    2. Identify Opportunities For Subconsultants

    3. Identify Subconsultant Firms For The Team

    4. Negotiate Teaming Agreements with Subconsultants

I. Negotiate a Teaming Agreement with the Lead Design Firm (Subconsultant Position)

    1. Identify Scope of Work

    2. Identify Staff Requirements

    3. Identify Labor Reimbursement Terms and Conditions

    4. Identify Expenses Reimbursement Terms and Conditions

    5. Identify Proposal Office Requirements

III. Design Build Statement of Qualifications

    A. Win Plan

    B. Design Team Qualifications

    C. LOI/SOQ Document Preparation Support

IV. Design Build Proposal

    A. Development of Scope and Budget for the Proposal Work

    B. Engineering Support to the Design Build Contractor

    C. Design Build Proposal Information

    D. Use of Task Groups

    E. Design Schedule

    F. List of Drawing

    G. Design Labor Hour Estimate

    H. Design Fee Estimate

    I. Computer Costs

    J. Design Team Staffing Plan

    K. Design Team Scope of work

    L. Design Build Contract Terms and Conditions

    M. Design Contract Negotiations

V. Mobilization

    A. Design Contract Execution

    B. Project Office Set-Up

    C. Project Manager Checklist

    D. Computer Requirements

    E. Design Project Work Plan

    F. CAD Procedures Manual

    G. Design Quality Management Plan

    H. Project Controls

    I. Human Resources

    J. Human Resource Procedures

        1. Temporary Housing

        2. Relocations

        3. Hiring

        4. Office Orientation

    K. Project Safety Plan

    L. Design Subconsultant Agreements

VI. Project Execution

    A. Design Management Meetings

    B. Discipline Management Meetings

    C. Technical Work Groups (TWG)

    D. Inter-Discipline Design Review Meetings

    E. Design Coordination Meetings

    F. Over-The-Shoulder Review Meetings with the Owner

G. Design Management

    1. Over-The-Shoulder Review Meetings With The Owner

    2. Contractor Plan Review Meetings

    3. Owner Plan Review Meetings

H. Project Controls

    1. Contract Compliance

    2. Extra Work/Change In Scope Items

    3. Schedule Status

    4. Cost Accounting

    5. Earned Value

    6. Invoicing

I. Quality Control/Quality Assurance

    1. Quality Control Process

    2. Quality Assurance Process

    3. Design Plan Submittal Process

    4. Design Plan Review Process

    5. Design Plan Release For Construction Process

J. Project Reporting

    1. Schedule Status

    2. Financial Status

    3. Design Accomplishments For the Reporting Period

    4. Design Activities For The Next Reporting Period

    5. Resolution Of Action Items From The Design Coordination Meeting

VII. Demobilization

    A. Staffing Plan

    B. Project Files

    C. Office Closeout

VIII. Project Close-out

    A. Accounting

    B. Project Profile Sheet

APPENDICES

    A. Sample Teaming Agreement

    B. Sample Go/No Go And Risk Analysis

    C. Computer Need Cover Sheet Form

    D. Sample Scope and Budget for the Proposal Work

    E. Sample Resource Loaded Schedule

    F. Sample Project Controls Workbook

    G. Sample Scope of Work

    H. Sample Design Build Agreement

    I. Project Manager Checklist

CASE STUDY: WALSH'S ALTERNATIVE DELIVERY IMPROVEMENT INITIATIVE

I want to share a case study on improving AD practices at Walsh—this was Walsh's Alternative Delivery Improvement Initiative (ADII). As Executive Design Director, I co-chaired the ADII from November 2017 through November 2018 alongside Michael Bauer, PE, another design director with the firm, based out of Dallas. We both reported monthly to Joe Lee and the executive team on our progress.

Together, we led a 15-member task team of AD experts from across the country. We developed comprehensive guidelines, tools, and training modules for a web-based platform called *WalshWorks*, built entirely on best practices. Over 200 tools were created. The team was organized into three working groups focused on:

- Positioning the team for success.
- Proposal efforts.
- Project execution and close-out.

Each group held weekly meetings, and we convened monthly meetings with the full task team to ensure alignment and consistency. As the tools and guidelines came together, the entire team contributed input throughout. Michael and I also led the development of the training component and created a regional training module. We presented our final product to the executive team in October 2018 and received approval to move forward. Final coordination with the *WalshWorks* platform administrator ensured that all systems were functioning properly.

3. Training

It's not enough to develop a best practices manual or an impressive website—you must also train your teams on *why* it was developed, *what's* in it, and *how* to use it. Those involved in creating the manual and who are strong communicators should lead the training effort. I recommend hosting regional training sessions and providing project-specific training modules for new AD Mega-Project teams.

Let me share a few training case studies.

CASE STUDY: AECOM REGIONAL WORKSHOPS – 2007

In 2007, while serving as Deputy Director and COO of AECOM's design construct group, I developed a training program in response to growing interest in design construct projects valued between $10 million and $50 million. I led full-day regional workshops in Pittsburgh on February 14 and Coral Gables on March 24. These sessions helped energize regional staff and generated interest in larger AD pursuits.

The session materials included:

- Workshop Agenda and Detailed Outline
- Design Construct Group's Role
- Design Build Philosophy
- Risk Assessment Matrix

To access these four session documents, scan the QR code below to get to my website and go into *Attachments To My Book*.

These sessions sparked enthusiasm and significantly improved relationships with the regions. Several of these trainings led to new project leads and larger AD pursuits.

CASE STUDY: WALSH REGIONAL TRAINING – 2018

As part of ADII at Walsh, Michael Bauer and I led the creation of a regional training module. The training covered the *why* behind the initiative, the available tools and resources on *WalshWorks*, and best practices for positioning the team for success, proposal development, project execution, and closeout. We ensured the training was interactive and emphasized how to navigate and use the web-based tools effectively.

CASE STUDY: I-395 SIGNATURE BRIDGE, MIAMI, FL – PROJECT-SPECIFIC TRAINING

In November 2018, we rolled out a project-specific training program for the I-395 Signature Bridge design build project in Miami—an $850 million venture. As part of ADII, Michael Bauer and I collaborated closely with Project Manager Rami Nasra, PE (now a project executive), to develop a tailored training session focused on:

- Project understanding.

- Team alignment.

- Execution strategies.

- Close-out planning.

Nearly 50 team members attended the one-day session, and the feedback was overwhelmingly positive. The training ensured the project launched with a clear focus and the best chance of success.

Chapter 9
The Future and Why the Business is Changing

1.   Factors Affecting Changes in the AD Mega-Project Business

The following are eight factors that have influenced changes in the alternative delivery (AD) Mega-Project industry.

a. Owners Moving from Design Build to P3

Many owners are shifting from traditional design build to public-private partnerships (P3s). This shift is driven largely by the increasing size of projects and the difficulty in securing enough upfront capital for initial construction. Agencies like FDOT, ADOT, Georgia DOT, LA Metro, LAWA, MTTA, TxDOT, North Carolina DOT, and Virginia DOT have all moved in this direction for several of their AD Mega-Projects.

Tolls have often been used as a revenue source to enable a "pay-as-you-go" model—ADOT being a notable exception. Working directly for a developer under a P3 arrangement is vastly different than working with a public DOT or transit authority. It requires a highly skilled, collaborative developer capable of navigating the financial and contractual complexities that come with these long-term projects.

b. Fluor, Skanska, and Granite Have Exited the U.S. P3 Market

In an article published by *Construction Dive* in October 2019, it was noted that many P3 contracts are structured around fixed-budget, fixed-schedule agreements. Contractors like Skanska and Fluor have concluded that these arrangements are simply too risky to ensure a profit.

In mid-2019, Granite Construction openly criticized the P3 model for negatively impacting its business. Later that year, Skanska announced it would no longer pursue major design build transportation P3s involving equity investment. These decisions came after a string of high-profile P3 projects, such as the $2.3 billion I-4 Ultimate project in Florida and the $2.8 billion U.S. Army Corps flood risk management project in Minnesota. "Because most P3 jobs are large in size and long in duration, they are valuable for firms that want to secure business growth for several consecutive years", said Ben Vaught, CEO of online procurement market DemandStar.

"While such large-scale P3s can provide steady revenue over several years, the risks often outweigh the benefits." Granite CEO James Roberts told investors that the P3 model had become nonviable for the company. He announced that Granite's heavy civil division would no longer pursue Mega-Projects. This was a major shift, given the company's previous involvement in large infrastructure efforts, including airports, highways, and transit systems.

A primary concern with these contracts is the fixed-price nature of the agreements. As unexpected issues arise—and they inevitably do—disputes often follow over who is responsible for the additional costs. According to Roberts, "The owner assumes that the contractor had those issues in their bid, and the contractor didn't assume that—so it ends up in a dispute."

This misalignment has become a critical issue. In 2019, four disputed projects resulted in a net loss of $97.8 million for Granite in the second quarter alone. Roberts stated, "We are contractually obligated to continue work on these jobs and to recognize the associated costs, regardless of whether we agree that the work we have been directed to perform is within the scope of our contracts."

Fluor CEO and Director Carlos Hernandez echoed Roberts' concerns. He cited, "The excessive risks passed to contractors as a key factor behind industry-wide struggles. Going forward, Fluor will only take on fixed-price work selectively—where there's a clear competitive advantage, a limited bid pool, or opportunities to negotiate directly."

Fluor also emphasized the importance of performing its own front-end engineering and design (FEED) work to fully understand project risks before committing. Similarly, Skanska announced that it, too, would limit its involvement in P3s—especially those requiring equity stakes—after a $100 million write-down on its P3 portfolio.

The exit of these three major contractors—Fluor, Skanska, and Granite—has significantly reduced the field of major players pursuing P3s in the U.S. market.

c. Larger Design Builders Struggling to Make Profits on Design Build Mega-Projects

I've heard from many of the larger design builders for years that they are struggling to make profits on design build Mega-Projects. I also witnessed this firsthand on many AD Mega-Projects while I was at Walsh, serving as their Executive Design Director.

Senior management at Kiewit has told me that they favor progressive design build over traditional design build. Progressive design build allows design builders to work with the owner to collaboratively establish and develop the scope of work on a project. In contrast, design build Mega-Projects require bidding a lump sum based on only 10 to 15 percent plans. You don't get to collaborate with the owner until after you're selected and your bid is locked in. Many of these design build contracts are very one-sided, heavily favoring the owner and shielding them from construction risks.

There's a tremendous amount of effort and cost required to put together a technical proposal and bid. On many AD Mega-Projects, this can exceed $10 million. With progressive design build, those costs are much less because you're working with the owner to establish the scope. Value engineering and ATCs can be developed with the owner, key stakeholders, and third parties during the pre-construction phase.

Owners are beginning to enjoy the more collaborative nature of the progressive design build process.

d. Major Contractors Willing to Underbid the Field by Identifying Loopholes in the Contract

Meanwhile, some major contractors are still willing to underbid the field by identifying loopholes in the contract and relying more on legal maneuvering than on their construction expertise or innovative solutions.

I've seen this firsthand on two projects:

- On the IH 635 Managed Lanes project (discussed in Chapter Four).

- On the Purple Line Subway Extension, Section Two for LA Metro, where the low bidder came in $500 million below the third-lowest bid and $400 million below the second-lowest bid on a $1.9 billion AD Mega-Project.

These kinds of practices are not only devastating and time-consuming for owners, but they also make other proposers hesitant to bid when they know that a low-bidder is likely to be prequalified or shortlisted on future projects.

e. Larger Contractors Moving from Construction to Program Management

Bechtel Infrastructure Corporation is one example of a firm moving away from the design builder role. When I was part of Construction and Transportation Solutions (2019–2022), we had many conversations and meetings with Bechtel's senior infrastructure team—including Jarrette Cantrell, David Blazdell, John Engstrom, John LaPilusa, and Hector Garcia. They informed us that they were no longer pursuing work as a design builder and were shifting focus to program and construction management (PM/CM) on major transportation infrastructure projects. They saw the design builder role as risk-heavy and less profitable.

We discussed opportunities with LaPilusa on the Second Avenue Subway Phase Two for MTA (from Dec 8, 2021, to June 29, 2022) and with Garcia, who was leading Mid-Atlantic efforts for Bechtel. This included the I-495/270 P3 with APM, where Garcia said Bechtel would transition into the PM/CM role, though the scope details were still being finalized.

On June 28, 2024, Santa Clara Valley Transportation Authority (VTA) selected Bechtel to provide construction management services for the $12.7 billion BART Silicon Valley Phase Two Extension. This six-mile expansion includes four new stations and 5.5 miles of tunneling, connecting North San Jose and Santa Clara residents with the rest of the Bay Area's BART system. Bechtel signed a 10-year contract to manage the project and will begin oversight later this year.

f. More Consultants Entering the Program Management Space

A few major recent awards show this trend continuing:

- On September 29, 2024, the Gateway Development Commission awarded a Delivery Partner contract for the $16 billion Hudson Tunnel Project (HTP) to MPA Delivery Partners, a joint venture of Parsons Corporation, Arcadis of New York, and Mace North America. The team will provide project management and construction management support, focusing on interface risk management, cost and schedule assurance, safety and quality, and innovation.

- On April 8, 2024, Amtrak selected ADVANCE, a joint venture of AECOM and Jacobs, as its Project Delivery Partner (PDP) for the $6 billion Frederick Douglass Tunnel Program in Baltimore—marking the first time Amtrak is using a PDP model. ADVANCE will handle design oversight, construction and contract management, and administrative support. The program includes a two-mile dual-tube rail tunnel replacing a 1.4-mile section of aging infrastructure, five bridge replacements, a new station, and other corridor improvements.

Amtrak has already awarded two contracts under the CMAR model: one to a Clark-Stacy and Witbeck JV for the tunnel's southern approach and West Baltimore Station, and another to a Kiewit-JF Shea JV for the tunnel itself.

g. Large Spanish Firms Entered the Business in the 2000s with a Very Different Culture

ACS/Dragados and Cintra/Ferrovial. Both companies are headquartered in Madrid, Spain.

Dragados USA has worked on many projects in the United States, including highways, bridges, dams, tunnels, and airports.

California High Speed Rail: Dragados USA is part of the joint venture that designed and built the first high-speed rail project in the US. The project includes a 65-mile route between Fresno and Bakersfield.

I-64 Hampton Roads highway: Dragados USA and Flatiron (now owned by Dragados) are building tunnels and bridges on this highway in VA.

SH 288 Toll Lanes: Dragados USA worked on this project in Houston, TX.

I-595 Corridor Roadway (P3) Dragados USA worked on this project in Broward Co., FL.

Bridges:

Harbor Bridge: Dragados USA worked on this project in Texas.

Okeechobee Road and Palmetto Expressway: Dragados USA worked on this project in Miami, FL.

Tunnels:

East Side Access: Dragados USA worked on this project in NY, NY.

Alaskan Way Viaduct Replacement: Dragados USA worked on this project in Seattle, WA.

Seattle tunnel: Dragados USA constructed a 1.7-mile tunnel in Seattle, WA.

From Cintra's website on 2/01/25, In 2004, Citra and Ferrovial entered the U.S. market by establishing their U.S. headquarters in Austin, TX. Today, they manage five major concessions representing a total investment of roughly €9 billion, the IH 635 Managed Lanes (P3), North Tarrant Express (NTE), and NTE 35W in North TX, the recently opened I-77 Express Lanes in Charlotte, NC and the I-66 Outside the Beltway project in Northern VA. They were recently awarded the NTE 35W redevelopment project, the 3C project.

I had direct experience in working with ASC and Dragados on the IH 635 Managed Lanes (P3) proposal as the proposal Manager for AECOM and was the Project Manager for AECOM on the I-595 Corridor Roadway (P3). I found that Dragados was arrogant and terrible at collaborating with their partners. They treated their subcontractors very badly and there were many complaints made by many of the local contractors to FDOT on the project. ASC was much more collaborative on the IH 635 Managed Lanes (P3). Dragados was impossible to work with and was very litigious.

My experience with Cintra and Ferrovial was as a competitor on IH 635 Managed Lanes (P3) where I found that their practices were underhanded and blatantly dishonest. Indirectly when I was with AECOM, where AECOM provided Lead Design services to Ferrovial on NTE. Ferrovial was only willing to pay their designers 2.5% of the construction value for Design Services. The only way to be able to make a profit in doing business with them was to manage the work on the ground with a small design management team and have all the production work done overseas. With most Design Builders on highway projects, we were able to obtain a 6.5-7.0% fee for Basic Design Services on AD Mega-Projects.

Both ACS/Dragados and Cintra/Ferrovial are very active in the U.S. in the AD and P3 Mega-Project space and highly competitive.

h. CM/GC and CMAR Have Not Been Used as Frequently

CM/GC and CMAR have been used in the U.S. since 2011. However, they are not used as often as Design Build and P3s. Organizations that actively support and promote CM/GC and CMAR project delivery methods include: the Associated General Contractors of America, the Construction Management Association of America and various large construction firms who regularly utilize these methods on projects, often highlighting their collaborative approach and potential for cost optimization. However, I believe that the support from these organizations is much smaller than the support of Design Build and therefore, is totally supporting this methodology and therefore has not received the recognition for the public and the agencies.

The Design Build Institute of America (DBIA) was established in February 1993. DBIA is a non-profit organization that provides education, resources, and advocacy for design build. They have been very successful in promoting design build and have seen a tremendous amount of growth since their founding. Total growth in design build construction spending is projected to be 22.5% from 2022 to 2026. Design build is anticipated to account for $1.9 trillion of construction spending in the assessed segments over the 2022 – 2026 forecast period. P3s have several organizations that have supported it, especially since design build has been used mostly as the method to construct the initial projects.

2. Projections as to How the Business Will Evolve

More and more, owners will be looking to the P3 model to help finance alternative delivery (AD) Mega-Projects. However, the space for developers is getting narrower, with only a few firms dominating the market. For P3s to become fully accessible and acceptable to all parties, significant changes will be needed on both the owner and developer sides.

Design build in its current form is not working particularly well for either owners or design builders. One potential shift is the use of a project delivery partner (PDP). While this has been used successfully in other countries, it hasn't yet been fully adopted in the U.S. That said, there may not be much difference between using a PDP and a PM/CM or General Consultant in terms of function. Progressive design build may be the answer—and it appears that more and more projects are beginning to lean in this direction.

3.   How These Changes Will Affect the Business for the Better

Let me share two examples that highlight some of these positive shifts.

In August 2024, the Maryland Transportation Authority (MDTA) Board approved a $73 million Phase One contract to Kiewit Infrastructure Company to act as the progressive design builder for the I-695 Francis Scott Key Bridge replacement. Proposals were evaluated by an MDTA selection committee, and the contract was awarded to the team deemed most advantageous to the state.

The project is slated to begin in 2025, with the replacement bridge expected to open by fall 2028. For this critical rebuild, MDTA is using a progressive design build process that brings the delivery team under one contract to provide both design and construction services. MDTA plans to foster collaboration across the project team, local communities, and stakeholders, promoting open communication and inclusive partnership opportunities—especially for small and disadvantaged businesses.

The two-phase process emphasizes flexibility and teamwork. Kiewit was selected for initial services to collaborate with MDTA and project stakeholders on defining the project scope and requirements. If Phase One is completed successfully, Kiewit will hold exclusive negotiation rights for Phase Two, which includes final design, engineering, and construction. If a Guaranteed Maximum Price (GMP) is not reached, MDTA retains the right to deliver the work using another contracting mechanism.

On July 22, 2024, the City of Englewood announced the selection of Elevated Englewood Partners (EIP) as the best-value proposer for the Englewood Transit Connector (ITC) project. EIP is a P3 consortium composed of Plenary Americas U.S. Holdings, Inc. (equity member), Tutor Perini Corporation (lead contractor), Parsons Corporation (lead designer), Woojin Industrial Systems (automated transit system supplier), and Alternate Concepts, Inc. (lead operations and maintenance contractor).

The ITC will design, build, finance, operate, and maintain a 1.6-mile automated people mover to connect the Metro K Line with key Englewood destinations, including SoFi Stadium, the Intuit Dome, and surrounding commercial and residential areas. The city has partnered with LA Metro and the County of Los Angeles to form the ITC Joint Powers Authority, which will oversee the project after contract award.

The project will not only enhance mobility but also help reduce traffic, lower emissions, and increase Metro ridership. With environmental approvals in place and a community workforce agreement signed with the LA/OC Building Trades Council, construction is expected to start next year.

However, while these projects represent progress, they don't yet tell the full story. Their success will depend on how well the involved parties manage process, procedures, communication, transparency, staffing, training, and day-to-day administration. These factors will ultimately determine whether this shift truly improves outcomes in the AD space.

4. Potential Changes with a New Trump Administration

a. Status of the Completion of the IIJA

Three years into the five-year, $1.2 trillion Infrastructure Investment and Jobs Act (IIJA), former President Joe Biden will pass the baton to President Donald Trump with a sizable chunk of money left to allocate.

The incoming administration will need to quickly staff up and get up to speed on the many programs under the IIJA. According to an analysis by the Washington, D.C.-based think tank Brookings, the funds are on track to be awarded in full within the five-year time frame—but that doesn't mean the money has reached the job sites yet. It will take years beyond the IIJA's expiration for all the associated projects to be completed.

It's possible that Trump may attempt to claw back some of the funds and reallocate them. As of the handoff, the Biden administration is leaving approximately $294 billion still to be awarded, including $87.2 billion in competitive grants—where the incoming Trump agency staff will have considerable discretion in determining the recipients, according to Brookings.

In anticipation of the transition, President Biden's team at the U.S. Department of Transportation worked overtime to get as much IIJA money out the door as possible before leaving office on January 20, 2025. In fact, $9 billion in funding or financing was announced in just the final week of his term.

In an official announcement, outgoing Transportation Secretary Pete Buttigieg noted that when Biden took office four years ago, he faced some of the most profound and wide-ranging transportation crises in modern history. Through his leadership, the administration passed a sweeping infrastructure investment plan—unlike anything since the Eisenhower era—with support from both Democrats and Republicans in Congress.

To date, the IIJA has led to $17.9 billion in grant announcements. However, the types of projects and funding priorities have varied significantly between administrations—and it's likely that pattern will continue under Trump.

	Obama (FY09-FY16)	Trump (FY17-FY20)	Biden FY21-FY25-1)	TOTAL (FY09-FY25-1)
Aviation	$0	$39,690,047	$24,650,000	$64,340,047
Bike-Ped	$310,946,765	$0	$1,821,856,633	$2,132,803,398
Port/Maritime	$623,767,218	$397,076,961	$387,182,040	$1,408,026,219
Railroad	$1,079,916,615	$282,535,733	$368,534,015	$1,730,986,363
Road-Bridge	$2,082,552,763	$2,777,567,441	$4,653,559,223	$9,513,679,427
Transit	$1,420,659,409	$348,860,917	$1,358,555,639	$3,128,075,965
TOTAL	**$5,517,842,769**	**$3,806,041,052**	**$8,589,687,550**	**$17,913,571,371**
Aviation	*0.00%*	*1.04%*	*0.29%*	*0.36%*
Bike-Ped	*5.64%*	*0.00%*	*21.21%*	*11.91%*
Port/Maritime	*11.30%*	*10.43%*	*4.51%*	*7.86%*
Railroad	*19.57%*	*7.42%*	*4.29%*	*9.66%*
Road-Bridge	*37.74%*	*72.98%*	*54.18%*	*53.11%*
Transit	*25.75%*	*9.17%*	*15.82%*	*17.46%*

Excludes $59.2 million of planning grants under Obama that were not coded with a modal type

b. Shared Perspective Based on the First Trump Administration and Projections for the Second Term

The incoming administration promises new policies that could affect permits, materials, labor, and project funding. Below are several key ways that President Donald Trump could influence the civil construction sector:

Potential Impact to IIJA Funding

It's reasonable to expect that the Trump administration will conduct a comprehensive review of the Infrastructure Investment and Jobs Act (IIJA) and may seek to roll back portions of the bill it considers excessive spending. However, many of the infrastructure programs that benefit the construction industry are expected to remain in place at least through fiscal year 2026. According to SmartBrief, dismantling these infrastructure investments—many of which address core transportation and water needs—is unlikely to be a high priority.

The Trump team is also expected to extend support for the Transportation Infrastructure Finance and Innovation Act (TIFIA), a long-standing tool to assist infrastructure funding.

More Focus on Traditional Infrastructure and Rural Areas

A new administration brings new priorities. Trump may seek to defund high-speed rail initiatives and has voiced criticism of electric vehicle programs. Expect a renewed focus on roads and bridges—traditional infrastructure—particularly in rural areas. Discretionary grants, which run through the U.S. Department of Transportation, will likely see a reprioritization of project selections. Emphasis may shift away from climate change mitigation and carbon reduction strategies seen under the previous administration.

Emphasis on P3s

During his first term, Trump insisted that infrastructure bills include major private-sector contributions. That same approach is likely to carry forward, with increased encouragement of public-private partnerships (P3s) and other mechanisms to attract private investment. While public opinion is often mixed on P3s, Trump ran on reducing government spending—making P3s an attractive tool for funding. He may view them as a necessary means to accomplish infrastructure goals without putting the entire financial burden on the federal government.

Weaker NEPA, Faster Permits

Expect the return of Trump-era executive actions aimed at expediting environmental permitting. In 2020, Trump issued orders weakening the National Environmental Policy Act (NEPA), Endangered Species Act, and Clean Water Act. These policies included concurrent reviews, page limits for federal agencies, approval deadlines, and consequences for missed deadlines. It's likely he will return to this approach early in his second term.

Trump has signaled continued focus on speeding up permits. In a December 2020 Truth Social post, he stated that any $1 billion investment in the U.S. would receive full expedited approvals, including environmental clearances.

There is also a pending Supreme Court case—Seven-County Infrastructure Coalition vs. Eagle County—that could significantly weaken NEPA if ruled in favor of the coalition. Meanwhile, contractors are pushing for revisions to the Build America, Buy America (BABA) program, which requires the use of domestically manufactured materials on federally funded projects. The current BABA waiver process is viewed as cumbersome and frustrating.

Increased Scrutiny on Spending: Waste and Fraud

Trump's administration is expected to prioritize oversight of federal infrastructure dollars. A proposed Department of Government Efficiency (DOGE) may take a central role in identifying waste, fraud, and abuse. Contractors should prepare to demonstrate robust cost-control systems and compliance mechanisms. Transparency and accountability in managing federally funded projects will be under the microscope.

5.   What's Beyond the IIJA?

CBO Says the Next Bill Needs to Fill $40B/Year Highway Trust Fund Deficits

The Congressional Budget Office (CBO) has projected a significant shortfall in the Highway Trust Fund (HTF). In its January 17 budget and economic outlook, the CBO forecasted that a five-year reauthorization from FY 2027 through FY 2031 will require at least $150 billion in general fund transfers—unless Congress raises new tax revenues or reduces spending.

In FY 2024, the "user-paid" deficit—the amount by which trust fund spending exceeded tax receipts—was $26.7 billion. This is projected to increase to $33 billion in FY 2026, the final year of the IIJA. For FY 2027–31, the CBO anticipates annual shortfalls of roughly $40 billion.

Mass transit outlays are projected at just $17 billion per year—less than half the amount of the deficit—so eliminating them from the trust fund would not close the gap.

Fuel Tax Declines

A major reason for the funding gap is declining gasoline tax revenues. Based on current CAFE standards and EPA greenhouse gas regulations discouraging internal combustion engines, the CBO projects receipts from the federal gas tax ($0.183 per gallon) will fall from $25 billion per year to just $15 billion by 2035. Diesel fuel taxes and increased trucking fees will not offset this decline, leading to a projected 14 percent overall reduction in HTF receipts.

In short, the Highway Trust Fund is not sustainable under current policies. Policymakers have debated reforms for more than 25 years, and the urgency to act is growing.

Trump's Funding Freeze Leaves IIJA, IRA Projects in Limbo

In a sweeping move, President Trump instructed federal agencies to halt the disbursement of IIJA and Inflation Reduction Act (IRA) funds—even those already authorized by Congress. The decision has thrown numerous infrastructure and climate projects into a state of uncertainty, with many in various stages of development now paused.

Trump's January 20 executive order—"Unleashing American Energy"—paused and initiated a review of all funding mechanisms. This has significant implications for both the IIJA and IRA, potentially resulting in delays, contract terminations, and broader economic disruptions.

While the full impact of the freeze may not be known for months, the uncertainty alone is causing concern among state DOTs, contractors, and project stakeholders. Billions in obligated funding may be at risk, even for projects already under construction.

Another major announcement that same week only added to the confusion surrounding the federal infrastructure agenda.

A January 27 internal memo from the Office of Management and Budget ordered a pause in all federal grants and loans starting at 5 p.m. on January 28. Federal agencies must temporarily halt funding and agency activities that may be implicated by the executive orders, including but not limited to financial assistance for foreign aid, nongovernmental organizations, DEI, gender ideology, and the Green New Deal, according to an administration memo. A federal judge temporarily blocked the effort on January 28.

U.S. District Judge Lauren L. Alicons put a stay in effect until February 3 while she considered arguments from the U.S. government and plaintiffs in the case of a nonprofit coalition that includes the National Council of Nonprofits and the American Public Health Association. There are many open questions about the scope and effort and effects of Trump's orders and how they will be implemented, but it's clear that they will affect the contractual and other legal rights of federal contractors. This will have a broad effect on federal contracts, grants, and other assistance agreements in the specified areas and will take time to unpack.

U.S. Transportation Secretary Sean Duffy Takes Action to Rescind "Woke" DEI Policies and Advance President Trump's Economic Agenda

On January 29, U.S. Transportation Secretary Sean Duffy authorized a series of actions advancing Trump's agenda to rescind policies, roll back certain regulations, restore economic growth, and ensure that all U.S. DOT policies align with the administration's priorities. These actions deliver on the President's commitment to rescind what were viewed to be harmful policies enacted under the Biden-Harris administration and reaffirm U.S. DOT's focus on safety, efficiency, economic prosperity, and regulatory reform.

Duffy's Work Recession Memorandum and Policy Realignment

Duffy signed the Work Recession Memorandum, directing secretarial officers and heads of operating administrations to identify and eliminate Biden-era programs, policies, activities, rules, and orders that promote climate change activism, diversity, equity, and inclusion (DEI) initiatives, racial equity, gender identity policies, environmental justice, and other partisan objectives. This action aligns with several of President Trump's executive orders, including Order 14148, which calls for the initial rescission of harmful executive orders and actions, and Order 14151, which ends what the administration considers radical and wasteful DEI programs and preferential government activities.

Lowering Costs Through Smarter Policies, Not Political Ideologies

Duffy also signed an order ensuring that all U.S. Department of Transportation (U.S. DOT) policies, grants, loans, and actions are grounded in sound economic principles, positive cost-benefit analysis, and pro-economic growth priorities. This directive aligns U.S. DOT operations with Trump's broader agenda to stimulate economic development and support American families by focusing on real, measurable benefits—moving beyond ideological considerations.

Rescinding the Greenhouse Gas Measurement Rule

Duffy approved the submission of a notice of proposed rulemaking to rescind the Biden-Harris administration's rule requiring state transportation departments to measure and establish declining targets for carbon dioxide emissions on federally funded highways. This rule, originally rescinded during Trump's first term, was reinstated under Biden, but later struck down by two federal judges who ruled that the U.S. DOT lacked authority to issue it.

This move signals a significant shift in the U.S. DOT's regulatory posture—emphasizing economic pragmatism over environmental mandates. By removing restrictive regulations and prioritizing economic growth, the department is positioning itself fully in line with Trump's mission to restore efficiency, emphasize merit-based opportunities, and enhance American prosperity.

Project 2025 – Chapter 19: U.S. Department of Transportation

Given the actions already taken, it is reasonable to expect that the Trump administration will follow the framework outlined in *Chapter 19* of the **Project 2025** document. Authored by Diana Furchtgott-Roth, this chapter lays out a roadmap for transforming the Department of Transportation—reducing regulatory burdens, prioritizing traditional infrastructure investments, and restoring the agency's focus on mobility, economic opportunity, and national competitiveness.

Conclusion

1.   Recap of Chapters and Key Points

Through my experience, I've found that a systematic approach to business development—by identifying your targets early and dedicating the necessary time and resources throughout the process—can lead to the greatest success.

Focusing on execution during the proposal phase also removes much of the guesswork later when you move into schedule development, pricing, negotiation, project execution, and close-out. This book presents that approach in detail, with best practices and real tools based on my successes and failures across many case studies. I've dedicated specific chapters to both owners and developers, and Chapter 9 addresses the major factors impacting changes in the alternative delivery (AD) Mega-Project business—including the potential impact of a new Trump administration.

The following is a recap of the key points of the chapters.

Prior to the RFQ

On most AD projects, the owner requires several years of internal work before releasing an RFQ. During this time, a significant amount of material is generated by the owner and their consultants—information that should be thoroughly reviewed to determine which projects best align with your team's capabilities, experience, and strategic objectives.

I recommend starting this due diligence at least two years before the RFQ is issued. Once a project is targeted, meet with your internal team and leadership to assess fit. This chapter outlines a comprehensive early-stage pursuit process that includes:

- Initial due diligence.

- Participation in preliminary planning, environmental, and community engagement meetings.

- Attending public committee and board meetings.

- Conducting background research.

- Meeting with the owner and your internal team.

- Preparing and updating go/no-go assessments.

- Developing a detailed pursuit plan once approved.

- Initiating and negotiating teaming agreements.

- Holding strategic planning sessions with your partners.

- Coordinating assignments and advancing additional due diligence.

Proposal Activities

This section focuses on positioning your team for success and profitability from the start of proposal development. It outlines how to build a strong foundation and includes:

- Creating a proposal work plan.

- Reviewing and validating the proposal outline.

- Developing a 30, 60, and 120 day startup plan.

- Estimating budgets and resource allocations.

- Monitoring progress and aligning proposal activities with project goals.

- Conducting value engineering and risk assessments.

- Finalizing your execution strategy.

- Preparing your bid and estimates.

- Negotiating your design agreement with the design builder.

- Engaging in negotiations with the owner and validating original assumptions.

Project Execution

The documents and plans developed during your proposal phase should carry over and guide your execution efforts. This continuity ensures that strategies and decisions are implemented smoothly.

Key items to carry forward include your execution strategy, startup checklists, staffing and recruiting plans, MWDBE/SDVOSB plans, risk register, and Monte Carlo analysis, financial plan, approved ATCs, project schedule, and final agreements.

This chapter covers topics such as:

- Transitioning from proposal to execution.

- Defining your role as principal-in-charge and project leader.

- Finalizing your engagement strategies (MWDBE, SDVOSB, community, political).

- Mobilizing staff and resources.

- Establishing project controls and invoice procedures.

- Creating a CAD/BIM manual and procedures.

- Expanding task and technical work groups.

- Creating tiger teams and peer review processes.

- Launching the full project execution plan.

- Continuing VE and life-cycle-cost analysis.

- Advancing your risk management strategy.

- Submitting and monitoring QA/QC and environmental compliance plans.

- Establishing safety protocols and review tracking systems.

- Confirming close-out procedures and responsibilities.

- Finalizing post-design service organization and project close-out framework.

Owner-Specific Processes

As an owner, the way you structure procurement, hire a general consultant and legal team, advise your diversity strategy, and collaborate with your entire team has a major impact on the success or failure of your AD Mega-Project. The way you incorporate value engineering, use partnering, apply risk management, and leverage alternative technical and financial concepts matters.

Your involvement in the design builder's task group meetings, your support during project close-out, and your ability to honor the requirements set up in the RFP and validate what the proposers have submitted—these are all critical. How you differentiate yourself during the developer and design builder selection process also shapes the outcome of your project.

Developer-Specific Processes

As the developer, you're the leader of any P3 project. Your ability to get to know and understand the owner, conduct thorough due diligence before starting, participate in soundings, and build the right team will determine your success. You must also engage in early risk assessments, make the go/no-go decision with care, and define your role in QA/QC.

How early you begin preparations before the RFQ matters. Your collaboration with the design build team, involvement in ATCs and AFCs, partnering with the owner, and commitment to MWDBE engagement are all essential elements that can significantly influence the project's success or failure.

Importance of Developing a Best Practices Manual and Training

The importance of developing a best practices manual and training program for your firm and project teams cannot be overstated. AD Mega-Projects are large and extremely complex. Throughout this book, I've shared experiences, best practices, and lessons learned—many of them through failures that ultimately made me and my teams stronger.

Many team members may be talented, but most have never worked on an AD Mega-Project. In my experience, only about 5 to 10 percent of a team typically has direct experience on these kinds of projects. When I assemble teams for an AD mega-project, I ensure that nearly all management-level personnel have been involved in AD mega-project work before. This significantly increases the likelihood of success.

However, just because someone has worked on an AD Mega-Project doesn't mean they know or follow best practices. That means 90 to 95 percent of your team may be unfamiliar with what it truly takes to succeed on an AD Mega-Project. No matter how good your management team is, success is unlikely without the proper tools and training in place.

If your organization already has a best practices manual and a rigorous training program for both your regional offices and project teams—congratulations. Your teams are likely operating efficiently, earning solid profits, and increasing your market share and reputation.

The Future and Why the Business Is Changing

This chapter also discusses the evolving nature of the AD Mega-Project business. It outlines the trends driving change, offers projections on how the industry will evolve, and explores how these changes can ultimately improve the business. It includes an analysis of the potential impact of a new Trump administration and provides a look at what might come next beyond the Infrastructure Investment and Jobs Act (IIJA).

2. Core Themes

Throughout the book, I emphasized several core themes essential to success in the AD Mega-Project space:

Selection of the Right Project

You must understand the owner, their consultants, how they do business, their views on risk allocation, and how they administer procurement. Have they delivered successful AD projects before? Do their contracts support fair compensation for changes? Is this project aligned with how your organization does business? Can you build trust with this team, and do you have sufficient time to conduct your due diligence?

Selection of the Right Project Team

Success depends not just on selecting the right firms but on having the right key personnel and SMEs who can deliver on this project, with this owner.

The Role of Strategic Positioning for Success and Profitability

Do you have the time, discipline, and the right team willing to work collaboratively to win, plan for success, and execute in a way that ensures profitability?

Preparing and Updating Your Go/No-Go Form Throughout the Project

A living go/no-go document will allow your team to make informed decisions throughout procurement—well before you've spent tens of millions on a proposal and bid.

Fostering a Cohesive Project Team

The team's culture, including that of the owner's team and how the prime contract is structured, must allow for transparency, truthfulness, and collaboration. Ask yourself: Will the owner work collaboratively with the team to achieve success during execution?

Developing Your 30, 60, and 120 day Startup Plan During the Proposal

This is a crucial tool that should be created during the proposal process and used immediately at the start of execution.

Developing Effective Project Controls

Effective project controls should begin before the issuance of the RFQ and carry through the proposal and execution phases. By implementing robust project controls early, you enable your team to track, report, schedule, plan, and strategize across the entire life-cycle of the project. This provides greater visibility into performance and allows timely adjustments to keep the project on schedule and aligned with its goals.

The Value of Risk Management Strategies Throughout the Project

Risk management should not be an afterthought. Like project controls, your risk strategy must begin prior to the issuance of the RFQ and continue through the proposal and execution phases. Once selected, the owner, developer, and contractor should commit to participating in structured risk management workshops and monthly risk meetings. These sessions help identify, assess, and mitigate risks in real time—fostering collaboration and minimizing surprises.

Start Your Close-out Activities Early

Close-out should not be treated as an end-of-project formality. Instead, incorporate your close-out activities as part of your 30, 60, and 120 day startup plan. Starting early ensures a smoother transition and reduces the risk of extended costs, delays, or disputes. Both the contractor and the owner should assign dedicated close-out managers who work collaboratively from the outset. Starting your close-out planning as early as possible significantly improves the likelihood of finishing your project on time and profitably.

3. Acknowledgment of Other Important Activities

There are many additional managerial, administrative, and technical tasks involved in project startup, proposal development, and execution that were not covered in detail within this book. Several of these important subjects will be explored further in future writing to provide a more comprehensive view and to support the continuing evolution of AD Mega-Project delivery.

4. Final Thoughts and Takeaways

Key Advice for Success

The success of your AD project depends on meticulous preparation and the validation of your team's assumptions throughout the process. Equally important is engaging your SMEs and maintaining clear, transparent communication with the owner, stakeholders, elected officials, and the community. Flexibility in adapting your plans as the project evolves is key.

We are now entering the fourth decade of delivering AD Mega-Projects in the U.S., and we've come a long way since the beginning. This delivery method has proven to be a powerful tool. Through continued learning, adaptation, and collaboration, we will continue to improve how we plan and execute these complex projects. The past three decades have brought us incredible projects made possible by alternative delivery, and the future is bright.

Encouragement

I encourage you and your organization to apply the strategies, case studies, and best practices shared throughout this book. Use them as a foundation to strengthen your own procurement and project execution efforts. Tailor them to fit your needs and improve how you pursue and deliver your AD Mega-Projects.

Closing Gratitude

I want to express my sincere appreciation for your time and engagement with the content of this book. I hope it serves as a useful resource and practical guide for you, your organization, and your project teams. If there is any way I can assist further—through training, advisory services, or speaking engagements—I would be happy to connect.

Thank you again.

Let's Stay Connected

I'm **Michael Shapiro, P.E.**, founder and owner of **Michael S. Shapiro Consulting LLC.** My work is all about helping teams improve how they operate, build relationships, and execute in the world of infrastructure and alternative delivery.

If something in this book sparked an idea or raised a question—or if you'd just like to chat more about how to improve your projects—I'd love to hear from you.

- **Email:** michaelshapiro.az@gmail.com

- **Phone:** 602-312-3097

- **Website:** https://msscllc.net

Feel free to reach out. Whether it's brainstorming ideas, running a workshop, or sharing lessons learned—I'm here to help.

www.ingramcontent.com/pod-product-compliance
Lightning Source LLC
Chambersburg PA
CBHW021550210326
41599CB00010B/385